THE TWILIGHT OF REASON

EMUNOT:
JEWISH PHILOSOPHY AND KABBALAH

Dov Schwartz *(Bar-Ilan University)*, Series Editor

EDITORIAL BOARD
Ada Rapoport-Albert (University College, London)
Gad Freudenthal (C.N.R.S, Paris)
Gideon Freudenthal (Tel Aviv University)
Moshe Idel (Hebrew University, Jerusalem)
Raphael Jospe (Bar-Ilan University)
Ephraim Kanarfogel (Yeshiva University)
Menachem Kellner (Haifa University)
Daniel Lasker (Ben-Gurion University, Beer Sheva)

THE TWILIGHT OF REASON

W. Benjamin, T. W. Adorno,
M. Horkheimer and E. Levinas
Tested by the Catastrophe

by Orietta OMBROSI

Translated from French by Victoria Aris

Boston 2012

With the support of the
Fondation pour la Mémoire de la Shoah
and the
Fondation du Judaïsme Français

Library of Congress Cataloging-in-Publication Data:

A catalog record for this title is available from the Library of Congress.

Copyright © 2012 Academic Studies Press
All rights reserved

ISBN 978-1-64469-667-5

Book design by Ivan Grave

Published by Academic Studies Press in 2012
28 Montfern Avenue
Brighton, MA 02135, USA
press@academicstudiespress.com
www.academicstudiespress.com

To Hurbinek

Table of Contents

Preface by Catherine Chalier ix

Foreword 1

Prelude
THE NOSTALGIA OF ODYSSEUS 11
    Regression: subjugated in order to subjugate 14
    The circle of the Same 21
    Why Odysseus? 26

Chapter I
FACING BEHEMOTH 29
I. The Jews, a problem in Horkheimer's analysis of anti-Semitism . . . 33
II. Anti-Semitism: a product of civilization, according to Horkheimer
    and Adorno 40
III. Hitlerism: paganism according to Levinas 47

Chapter II
ON THE THRESHOLD: WALTER BENJAMIN 55
I. From the *before* to the *after*: catastrophes 61
    1. Catastrophe and technological progress 62
    2. Catastrophe and the historical *continuum* 66
    3. Catastrophe and redemption 75
II. From the *after* to the *before*: flashes of remembrance . . . 81
    1. Dialectic of remembrance 83
    2. Dialectic of memory and forgetting 87

Interlude
A PHILOSOPHY OF TESTIMONY 93
    Silences of the witnesses 97
    Words of the saved 107
    The *here* and the *now* of testimony 111

Chapter III
THOUGHTS OF EXILE:
THEODOR W. ADORNO AND MAX HORKHEIMER 117
I. Adorno: a "sad knowledge" 122
    1. Philosophical thought *after Auschwitz*: a truth of feeling . . 123
    2. Ethics of physical suffering 129
    3. Theoretical thought in the face of pain and death 135
    4. A death worse than death 139
    5. Education *after Auschwitz*, or against coldness 142
II. Horkheimer: between lucid despair and mute hope 147
    1. Reason and its shadow: self-destruction 150
    2. Reason and nomination 156
    3. A Jewish intellectual *after Auschwitz* 159

Chapter IV
"THE PRESENTIMENT AND THE MEMORY OF THE NAZI HORROR":
EMMANUEL LEVINAS 165
I. Philosophizing *after Auschwitz*: three lessons 170
II. A subjectivity of flesh and blood 176
    1. Subjectivity as sensibility 180
    2. Subjectivity as vulnerability. 183
    3. Subjectivity as persecution 186
III. A humanism of the "suffering servant" 192
    1. Auschwitz as a paradigm of useless suffering 192
    2. Ethical resistance *afterwards* 195

Conclusion 199

Indicative Bibliography 212

Preface

A long lament, weak and already fading away, but still sometimes audible to those who continue to listen and who feel the terror of living when the thread that links them to the past is soaked in blood and opprobrium, dereliction and hate, is once again spreading across Europe's soil. Its breath is made up of the indefinable and insistent echo of millions of words that were stammered, murmured, prayed or cried in absolute despair during the persecution, physical abuse and murder which, during the twentieth century, touched the abyss at the heart of a civilization where the most noble concepts prevailed. For several years, philosophy, theology, science and technology, literature and the arts — so subtle and flourishing, and endowed with a past rich in ideas, creations and discoveries — which were the pride and passion of this civilization that strove so fiercely against obscurity, were commanded to serve inhumanity or to disappear. All the barriers erected by reason and the mind against man's dark and dreadful depths yielded, one by one, to the irresistible current of a terrifying barbarity that perpetually annihilated them. Books were burned, words became murderous slogans, thoughts were snuffed out in minds, and, crucially, sensitivity and emotion were perverted. Moments of compassion towards the tortured vanished behind a dark veil.

Orietta Ombrosi's book speaks of this terrible history, the unprecedented violence and apocalypse that still cast a terrible shadow on the present. However, it does not recount the events woven through this history; it declares strongly, and without concession to those who feel it is high time to turn the page as other tragedies require our attention, that philosophy does not emerge unscathed from this disaster. This insistent thought makes its way through the pages that follow because the author has lent an ear to the long lament just mentioned. It seems to me that, in doing so, she compels us to reflect on what effect this history had on reason, as terrible as it may be, and does so in a demanding and implacable way that is incompatible with relativism or eagerness to close the chapter. And yet, to reflect on this question does not by any means allow the suffering and perils that filled the twentieth century to escape from their own time. On the contrary, to consider the injuries of that period, to hear the lament of the European Jews murdered along with millions of other human beings, all equally powerless and equally innocent, as a question addressed to philosophy is — perhaps, anyway — to preserve opportunities for reason and philosophy, and even hope.

Some of the philosophers gathered in this book sensed this disaster and suffocating and cruel interruption of the taste for thought, for loving and living, even before they existed within the grasp of perception and grief. They saw what would happen, what could not be prevented from happening. Not because they had some particular gift, but quite simply because they had not supported logical and scholarly abstraction or even haughty coldness against the evidence of events and the suffering of flesh-and-blood individuals under the pretext of faithfully exercising a speculative reason that remains resolutely deaf to such things, or by claiming to prefer neutrality to human faces. Emmanuel Levinas, in the following pages, explicitly mentions this "presentiment of the Nazi horror," a presentiment, he says, that was then ingrained in him like dread or a "tumor in the memory" whose unfathomable sadness he wanted to put to use in a philosophy that rebelled at offering the slightest security to dialectics and the ruthless alliance that necessarily binds it up with evil. This does not mean, however, that he supported irrationalism, which he opposed very early due to its dangers and its complicity with what he considered to be an arrogant and sectarian paganism inclined to celebrate the coarseness of the cult of imprisonment in a nature with no afterlife. Walter Benjamin, who was a victim of persecution — though he never knew the immense extent of the *Shoah*, as in fear of being arrested and deported he committed suicide in Port-Bou in 1940 during his flight to Spain — also felt the premonition of an inexorable disaster. Thus in his analyses on the concept of history, his final manuscript, it seems that there is an insistent reflection on disaster. Written with an urgency that makes us feel the threat to the author's very survival, some of Benjamin's theses can indeed be read, quite rightly, as a terrible premonition of the imminent end of days. This at least is the perspective of Ombrosi's interpretation, a perspective that is tenaciously and perceptively held: there is certainly a difficulty in the fact that, according to Benjamin, the disaster is that things last, i.e. that they always remain subject to the control of time, even though this book supports the fact that the *Shoah* forces us to view it as a rupture that must be thought of in terms of a before and an after. However, the hopeless yet fervent care that Benjamin takes in entrusting to the men of today the task of opening up the questions of the past in order to once again give a voice to those who were humiliated and broken by the uncontrollable momentum of exploitation and domination, to bring into the world a little of his enigmatic messianism, constitutes a way for him, too, to unite a before and an after — an after that could save a little of the broken hope of the before. But can this still be said, in light of what went before?

Benjamin cannot answer this tragic question, unless time, which stopped so brutally for him on the threshold of a world where he would perhaps have been able to follow his path, is his only response to the immense disaster that he sensed without having the time to deal with it in his work: the interruption is endless. No remembrance will ever save the terrorized thoughts, the little words murmured to children and the gestures of tenderness on the edge of madness, when the bodies went up in smoke.

But this conclusion is called into question again, to a certain extent, by Adorno and Horkheimer, who had to go into exile to survive the murder that was destined for them. By dedicating his philosophical work to "those who died in unspeakable torments," Horkheimer also gives all the "Jewish intellectuals who escaped death by torture under Hitler"[1] this same duty. But in doing so, he paves the morally imperative and instantly conceivable way for a link with this past. The fact that, for him as well as Adorno (and Benjamin before them), the ideology justifying persecution and then extermination was forged in his native language certainly intensifies the horror that gripped him. We can suppose that this also burdened him with an immense responsibility. However, even though no one can imagine what happened in those years when millions of lives were interrupted at the same time, and though no language or thought can contribute to it, Adorno and Horkheimer nonetheless maintain that philosophy must henceforth make the unimaginable the

---

[1] Max Horkheimer, *Notizen 1950-1969 und Dämmerung* (Frankfurt: Fischer Verlag, 1974), 273.

very foundation of its activity. It is what forces us to see in the rupture that took place — a rupture whose radicality must remain impossible to attenuate using the weapons of historical dialectic or any kind of theodicy — the unfathomable point that must now be confronted by thought. It is vital to both the crisis of modernity and the fate of western civilization.

Adorno and Horkheimer, like Levinas in another way, in fact believe that the extreme nature of the crime committed — to exterminate the whole of a people, however far away they thought they had found refuge, without there being the least strategic or political interest in doing so — poses an incommensurable challenge to thought. The extermination was indeed carried out in a methodical, rational and technically very effective manner while being without reason in regard to the objectives of war. In a study entitled "After Auschwitz,"[2] Adorno explains on this subject that the new categorical imperative that applies henceforth — to think and act so that the disaster is never repeated — involves a radical revision of what was previously the pride of culture. He particularly highlights that if reason, with the best concepts that it was able to create over the course of history, such as freedom, failed to prevent or stop the barbarity, it is because these concepts were unable to "touch and transform men." This is a point particularly emphasized in Orietta Ombrosi's book. Criticizing the tragic impasses of instrumental reason, reason that acts to dominate things and men, and whose dark depths were revealed by Nazi excesses — according to Adorno and Horkheimer — is only one aspect of these philosophers' work. They do not heedlessly attack reason; they have no predilection for spontaneity and its unsophisticated and dramatic savagery. Adorno, in particular, seeks to think of reason that will remain open to emotion, to sentiment and to suffering; the suffering of human subjectivity, too often forgotten due to system, objectivity or even abstract universality, but also, and above all, the suffering of the fragile and mortal bodies about whom Orietta Ombrosi writes so profoundly. This is the heart of this new imperative; its cognitive contents and its presumed necessity and universality are in fact subordinate to what still remains factual, contingent and empirical — namely human suffering. All this, explains Adorno, without negating the necessity of principles and the primacy of justice, requires compassion.

---

[2] Theodor Adorno, *Negative Dialectics*, trans. E.B. Ashton (London: Routledge, 1973), 361.

Opening up reason to its other — the body, emotion, the face — is equally central for Levinas. He refuses, just as much as Horkheimer and Adorno, to have to choose between reason and irrationality. He does not set out, any more than they do, to attack reason under the pretext of redeeming the position of emotion or feeling. Instead, he considers the significance of a reason called upon to listen to the cries of wretchedness and human vulnerability that are incommensurable with thematic concepts and developments. Resolutely opposed to any attempt to give sense to the suffering, lament, or mourning of the other (he sees this as immoral), Levinas believes, on the contrary, that the thought that a sense of suffering exists is only preserved by the major discomfort provoked in the ego by this suffering, including the feeling of no longer having the right to live in complete innocence and irresponsibility. And this is the only sense that *should* survive, especially at the haunting and fatal times when countless people allowed themselves to be seduced by nihilism, took pleasure in fuelling and increasing hate and, more banally but no less dangerously, rushed to attend to their own business, indifferent to the fate of others.

The three lessons that can be communicated to younger generations — to those who come after the catastrophe, with the formidable burden of thinking and living humanely in memory of this heritage — which he draws from his experience of persecution, and which are so ably presented in this book, are remarkable in this respect. I will mention just one of them in this preface: to teach newcomers how to preserve in themselves an interiority that can live in harmony with concern, especially as the very idea of interiority is derided by the advocates of realism. Levinas obviously is not speaking of an interiority that retreats from the world the better to spare itself any contact with its injuries and horrors. He refers to an interiority fed by words that make it responsible for the other, and which give it the strength to remain alone when institutions and high rational maxims no longer protect humans. In particular, he explains, it is the words that the Jewish people listened to in their books that gave them the certainty that we must shelter, in the consciousness, the little Good that remains when magnificent civilizations collapse and would rather allow the screaming of exterminatory language, without hesitation, than look after the persecuted.

Orietta Ombrosi rightfully gives an important place to what she and Ricœur call a "philosophy of testimony." The defeat of reason, which her book seeks to consider, must in fact contemplate the excess of what testimony says on the logic of the concept. But if testimony is part of an attestation that remains irreducible to the sometimes implacable and cold, and often daunting necessity for the internal coherence of reasoning determined by logic; if it requires an interpretation that does more than comply with the rigor of a demonstration, this does not mean that it is impertinent to summon it to the field of philosophy. This, at least, is the argument that Orietta Ombrosi's book defends, with a remarkable perseverance.

Testimony requires the philosopher to face the implacable finiteness of thought. It creates an opening in his attempts to develop a speculative, systematic discourse, and often tends to neglect Kantian wisdom as to the limits of what pure reason can know. It calls each person back to the physical: the witness saw; he heard; he remembers, whether well or badly; he says, in rough, hurt and uncertain words, what often no-one wants to hear. Not out of spite or callousness, however, but because, in the case of those who escaped the *Shoah*, what a witness says always exceeds traditional and reasonable thought and remains unimaginable by it.

The fact that this tragedy left its mark branded on reason and language, that it destroyed the dynamism of concepts by revealing their inability to curb the furious momentum of the ideologies that deny reality, is what creates memory from the words of the witness. But it is also why they are so often met with deafness or doubt from those who prefer unreality or speculation that is not based on the fragility of things, or even the world of pure ideas — pure in tragedy, pure in the unfathomable cruelty of which men are capable, but also pure in compassion towards those who suffer. However, as the testimonies of the camps show, if some prisoners attempted — until then — to say and communicate fragments of poems, prayers or memories of old reading, even though they were imprecise and already being overtaken by the night, was this not because they felt the *vital* necessity of taking care of language in circumstances so horrifying that they at the same time forbade any appeal to reason and logic to do so? For we must remember that there was no "why" in the camps. And yet these acts of spiritual resistance, the moments where the prisoners attempted, in a very small way, to save language from drowning in the surrounding madness and in the paralysis caused by terror, are precisely those which must be evaluated by a philosopher if he wants to think differently to how he did before the disaster. In short, there, where the executioners attempted to strip death of its human sense by making people fear a fate worse than death, as Adorno says, these testimonies are a way of still caring for the human.

The defeat of reason is not irrevocable. Moreover, it would be dangerous if it were. But as the philosophers in this book say, each in their own way, the reason at work in the philosophical exercise is called upon to open itself to human suffering, without seeking to alleviate it through dialectical or theological explanations abstract and indifferent to the fate of individuals. It is required to listen to testimony that painstakingly attempts to make this suffering heard. Even at the price of having to immediately deny what concepts and theories allow them to confidently say and express, the philosophers must therefore open themselves up to the extremity of this plea. But what does this mean? This, no doubt: that their works and their lessons testify, even in the rationality that they rightly seek to preserve, to the suffering that requires them. It seems to me that to think of the suffering of yesterday and of now, and to respond to it with a feeling of immense responsibility, not chosen but inevitable, without fleeing to the unreality of speculative constructions that require nothing of anyone, is the task that the philosophers in this crucial book suggest. Here, despite the darkness, there is perhaps a thrill of hope.

Catherine Chalier
Paris, July 2007

Foreword

Jerusalem remembered
in the days of her affliction and of her miseries
all her pleasant things that she had in the days of old,
when her people fell into the hand of the enemy,
and none did help her.

Lamentations 1:7

"The thought of the disaster"[1] (Maurice Blanchot) is at the heart of this reflection on *reason* put to the test by the Disaster that rained down on European Jews during the period of Hitler's rule. The thought of the disaster on the one hand means to philosophically understand and know *why* it happened in civilized Europe, cultivated by and emerging from the ideal of human reason, and developed by the values of progress and the Enlightenment; on the other hand, it means to think about the possibility of a future for philosophic thought. Indeed, is it still possible to philosophize in the devastation of the "post-disaster"? Is it still possible to find meaning? If so, *how* do we do so? *How* should we think?

What remains of this disaster, what it leaves us with — aside from disillusion and nihilist disenchantment — is the need to find an "ultimate propriety" in thought and knowledge; to restore a dignity to them, *at least* in the research that belongs to them, the research *of* knowledge; and, to start with, to know what happened in the extermination camps, and before that, what allowed their conception and construction. Indeed, as Blanchot says: "[H]ow can we accept not to know? We read books on Auschwitz. The wish of all, in the camps, the last wish: know what has happened, do not forget, and at the same time never will you know."[2] On the one hand, therefore, the thought of the disaster is taken in this book as an attempt to understand *why* Nazi barbarity emerged at the heart of civilized Europe, and especially to understand this "why" *philosophically* — i.e. to decipher the philosophical reasons involved in the irrationality created and devised in Nazi Germany. On the other hand, the thought of the disaster is developed here into an attempt to think about

---

[1] Maurice Blanchot, *The Writing of the Disaster*, trans. Ann Smock (Lincoln: University of Nebraska Press, 1995), 5.

[2] *Ibid.*, 82.

the *how* — *how* can a future emerge for thought and once more be allowed to confront the preliminary to philosophical practice that is an inquiry into the Disaster and the suffering caused, thus affording it the intended dignity.

It is through this confrontation that this book gathers together the thinking of Max Horkheimer (1895-1973), Theodor Wiesengrund-Adorno (1903-1969), and Emmanuel Levinas (1906-1995), along with that of Walter Benjamin (1895-1940), who was already concerned ahead of time. All these philosophers, each in their own way and with varying forcefulness, had the courage, the strength, the perception, and sometimes simply the desperation to strive to understand what happened, to allow themselves to be questioned by the event and by the shock that it produced, to face questions which by their very nature challenged their own right to exist as philosophical questions. Moreover, my selection of these sometimes greatly differing authors is justified by their vehement sense of the necessity of *testifying* to the suffering and death imposed on the victims of the gas chambers, the necessity of subjecting their personal thoughts to the ordeal of this scandal and facing this danger. They felt the urgent need to deal in their thinking with the cries and agony of those who died at Auschwitz. It is with attention to this injury that I have attempted to examine them.

This book therefore does not belong to the history of philosophy or the history of ideas, nor historiography, but is instead on the fringes, the margins of the *philosophy of history*. The Extermination becomes the "object" on the basis of which a philosophical discourse can (or cannot) take place, the object from which a critical self-reflection of *reason* and its discourse — and an alternative — can be developed. This self-criticism will be tackled principally in the *Prelude*, and the alternative will be outlined and explained in the *Interlude*.

The discourse that I will develop here will therefore attempt to explain the historical event by way of abstract, theoretical, and hermeneutic means. History, this unique history, will also be asked to throw a somber light on philosophy and philosophical reason. For these reasons, we can speak here of the *philosophy of history* in the objective *and* the subjective genitive sense. More precisely, a philosophy *of* history (in the objective sense), as a reflection on the historical event, will take on the traits of a *philosophy of testimony* which, for these philosophers (as we will see), on the one hand *testifies to the disaster* — through the testimony of the suffering at Auschwitz — and on the other *identifies with the testimony* by addressing *us*. The subjective genitive sense, meanwhile, is justified by the fact that history, the Extermination in this case, imposes itself on philosophy in general and this line of thinking in particular, shaking them up and putting them to the test.

Furthermore, this book must be considered within the interpretive landscape pioneered by the philosophers of the Frankfurt School, sharing with them the idea that the Extermination represents a *rupture* or even a *caesura* in history, while also being *one* possibility of the dialectic of the Enlightenment that shows that *reason can* go so far as to self-destruct, and that enlightened civilization *can* succeed in reverting to barbarity.

The milestones of this analysis are reformulated by Dan Diner in his interpretation of the "breakdown of civilization" (*Zivilisationsbruch*)[3]. According to Diner, along with the Holocaust (this term expresses both memory of and thinking about the event), we must deal with a radical reversal of the values of the west's enlightened culture, which is precisely what makes the phrase "breakdown of civilization" pertinent. Furthermore, this formula brings into play an intellectual comparison that simultaneously covers history, epistemology, philosophy and anthropology. But the most original aspect of this interpretation, which justifies its revival here, is that the idea of the "breakdown of civilization" allows two generally very distinct and often opposite approaches, namely the singularist and universalist approaches, to be united in their least extreme forms: the first being that which considers the Event from a singular perspective, as the unique experience collectively undergone specifically by the Jews who were exterminated solely for being Jews; the second going beyond the fate of the Jews as such and aiming to make a singular case a universal one, pertaining to humanity and its heritage, as something that should never again happen. Diner reconciles these two perspectives by applying the interpretive key of the "breakdown of civilization" to each: with regards to the Jews, in the sense of a *never before*; with regards to humanity, in the sense of a *never again*. Thus, a crime against humanity, undergone and experienced primarily by the Jews, is interpreted from a perspective that focuses on the victims and, at the same time, is expanded to a universally valid anthropological perspective.

---

[3] Dan Diner, *Zivilisationsbruch: Denken nach Auschwitz* (Frankfurt am Main: Fischer, 1988). See also *Beyond the Conceivable: Studies on Germany, Nazism and the Holocaust* (Berkeley: University of California Press, 2000).

In this book, these two perspectives touch and move apart, meet and separate, revealing a tension, an "uneasiness" between their two poles that is never resolved. As the monographic sections show, the singular point of view is central, as we will hear the *testimonies* of philosophers, all Jewish, who are in the "difficult" situation of having survived and wanting to talk of the *singularity* of a suffering which they did not physically experience and which, at the same time, *singularly* concerns them as Jews. On the other hand, the universal point of view is equally recognized, despite everything — despite the rigorous criticism that the authors in this book put forward with regards to the universalist view of history — because their reflections, beginning with the Event and its unique suffering, concentrate on universally valid philosophical ideas: the idea of instrumental or identifying reason, the principle of self-preservation, and the coldness that are at the very foundation of civilization, but also remembrance, solidarity, responsibility and compassion, i.e. the ideas that allow these philosophers to think *differently*. These are ideas that should be universally considered, especially *afterwards*, *after* the "breakdown of civilization," so that the horror will *never again* occur. It is as though the universalist view reemerged at the moment of thinking *afterwards* and of considering, as these philosophers have done, *how* to overcome the total confusion and the loss of all sense — sense of the human, sense of reason, sense of God — without giving in to the temptation to succumb to the emptiness of grief.

But, paradoxically, this universalist view re-emerges from an anchoring in a singularity, that of a *here* and *now*: the *here* and the *now* of *testimony*. And it is precisely through the prism of *testimony* that I will interpret the works of these authors that are sometimes poles apart, an interpretation which will allow me to bring them together and to include Benjamin — even though he never knew the ultimate consequences of Nazism — due to the revolutionary power of his philosophy of history which teaches us that, in the historical past, nothing is lost.

The destruction of the European Jews, like the title of Raul Hilberg's now-famous book, therefore dominates philosophical discussion because a certain idea of *reason* perished in the death chambers along with the body of Israel. Indeed, the Disaster signals the twilight of *reason*, as it does all reasons, but especially of the *reason* that is expected to be the source of civilization, of progress, of deliverance, of freedom and of human rights. The "Passion of Passions"[4] of the Jewish people (to use Levinas's exaggerated phrase), accomplished in the middle of the twentieth century, at the heart of a Europe that had been Christianized for a thousand years and long nourished by spiritual values, sets a test for *reason* and its most appropriate discourse (philosophy): to confront itself, to challenge itself, analyze itself from within, and make its *mea culpa*, even if it is in the form of a lament.

It is a spoken or even written lament over the desolation and devastation that it legitimized, and against which it did not sufficiently protect itself during this century of horrors. It is a lament over *reason*, then, which, in the solitude and misery of its ruins, can only call upon its own resources by seeking a new course for a renewal of thought within itself, in the unexplored cracks of its possibilities and alternatives. It is a lament over *reason* at nightfall which can give life to the dawn of a new day.

But do we not picture *reason* too unequivocally in this foreword, even in the very title? Can we, in fact, talk of *reason*? Would it not be more appropriate to decipher a plurality of senses of *reason* — more relevant to talk of reasons in the plural?

Firstly, the singular use of this term owes itself to the authors' legacy: "complete reason or peace among men,"[5] says Levinas in the preface to the German edition of *Totality and Infinity*; and it is necessary "for enlightenment to reflect on itself if humanity is not to be totally betrayed,"[6] write Horkheimer and Adorno in the introduction to *Dialectic of Enlightenment*. The sense given by these same authors to the term *Aufklärung* includes the Enlightenment, enlightened thought, progressive thought, certainly, but also informed reason, reason which distinguishes between the subject and the object — in a word, theoretical reason. Likewise, for Levinas, the reason that must be challenged, or rather, that which does not exhaust the entreaties of the sensible, is theoretical reason that uses an adequation process. It is this reason which is primarily

---

[4] Emmanuel Levinas, *Difficult Freedom. Essays on Judaism*, trans. Seán Hand (Baltimore: Johns Hopkins University Press, 1997), 158.

[5] Emmanuel Levinas, *Totalität und Unendlichkeit: Versuch über die Exteriorität*, trans. Wolfgang Krewani (Freiburg: Karl Alber, 2008), ii.

[6] Max Horkheimer and Theodor Adorno, *Dialectic of Enlightenment*, trans. E. Jephcott (Stanford: Stanford University Press, 2002), xvii.

examined by these authors and whose rights are challenged by the Disaster. Hence the necessity, as we will see, for them to conceptualize, to think of, to *witness* an *other reason*: a reason fractured by an interruption (Benjamin), a reason that is "non-identical" and affected by sentiment (Adorno), a non-instrumental reason that names its objects (Horkheimer), or even a reason open to transcendence (Levinas).

Furthermore, while it is true, as Edmund Husserl said in 1935 in his lecture *Philosophy and the Crisis of European Humanity,* that "reason is a broad title,"[7] it nonetheless seems appropriate to speak of *reason,* in the sense of *ratio,* when this term, or rather this concept, runs up against the upheaval and crisis in Europe during the 1930s. Indeed, Husserl writes: "I too am certain that the European crisis has its roots in a misguided rationalism. [...] Rationality, in that high and genuine sense [...] the primordial Greek sense which in the classical period of Greek philosophy had become an ideal, still requires, to be sure, much clarification through self-reflection; but it is called in its mature form to guide [our] development. On the other hand, we readily admit [...] that the stage of development of *ratio* represented by the rationalism of the Age of Enlightenment was a mistake"[8]. Although these reflections by Husserl lead in a distinct direction, it seems clear that this extract anticipates and identifies the question that our authors will later intensify. It is this *reason,* inherited from the Greeks and refined by the Enlightenment, a *reason* that should develop the maturity of men, liberate them and guide them in their moral and intellectual progress, which has been led astray. Which has failed. Which has fallen.

In short, even if we allow the existence of other notions of reason, such as contemplative reason in the Platonic sense of the term — reason which contemplates the immutably beautiful order of the stars — or practical reason in the Kantian sense — capable of being determined by the autonomy of will — we cannot avoid recognizing that, for those swept away by the storm, all of *these reasons* lose their sense and are insufficient. Robert Antelme, who was there, says: "You can burn children without that disturbing the night. The night is unmovable around us [...]. Above

---

[7] E. Husserl, "Philosophy and the Crisis of European Humanity" in *The Crisis of European Sciences and Transcendental Phenomenology*, trans. David Carr (Evanston: Northwestern University Press, 1970), p. 290.

[8] *Ibid.*

us, the stars too are calm. But this calm, this immobility are neither the essence nor the symbol of a preferable truth; they is the scandal of nature's ultimate indifference."[9]

I will attempt, over the course of this deliberation, to speak of a *reason* that is unlike this indifference, unlike the silence all around us — silence of the cosmos or silence of God, but certainly also the silence of *reason* and of all its reasons — in other words, a non-indifferent *reason* which, to paraphrase Levinas, does more than think; it thinks while *testifying*, and testifies while thinking of its own injuries, and above all bears witness to the injuries inflicted during history's night.

It is a *reason*, in short, that testifies to the suffering and death of the "unnamed," even if only to the death of a single person, the "nameless" child spoken of by Primo Levi, the child of death who was born in and died at Auschwitz at the start of January 1945, "free but not redeemed."[10]

---

[9] Robert Antelme, *The Human Race*, trans. Jeffrey Haight and Annie Mahler (Evanston: Northwestern University Press, 1998), 111.

[10] Primo Levi, *The Truce*, trans. Stuart Woolf (London: Bodley Head, 1965), 23.

Prelude

The Nostalgia of Odysseus

All philosophy is nostalgia.
Novalis

"*Considerate la vostra semenza: fatti non foste a viver come bruti, ma per seguir virtute e canoscenza.*"[1] These are the lines of the song of Odysseus [Ulysses] from *Inferno* in Dante's *Divine Comedy*, which return to Primo Levi's mind at the deepest point of his despair at Auschwitz. The chapter entitled "The Canto of Ulysses"[2] in his book *If This Is A Man* tells of Levi's attempt to translate this song from *The Divine Comedy* and, even more, to highlight the importance of these verses to a French prisoner named Jean — *il Pikolo* in the chemical *Kommando* — because "it's absolutely necessary and urgent that he listen [...] before it's too late." It is not simply a case of a struggle to reaffirm the spirit against the inexorability of time and history, an attempt to draw out the detainee's humanity, desperately clinging on to a fragment of poetry, but something more — perhaps a "gigantic" intuition capable of understanding or foreseeing *why* he, *Pikolo* and all the others who were deported to and killed at Auschwitz-Birkenau: "I must tell him [...]," writes Levi, "something gigantic that I myself have only just seen, in a flash of intuition, perhaps the reason for our fate, for our being here today..."[3]

But what had Levi "seen" by remembering the verses of Dante's song of Odysseus? What had he understood? What was the "explanation" for their destiny? What was the relationship, the association, between

---

[1] Dante, *The Divine Comedy: Inferno*, trans. Longfellow, canto XXVI, vv.118-120: "Consider ye the seed from which ye sprang; ye were not made to live like unto brutes, but for pursuit of virtue and of knowledge."

[2] Primo Levi, *If This Is A Man*, trans. Stuart Woolf (London: Penguin, 1979), 115.

[3] *Ibid.*, 121.

Odysseus and that bleak place called Auschwitz?[4] The association between the foundering of Odysseus's and his companions' ship and that of Levi and the others?

For Dante, who did not read the *Odyssey* directly, the figure of Odysseus was undoubtedly characterized by shrewdness, particularly demonstrated in his verbal skills, but principally by an inexhaustible thirst for knowledge and travel, as revealed in the twenty-sixth canto of *Inferno*. And yet Levi, in his recitation, appropriates Dante's image of Odysseus, inviting his companions to recover and to keep their human dignity: to not relinquish knowledge, to not despair of rationality, to continue to be captivated by the longing for the unexplored, by *"l'alto mare aperto"* (the "high open sea"). However, in living through the concentration camp experience, "living" at Auschwitz III-Buna-Monowitz, how could he avoid measuring the gap between the myth of reason as the eminent dignity of man, embodied by Odysseus, and the reality of the madness in which he found himself? Levi perhaps caught a glimpse of the true connection between the reason narrated by this myth and the madness established at Auschwitz-Birkenau. Perhaps.

REGRESSION:
SUBJUGATED IN ORDER TO SUBJUGATE

The "gigantic" intuition that Levi had during the winter of 1943-44, and which we will never know, is perhaps comparable to that which Max Horkheimer and Theodor Adorno develop in their shared work — *Dialectic of Enlightenment* (*Dialektik der Aufklärung*), also written during those years and published in 1947, the same year as *If This Is A Man*. Starting with the mythical character of Odysseus, a symbol of reason and enlightened western civilization, the two Jewish German philosophers try to understand and explain why the irrational event of the Extermination of European Jews occurred in civilized Europe, a Europe born of the ideal of human reason and raised with the values of progress and Enlightenment. A first attempt to theoretically understand the Event while the gas chambers were still working, *Dialectic of Enlightenment* is

---

[4] Cf. François Rastier, *Ulysse à Auschwitz. Primo Levi, le survivant* (Paris: Cerf, 2005).

the result of an attempt to rethink the culture and civilization that were not able to prevent this fracture in history using the lucidity of critical theory. In this book, the authors strive as *philosophers* to become aware of the "tireless self-destruction of enlightenment"[5] and to show why *reason* — enlightened thought, progressive thought, the tradition of the Enlightenment, *ratio* — and, more generally, philosophical thought can sit side by side with barbarity.

Thus, the aporia faced by these philosophers is to decipher reason's "own share of guilt" and so to keep it from "its last remaining innocence,"[6] using reason itself. "Humanity is not to be totally betrayed"[7]; it must not be betrayed again, and so it is necessary to consider and explain the "seeds" of the regression of Enlightenment (*Aufklärung*) in new forms of mythology, even if they are pagan or nationalist like those suggested by Nazism. The central aim of these philosophers is therefore to update the mechanism by which reason can regress into mythology, or even worse, barbarity: "the cause of enlightenment's relapse" must be sought in "the fear of truth which petrifies enlightenment itself."[8] The destructive mythology of reason is therefore hidden within it, more or less somnolent. There is not a radical opposition between reason and myth, as believed by the Enlightenment — for whom the complete demythification of reason was not only possible, but the condition of all progress — but rather a dialectic, a complicity; there is a mythological nature in reason and a rational nature in myth. But if this dialectic of reason explains the transformation of reason to myth, or the proximity between the two, what about the conversion into domination, and specifically into barbaric domination?

According to what the two philosophers wrote at the start of their book, "[e]nlightenment, understood in the widest sense as the advance of thought, has always aimed at liberating human beings from fear *and* installing them as masters." And yet it is precisely in this link between the two purposes, in the "*and*," that the transformation occurs. When fear is internalized or repressed, instead of being liberated, it is diverted and

---

[5] Horkheimer and Adorno, *Dialectic of Enlightenment*, xiv.
[6] *Ibid.*
[7] *Ibid.*, xvii.
[8] *Ibid.*, xvi.

sublimated into the desire to dominate, into an appropriation of all that causes it, into a hold over all that creates it, whether untamed nature or different, even dissociated human beings. Hence the domination over nature and man. Put more subtly, what is repeated in this movement is the fear of the outside, the heterogeneous, the fear of alterity which forces reason to favor the identity, *by returning* the outside and *the other to the same*. Therefore by sublimating and distorting the fear of the *other*, whether it is the exterior world of nature or men, reason begins to consider this world as *its own* world, as its prey, because "nothing is allowed to remain outside, since the mere idea of the 'outside' is the real source of fear."[9] Reason frees itself from the fear and terror of the outside only by making itself sovereign and dominant, or even "totalitarian."[10] In addition, this very *reductio ad unum* that belongs to reason gives it access to totalitarian domination in the sense that nothing more can remain outside of it, or nothing outside is allowed to remain as such; everything must be returned to the same. Thus, "by subjecting everything *particular* to its discipline, it left the uncomprehended whole free to rebound as mastery over things against the life and consciousness of human beings."[11] Through this pattern of reducing and dominating the *other*, which is present in its way of processing, knowing and thinking, reason can therefore become inhuman or even barbarous.

Offering a criticism and polemic review of almost all western philosophy, Horkheimer and Adorno undertake an analysis of the *Odyssey*, one of European civilization's fundamental texts, which "bears witness to the dialectic of enlightenment."[12] According to the philosophers, this text is not only one of the first representative documents of western civilization; it is also the one which most clearly exposes the dialectical link between myth and enlightenment, and they dedicate an entire chapter to its protagonist: "Odysseus or Myth and Enlightenment." Not only is the *Odyssey* built on the reciprocal balance between the form of the epic

---

[9] Horkheimer and Adorno, *Dialectic of Enlightenment*, 11.
[10] *Ibid.*, 4.
[11] *Ibid.*, 33.
[12] *Ibid.*, 35.

and the mythological content,[13] but the relationship between myth and enlightenment represented by Odysseus becomes clear within the tale itself. Homer's hero oscillates between the myth of the prehistoric era and the enlightenment of the liberal and bourgeois era of modernity, whose fundamental characteristics he embodies, even though the "bourgeois" concept, which appeared at the end of the medieval era, cannot be attributed to Homer's character without being anachronistic. Odysseus remains in the space of the mythological world, and at the same time crosses time in the development of his awareness. While travelling the seas and distant lands meeting fabulous characters, he becomes more and more similar to modern man who thinks only of being, of maintaining and preserving his established human condition: "The contrast between the single surviving ego and the multiplicity of fate reflects the antithesis between enlightenment and myth. The hero's peregrinations from Troy to Ithaca trace the path of the self through myths, a self infinitely weak in comparison to the force of nature, and still in the process of formation as self-consciousness."[14] Odysseus' wanderings represent the course of development of the consciousness of an *ego*, through experience and knowledge of mythical places and persons. In addition, his countless adventures and his resourcefulness form the concrete basis of his knowledge — a knowledge that allows him to survive, to recklessly face any danger and, more, to establish his *ego*.

The incident with the Sirens' seduction is one of the clearest examples. The Sirens represent the temptation to lose oneself, and to lose oneself in the past; their song and their voices invite him to listen and learn, or perhaps re-learn. They know everything about the past, everything that happens on earth, including Odysseus's recent past, the Trojan War. But as a price for this knowledge, this opportunity to hear and see the

---

[13] Walter Benjamin had already highlighted that Odysseus, more precisely the Odysseus in Kafka's narrative "The Silence of the Sirens," "stands at the dividing line between myth and fairy tale. Reason and cunning have inserted tricks into myths": cf. Walter Benjamin, "Franz Kafka: On the 10th Anniversary of his Death," trans. Harry Zohn, in *Selected Writings II* (Cambridge: Belknap Press, 2005), 799.

[14] Horkheimer and Adorno, *Dialectic of Enlightenment*, 38.

past again, to remember it and plunge into it, the Sirens demand the sacrifice of his future and his life. In the myth, the temptation to lose the *ego* through the promise of happiness is associated with the strength of preservation of this *ego*; here the temptation of self-destruction reinforces self-preservation. The more Odysseus, bound to the mast, is seduced by the skill and the charm of the Sirens' song, the more his companions tighten the bonds. After having witnessed the temptation of forgetting oneself and any desire to return home in the land of the Lotophagi, and having seen his comrades transformed into pigs on Circe's island and known the peril of a return to animal life, Odysseus knows very well that only his reason can preserve and save him. He can only save himself by resisting the seductions of pleasure and illusion, by a renunciation and a "mutilation" of the self. Thus, he saves himself and keeps his identity. His patience, his self-control, his sangfroid, and also his *coldness* make Odysseus the model of a hero who loses himself in order to rediscover and preserve himself: "[the self] takes on its solidity only through this antithesis, *and its unity through the very multiplicity which myth in its oneness denies.*"[15] His inflexibility towards temptation and passion allows him to preserve and save himself and thus to recognize himself in his *ego* and join his unity.

And yet guile is the most subtle method that Odysseus possesses with which to identify and to preserve himself. It is the absolute weapon, the most precious ability to protect himself in any circumstances and, whatever the conditions of the struggle, to ensure victory and domination over the *other*. Horkheimer and Adorno highlight its most fundamental aspects: cunning is revealed first in the deception presupposed in the sacrifices to the gods, then in the formalism of the language and in the rhetoric; it is finally manifested as the means of exchange peculiar to *homo œconomicus*. But what Horkheimer and Adorno find strange is that "even Odysseus is a sacrificial victim,"[16] a victim sacrificed in order to suppress sacrifice. With Odysseus, there is a transformation of sacrifice into a sacrificed subjectivity, i.e. into a subjectivity whose *ego* consists of and is based on the renunciation of a part of its nature in order to achieve a stronger reaffirmation of self, a sacrificed subjectivity whose sacrifice is offered to itself. Once more, the domination of the self which saves

---

[15] *Ibid.*, 38 [my emphasis].

[16] *Ibid.*, 43.

the man's life, which protects and preserves him, is at the same time a "mutilation" of this life, a patient self-control. Odysseus thus becomes the model for the history of civilization that is a history of "renunciation": man's renunciation of his passions and domination of his own nature; in a word, the renunciation of man's inner nature — such is the price of achieving domination over all of nature and other men. This denial, "the core of all civilizing rationality,"[17] "the principle of bourgeois disillusionment, the external schema for the internalization of sacrifice, is already latent [...] in the assessment of power relationships that admits defeat in advance and makes survival virtually dependent on death."[18] Cunning reason must always calculate its own impotence towards nature and evaluate the power relationships so that it is not overcome itself. Its partial adaptation to the superiority of nature depends on the fact that it can only subdue and dominate nature thanks to its assessments and the coldness of its calculations detached from the instinctive and the natural. It is as if reason had to pay tribute to nature by offering up the natural in man in order to become the *master* of the whole realm itself.

The traits of cunning[19] — such as polymorphia, deception, the art of speech, equivocation, inversion, flexibility, reversal, preservation — that can be drawn from these reflections, which are not exempt from Marxist rhetoric, refer to the attributes of flexibility, obliqueness, the curve. They evoke the image of a circle — the perfect shape of identity, as it is completely inverted and closed in on itself, at the same time both mobile and motionless in its rotation, without beginning or end, totally enclosed, absolute. They follow the example of Odysseus, who is absolutely steadfast in himself and whose core aim consists of persevering in his being, who accomplishes a voyage where the start and end coincide, who travels a totality, who in his motionless identity is shaped by the mobility of places, experiences and disguises, who turns inward without meeting anyone, and, finally, who remains in the clutches of his solitude. But Odysseus's circle of guile is the same as that of his voyage.

---

[17] *Ibid.*, 42.

[18] *Ibid.*, 45.

[19] Cf. Marcel Detienne and Jean-Pierre Vernant, *Cunning and Intelligence in Greek Culture and Society*, trans. Janet Lloyd (Chicago: University of Chicago Press, 1991).

In fact, the *Odyssey* is entirely constructed around the theme of return. From the start, *nostos* is the key word that resounds through the tale, to the extent that this word is repeated four times in the first twenty lines, and the very structure of the work indicates that the center, the aim of the voyages and of its hero, is only to return to Ithaca, the island of his birth and his place of origin.

Without ambiguity, Odysseus pursues "self-preservation, of returning to his homeland and fixed property. All the adventures Odysseus survives are dangerous temptations deflecting the self from the path of its logic."[20] And Horkheimer and Adorno add that "it is a yearning for the homeland which sets in motion the adventures by which subjectivity, the prehistory of which is narrated in the *Odyssey*, escapes the primeval world."[21] Once again, the principal object of Homer's work is, for them, the history of subjectivity, which seeks to establish and preserve itself, using its rationality and guile, by quickly leaving the prehistoric world of myths and launching itself towards modernity. They uphold that nostalgia,[22] "homesickness," colors the entirety of Odysseus' voyage, as much during his journey into the unknown as during his return towards the place of his birth, and they explain that all nostalgia and all regret at the loss of the original state are based on the concept of homeland.

These are the reasons why the figure of Odysseus interests these philosophers. But why examine them on the subject of Odysseus, and why dwell on this character beyond the tale of his adventures? Why open this book's reasoning with a discussion about Odysseus? What does he represent? What issues does he represent here? Furthermore, what has the hegemony of this archetype in the west made us forget in the twentieth century? And above all, how is Odysseus linked to the events that mark its history?

---

[20] *Ibid.*, 38.

[21] *Ibid.*, 60.

[22] See the analysis on the nostalgic Odysseus by Vladimir Jankélévitch, *L'irréversible et la nostalgie* (Paris: Flammarion, 1976).

THE CIRCLE OF THE SAME

A response to these questions brings us to Emmanuel Levinas who, in several texts, convincingly demonstrates that Odysseus's journey, that of his longing, is the model and foundation of thought, of the very act of thinking, and more generally, of all western philosophy and of all its metaphysics. He explains the univocity of the pattern whose prototype is Odysseus, which consists of ignorance of the Other in the identification of the Same. Thus, the preface to *Totality and Infinity* evokes a thought that is "closed in itself despite all its adventures — which in the last analysis are purely imaginary, or are adventures traversed as by Ulysses: on the way home."[23]

But is it possible to speak of a thought closed in itself? Is it not a characteristic of thought to seek what is other than itself, to open itself to what is different, to travel towards the unknown, to dive into the new? Is it an illusion to believe that thought, as an ability to know, discovers the alterity of the world? What does it mean for thought to return home? And what is thought's "home"? Thought or reason?

The first paragraphs of the essay *"La trace de l'autre"*[24] can help to answer these questions. Here Levinas considers knowledge on the basis of identification par excellence, the *ego*. Firstly, it must be said that the *ego* is "the being whose existing consists in identifying itself, in recovering its identity throughout all that happens to it,"[25] i.e. that it is identity par excellence, or that its content is identity. This is not a simple tautology, comparing the *ego* to itself and reformulating the *ego* in other terms, but rather an egoism that proclaims: "The *outside of me* is *for me*."[26] First, what is "outside of me" is the world that I feel to be foreign, and yet the first way of being me is to stay in this world, to become identified as at home there. The *ego* succeeds in transforming an initially foreign world into a habitable world, into a place where everything is at hand,

---

[23] Levinas, *Totality and Infinity: An Essay on Exteriority*, trans. Alphonso Lingis (London: Kluwer Academic Publishers, 1979), 27.

[24] Emmanuel Levinas, "The Trace of the Other," trans. Alphonso Lingis, in *Deconstruction in Context: Literature and Philosophy* (Chicago: University of Chicago Press, 1986), 345-359.

[25] Levinas, *Totality and Infinity*, 36.

[26] Levinas, "The Trace of the Other," 345.

into a house where everything belongs to it, into a country where it can do everything and possess everything. It is through this solidification of egoism, this transformation of the world into "my" place, this changing of the world's alterity into "my" world, that the *ego* becomes and recognizes itself as the Same.

Secondly, the ability to identify every object in myself and bring them back to me is due to the fact that I say *me, me ipse,* myself; all that is outside of me — that which is foreign to me, the world, the being — is encompassed in this return to me, and is embraced by my knowledge, its strangeness neutralized, without my identity being altered by it. This means that through knowledge the being, as thought's *other*, becomes the *property* of thought and the known is understood and thus acquired or possessed. In short, the Other becomes *of* the Same. Reason, in its gnoseological guise, is therefore the way in which an exteriority fits into an identified and identifying interiority; it is the connection between the Same and the Other where the Other is reduced to the Same by being deprived of its foreignness and by becoming the property of the Same. The being, the alterity of the being, is offered (in the sense of being given) for the taking, is allowed to be taken and "laid hold of" in the presence of the same. In perception, in comprehension and in the concept, knowledge is a "laying hold" of, a taking hold, an appropriation, a satisfaction, a pleasure for a selfish, "greedy and hegemonic"[27] *ego*, an *ego* that makes all being its being. However, not only does the being enter the same by becoming the subject, but it is as if every experience of the heterogeneneous, of the being's alterity, and of the *other* than being, had drawn its sense from the *ego*; in other words, as if the *ego* could explain all facts and all experience, as if the basis of sense was already in me, in short, as if sense's position of significance had always coincided with the being's adequacy to thought. Again, this adequacy or correlation between the being and thought makes it possible to say that we learn only what we already know, and that nothing new or transcendental can alter or increase the knowledge of the Same. Using Levinas's reference to Plato's *Timæus*, we can say that "the circle of the Same surrounds that

---

[27] Emmanuel Levinas, "Transcendence and Intelligibility" (1984), trans. Simon Critchley and Tamra Wright, in *Emmanuel Lévinas: Basic Philosophical Writings* (Bloomington: Indiana University Press, 1996), 152.

of the Other,"[28] and, in language astonishingly close to Adorno's, that "the circle of identification — which in the end always identifies itself alone — was drawn by a thinking that tolerates nothing outside it; its imprisonment is its own handiwork."[29]

And yet, according to Levinas, western philosophy is structured around the same circular movement of knowledge, the same process of return, because it wishes to neutralize and absorb every Other in the Same. As he writes: "Philosophy's itinerary still follows the path of Ulysses [Odysseus] whose adventure in the world was but a return to his native island — complacency in the Same, misunderstanding of the Other."[30] Western philosophy is a philosophy of the identical and the identity, and of totality, allergic to the Other that remains absolutely Other and that brings the heterogeneous back home and gives it autonomy.

In the same way, in a very important section of *Totality and Infinity*, Levinas attaches the philosophical figure of Socrates to the mythical model of Odysseus, as a symbol of western thought which progresses by identifications: "Western philosophy has most often been an ontology: a reduction of the Other to the Same by interposition of a middle and neutral term that ensures the comprehension of being. This primacy of the Same was Socrates's teaching: to receive nothing of the Other but what is in me, as though from all eternity I was in possession of what comes to me from the outside [...]. Cognition is the deployment of this identity. [...] To know amounts to grasping being out of nothing or reducing it to nothing, removing from it its alterity." And Levinas concludes: "The ideal of Socratic truth thus rests on the essential self-sufficiency of the Same, its identification in ipseity, its egoism. Philosophy is an egology."[31] Odysseus and Socrates, eminent figures in ancient Greece, can therefore be taken as the models on which western

---

[28] Levinas' quotation is imprecise. Cf. Plato, *Timæus*, trans. Benjamin Jowett (Echo Library, 2006), Volume X, 39a: "moving in the motion of the diverse, which is diagonal, and passes through and is governed by the motion of the same." Cf. also 35b, 36c, 40b.

[29] Adorno, *Negative Dialectics*, 172.

[30] Emmanuel Levinas, *Humanism of the Other*, trans. Nidra Poller (Chicago: University of Illinois Pres, 2003), 26.

[31] Levinas, *Totality and Infinity*, 43-44.

philosophy is based, and as representatives of rationality itself whose "work" consists of overcoming all alterity.

But why does Levinas, who was certainly fascinated by Plato and sufficiently influenced by his thinking to continue it and develop from it the idea of the Good beyond the Being, discuss the concept of Socratic truth? Why is Socrates brought into this discussion about the stance and workings of western philosophy? In what way is this master alleged to have failed? The answer seems clear: in his hypothesis of knowledge as *anamnesis*, Socrates showed the self-sufficiency of knowledge. Man cannot know anything new, or anything that he has not already seen, because the truth has always been there, implicit and hidden in him. We merely have to re-discover it, although this requires effort and the work of a whole lifetime. But all that is external, the alterity of all others, and of the absolutely Other as well, is reduced and returned to me in this circularity of knowing. The transcendence of the Other, transcendence as the Other, has no place in the Socratic truth.

Levinas therefore associates the figure of Socrates with that of Odysseus to make them at the same time the models of reason — and knowledge — and western philosophy. The maieutics and logic of one and the travels of the other reflect the ideal of a knowledge whose founding principle is an *ego*, i.e. a self-sufficient freedom which only knows how to return the Other to that which it has already seen and known, the expanse of ideas or the rocks of the beloved island. The *ego*, which knows how to speak in the nominative, i.e. how to say "I," reduces the distances that separate the Other and others by methods that it always has within itself, whether by using the generalization of the concept that annihilates all individuality or by extending the oppressive terror that leads a man to remain under the domination of another. The neutralization of the Other in and by the Same is violence against the Other, whether it is *other* through the alterity of things, animals or, even more, *other* through human alterity. In any event, the identifying procedure is the expression of a violent and totalizing egoism, of a power "by essence murderous of the other"[32] and of the ideal of satisfied man to whom nothing is forbidden. Thus, for Levinas, European philosophy in general is a philosophy of the being, a philosophy of identity, of autonomy, of totality, a "doctrine of absolute knowledge" and of satisfied man, a movement of return, a nostalgia, an "egology," a *logos* of the *ego*.

---

[32] *Ibid.*, 47.

The French philosopher does not stop there. Metaphysics, in its most general form, a form that it has held throughout the entire history of philosophy, is also a movement that travels this same circle. It leaves a "home" and goes towards a foreign "beyond-the-self," towards an Other in the eminent sense, towards the absolutely Other. Metaphysical desire has been interpreted as a fallen or incomplete being's need for a better world, as the consciousness of what has been lost, as the need to see the invisible, as a striving towards union, as a longing for return: "As a stage the separated being traverses on the way of its return to its metaphysical source, a moment of a history that will be concluded by union, metaphysics would be an Odyssey, and its disquietude nostalgia."[33] And the reproduction and repetition of this pattern of movement of metaphysics in Christianized western culture was primarily thanks to Plotin. Neoplatonism, which exalts the unity of the One and suggests an "understandability of return," influenced not only western philosophy, but also, through Christianity, European culture that draws its roots from that religion because it offered monotheism "an itinerary and stations capable of corresponding to mystical tastes and the needs of salvation."[34] Religious piety, therefore, follows the same itinerary of return as knowledge as such in striving in its own way to achieve unity and attempting to be one with the One.

Christianity and philosophy since antiquity both remain strongly influenced by Neoplatonism, but despite this common basis, each took a different path. For the Christian religion, the influence of Neoplatonism signified the reduction of God to Greek classification and the metamorphosis of piety into nostalgia and the need for salvation; for philosophy, it signified above all the renunciation of God's transcendence and of his inadequacy to reason: "the God of the philosophers, from Aristotle to Leibniz, by way of the God of the scholastics, is a god adequate to reason" that should not disturb the consciousness "which finds itself again in all its adventures, returning home to itself like [Odysseus], who through all his peregrinations is only on the way to his native island."[35]

---

[33] *Ibid.*, 102.

[34] Emmanuel Levinas, *Entre Nous: thinking-of-the-other*, trans. Michael B. Smith and Barbara Harshav (London: Continuum, 2006), 116.

[35] Levinas, "The Trace of the Other," 346.

Odysseus and Socrates, luminaries of Greek thought, contributed to making the myth of return one of the paradigms of western thought. Conversely, Levinas invites a line of thinking, in and by his philosophy, that imagines a movement without return, "*a movement of the same unto the other which never returns to the same*:"[36] "To the myth of [Odysseus] returning to Ithaca, we wish to oppose the story of Abraham who leaves his fatherland forever for a yet unknown land, and forbids his servant to even bring back his son to the point of departure."[37]

WHY ODYSSEUS?

As I have attempted to show, Horkheimer and Adorno, but also Levinas, through their different approaches, all address the figure of Odysseus as the prototype of modern rationality and subjectivity. Horkheimer and Adorno emphasize the aspects which make the Homerian hero not only the representative of the *ego*'s founding reason, of cold reason mastering all passions in order to ensure the preservation and fulfillment of its unity, but also the model of instrumental reason capable of dominating every situation and mastering the *other* by the most varied methods. Levinas, whose analysis goes even further, sees in this mythical figure and his circular voyage symbols of the west's way of thinking, based on ignorance of the Other in the identity of the Same and, more generally, a symbol of philosophy and one of its branches, metaphysics. In all cases, for these three philosophers, it is a modern reason, admittedly presenting various aspects but always associated with a subjectivity whose aim is its preservation.

However, what is important to me here is not to confirm how similar or different their thinking is, but to show *why* they place emphasis on Odysseus.

Without a doubt, this hero is one of the starting points for criticism, conducted in the form of a self-criticism, addressed to western philosophy and more generally to western classifications. It may be surprising that this criticism begins with a criticism of Odysseus. And yet, despite the surprise, it reveals at least two aspects that are closely linked and important to my topic. First is the need to distance oneself from an almost

---

[36] *Ibid.*, 348.//
[37] *Ibid.*

exclusively Greek source of thought and philosophy, felt particularly by Levinas. To say this does not mean to think that philosophy was born and developed in Greece — that would be tautology — but that it has not allowed any *other* voice to intervene in what it *says*. And this, in turn, not only means that philosophy has not paid attention to a different voice, in this case Jewish, but above all that it has forgotten the *other* as an object of its journey — all the philosophers agree on this — just like Odysseus, who in fact met no one during his odyssey. Secondly, criticism of Odysseus implies criticism of totality, present since the dawn of civilization and expressed by the hero's nostalgia, by his travelling in order to return, by his return voyage, and especially expressed by the totality that rejects the *other* implicit in Odysseus's reason, or in his reasons if you prefer, which share the unambiguousness of identifying modality. *Odysseus* is therefore a model of this identifying — and consequently totalizing — reason, a model of reason as domination, which places any alterity at the service of identity until it is overpowered, subdued and made identical to the self.

That is a partial answer — now another question.

Why did Horkheimer, Adorno and Levinas undertake this struggle against totality? Despite the differences in their approach — the Frankfurt School subscribing to a Marxist-inspired socio-cultural and political perspective, Levinas drawing on the philosophy of Judaism — it is a trauma rather than a theme that links them. Their thinking was marked, stigmatized and injured by the "fracture of civilization" represented by the destruction of European Jews, which was, in my opinion, the starting point for this philosophical criticism of the West in the form of a criticism of rationality and totality.

Their criticism towards western rationality and their effort to suggest reason or thought that is *other*, that goes beyond its own contents of identity and totality, and to think of the *other* in thought, the *other* as "content," no doubt arise from the painful observation of the complicity that can be established between the identifying and totalizing modality of reason on the one hand and of violence on the other. In other words, for these philosophers, the risk of violence is already present in the model of rationality which was offered to the west after centuries of the history of philosophy and through Christianity and the Enlightenment to the extent that Horkheimer and Adorno were able to write, in a highly provocative and extreme manner, that "[e]nlightenment is totalitarian"[38] and that it "stands in the same relationship to things as the dictator to human beings. He knows them to the extent that he can manipulate them."[39]

If, then, the seed of the totalizing (violent, not to mention totalitarian) temptation is present in reason, whether it is the reason of the *Aufklärer* or the very structure of knowledge — if, then, there is a possibility of even just *one* inhuman version of reason, it is *at least* justifiable that philosophers who experienced Nazi persecution during their lives as intellectuals of Jewish origin would explore the potential contamination by violence and investigate it down to its "marrow." Their effort, and mine, to understand, or even explain, starting from its dawn, how even the most advanced civilization can produce and spawn barbarity, and Enlightenment can deteriorate into darkness, is therefore justifiable.

---

[38] Horkheimer and Adorno, *Dialectic of Enlightenment*, 4.

[39] *Ibid.*, 6.

Chapter I

Facing Behemoth

"In the Jewish eschatology—of Babylonian origin—Behemoth and Leviathan designate two monsters, Behemoth ruling the land (the desert), Leviathan the sea. The land animals venerate Behemoth, the sea animals Leviathan, as their masters. Both are monsters of the Chaos. [...] It was Hobbes who made both the Leviathan and the Behemoth popular. [...] His *Behemoth* [...] depicts a non-state, a chaos, a situation of lawlessness, disorder and anarchy. Since we believe National Socialism is—or tending to become—a non-state, a chaos, a rule of lawlessness and anarchy, which has 'swallowed' the rights and dignity of man, and is out to transform the world into a chaos by the supremacy of gigantic land masses, we find it apt to call the National Socialist system: *The Behemoth*.

Franz Neumann

"We were all possessed, so to speak, of the idea we must beat Hitler and fascism, and this brought us all together. That included all the secretaries and all coming to the Institut and working there. This mission really gave us a feeling of loyalty and belonging together."[1] Horkheimer's secretary in New York, Alice Maier, thus recognized intellectual solidarity in the struggle against fascism by the members of what we now call the Frankfurt School as a priority for the members of the Institute of Social Sciences, which moved from Frankfurt to New York in 1934 following Hitler's rise to power. It was a solidarity that took shape at the end of the 1930s and the start of the 1940s, and whose coherence, or unilaterality, is difficult to demonstrate as the group moved through a strange and wide collection of interpretations of National Socialism and anti-Semitism. Differences between stances, which had already been marked since the start of the period of American exile, were very strongly accentuated by the arrival of new recruits in New York, but what connected them — the necessity of fighting against Nazism — remained unchanged.

Horkheimer confirmed this in an interview given shortly after the death of his friend and colleague Adorno, in 1969: "I believed that National Socialism could only be eliminated by a revolution, a Marxist revolution. My Marxism, being revolutionary, was a response to the tyranny of right-wing totalitarianism."[2] The first critical theory might have

---

[1] Martin Jay, *Dialectical Imagination. A History of the Frankfurt School and the Institute of Social Research, 1923-1950* (Boston: Little, Brown, 1973), 143.

[2] Max Horkheimer, *Die Sehnsucht nach dem ganz Anderen. Ein Interview mit Kommentar von Helmuth Gumnior* (Hamburg: Furche-Verlag, 1970), 54.

lost its "revolutionary" fervor, but Horkheimer continued to identify the goal pursued by he himself and the group surrounding him as a single and identical one — that of fighting against the "tyranny of right-wing totalitarianism."

However, it must be noted that several members of the Institute, primarily his *spiritus rector*, found it difficult to grasp the threat that bore down specifically on European Jews. Indeed, Horkheimer attributed the closure of the Frankfurt Institute in 1933 to its Marxist orientation, and not to the exclusively Jewish origins of its members. It was not until several years after the Institute's move to the United States that its members arrived at an analysis of anti-Semitism linked to the specificity of Nazism, and overcame their "ideological" reticence. In 1939, in an article nonetheless entitled *"The Jews and Europe"* (*"Die Juden und Europa"*), Horkheimer once again gave an analysis of German anti-Semitism that was interpreted in the general category of the crisis of liberal capitalism and categorized as "State capitalism"!

However, despite its limits, this text by Horkheimer marks the start of a crucial period, during which the Institute made an important change. As German troops achieved dazzling successes, and violence against Jews increased, anti-Semitism became a central theme of research for the Institute of Social Sciences — and would remain so until the end of the decade. In 1941, the journal *Studies in Philosophy and Social Science* published the *"Research Project on Anti-Semitism,"* with contributions from various authors, including Otto Kirchheimer; in 1942, Horkheimer's essay, *"The Authoritarian State,"* appeared, as well as the first edition of Franz Neumann's book, *Behemoth: The Structure and Practice of National Socialism*, which provoked a veritable internal conflict; in 1944, Adorno published *"Anti-Semitism and Fascist Propaganda,"* and, in collaboration with Horkheimer and Leo Löwenthal (at least partially), wrote the chapter "Elements of Anti-Semitism: Limits of Enlightenment," which would later be included in *Dialectic of Enlightenment*. Dating from the same period is also the ambitious program *Studies in Prejudice,* published between 1949 and 1950, which comprised a volume by Paul Massing, *Rehearsal for Destruction;* another volume written by Leo Löwenthal and Norbert Guterman, *Prophets of Deceit*; and the better-known *The Authoritarian Personality*, written by Adorno and three members of the Berkeley Public Opinion Study Group, where anti-Semitism was the starting point for research into the typology of the authoritarian personality.

As these bibliographic notes illustrate, the question of anti-Semitism was therefore gradually accorded a key position by the Institute. More importantly, it was imposed with such force that it compelled its members to abandon their doctrinal lines and Marxist categorization, and consequently to no longer consider anti-Semitism purely as a by-product of the capitalist crisis. Confronted with "real" anti-Semitism, the Frankfurt School members exiled in America, starting with Horkheimer, moved away from Hegelian-Marxist *theory* as and when the concentration and extermination camps were discovered. Before Hitler, left-wing German intellectuals (including Jews) were all convinced that "the more radical the Marxist, the less interested in the specificity of the Jewish question."[3] After the discovery of the gas chambers, Horkheimer broke ranks and entirely reclaimed the uniqueness and specificity of the "Jewish question," as if the effect of this discovery was to undermine all categorization and allow the question to be tackled from a closer, more "subjective" and unique point of view where the Jewishness of the author and certain premises of Judaism were drawn together, investigated and discussed under a never-ending strain and anxiety that became increasingly explicit over the years.

I. THE JEWS, A PROBLEM IN HORKHEIMER'S ANALYSIS OF ANTI-SEMITISM

Being unable to follow the developments and differences in the Institute members' interpretation of National Socialism and anti-Semitism, and leaving aside the dispute over National Socialism and "State capitalism" which had Horkheimer, Friedrich Pollock and the inner circle on one side and Neumann and the "new recruits" on the other,[4] it is preferable

---

[3] Martin Jay, "The Jews and the Frankfurt School: Critical Theory's Analysis on Anti-Semitism," in Jay M. Bernstein, *The Frankfurt School: Critical Assessments*, vol. 6 (New York & London: Routledge, 1994), 236.

[4] On the subject of this dispute, see Jay, *Dialectical Imagination*, 152-158 and 165-168. Cf also chapter 4.4, "Disputes on the theory of National Socialism," in Rolf Wiggershaus, *The Frankfurt School: Its History, Theories and Political Significance*, trans. Michael Robertson (Cambridge: MIT, 1995).

to immediately consider Horkheimer's article *"The Jews and Europe."* This article is in fact one of Horkheimer's last "predominantly Marxist"[5] essays, and one which appeared quite limited in the eyes of those who were expecting an analysis of anti-Semitism relating to the historical situation of the rise of Nazism and the persecution of German Jews already underway while it was being written. But as the French translator says, "despite its limits, this text, written in 1939 by an exiled Jew, remains an extraordinary *testimony* to the fear of those who were still vaguely becoming aware that fascism was signing their death warrant. The eyes of the survivors were not opened until 1945, when the death camps were seen"[6]. The irony of history means that this growing awareness, sensed through fear, was coupled with the difficulty of understanding the nature of Nazi anti-Semitism, which in Horkheimer's eyes is explained solely by the Marxist framework's economic classifications, which remain partial and yet do not completely invalidate "the urgent writing of a man determined to promote clarity." Horkheimer himself realized the limits of this article and initially decided not to include it in the anthology entitled *Critical Theory*. Nevertheless, he continued his research and directed that of his colleagues until the attempt to explain anti-Semitism in the chapter dedicated to it in *Dialectic of Enlightenment,* a book whose clarity condenses all the power of critical theory.

"Whoever wants to explain anti-Semitism must speak of National Socialism. Without a conception of what has happened in Germany, speaking about anti-Semitism in Siam or Africa remains senseless. The new anti-Semitism is the emissary of the totalitarian order, which has developed from the liberal one,"[7] begins the article *"The Jews and Europe."* If the title leads us to expect that attention will be paid to the fate of European Jews after the promulgation of racial laws in 1935 and at least to the fate of Jews in Europe, the premise also leads us to

---

[5] Jay, *Dialectical Imagination*, 329.

[6] Max Horkheimer, "Pourquoi le fascisme?" (*"Die Juden und Europa"*), French trans. and introduction Jean-Louis Schlegel, *Esprit*, no. 5 (1979): 62.

[7] Max Horkheimer, "The Jews and Europe" in *Critical Theory and Society—A Reader*, trans. Mark Ritter (New York & London: Routledge, 1989), 77.

think that anti-Semitism will be considered in relation to the situation in Nazi Germany. But this beginning immediately changes direction when another condition narrows the field of analysis: "[W]hoever is not willing to talk about capitalism should also keep quiet about fascism." Here the terms "fascism," "National Socialism," and "totalitarianism" are not differentiated, and the question is connected to an analysis of capitalism, specifically German capitalism, where Jews are relegated to the sphere of monetary circulation. The text's logic, associating anti-Semitism with Nazism/fascism and the latter with capitalism, merely follows an analysis of the process that pushed Germany to "absurdity" in the totalitarian order through the *leitmotif* of capitalism, which becomes the real object of this article where the initial question is carried over into the final paragraphs.

In sum, Horkheimer's reasoning, very close to that of Pollock, is that totalitarian order is nothing more than a liberal system without any brakes, or, if you prefer, an exacerbation of liberalism, even if it recognizes a different degree of oppression and dehumanization for productive forces, a degree "which leads to the annihilation of the humane."[8] But according to the philosopher, "this only continues a process that had already assumed a catastrophic dimension." National socialism only releases the brakes that held back the liberal-capitalist phase, producing new forces where the individual loses his false securities, where the masses are transformed into a powerful tool, where all of culture's lies are obvious and useless, where bureaucracy has the right of life and death, where the state's reason is the final, definitive reason, and where "fear of unemployment is supplanted by fear of the state." And yet, in this new form of an old "vice," Jews are susceptible to persecution because they control the sphere of monetary circulation, which, in the new order, passes into the direct control of the ruling class. In this discussion, attention on anti-Semitic measures in Germany is therefore completely brushed aside and anti-Semitism is reduced to an attempt to destroy those who control the sphere of monetary circulation, i.e. the Jews are relegated solely to the economic function: "The Jews are stripped of power as agents of circulation, because the modern structure of the economy largely puts that whole sphere out of action. They are the first victims of the ruling group that has taken over the canceled function. The governmental manipulation of money, which already has robbery

---

8   *Ibid.*, 88.

as its necessary function, turns into the brutal manipulation of money's representatives."⁹

Although some allusions are made to the "desperate situation" of those who must cross borders and go into exile, to "today's refugees," Horkheimer speaks of "dominant classes" and of "victims of social injustice" experienced by both Gentiles and Jews, and his point verges on the absurd when he writes that "probably those affected are not so innocent after all."¹⁰ Here, then, the presumed culpability of the victims, the Jews, is once again recognized in their complicity with the liberal "class." Moreover, the National Socialist plan is clear to Horkheimer: to throw what remains of German Judaism in with the *Lumpenproletariat*, in other words to proletarianize its representatives, to isolate them, to arouse competitiveness against them among the workers (the other "inferiors") — in short, to provoke "the vague, aimless hate of the crowd."

The philosopher thus creates a twofold simplification, with regard to anti-Semitism and with regard to the Jews, as Gershom Scholem highlighted in his severe criticism of this article.¹¹ Scholem's criticism was in the form of a response to Benjamin, who, for his part, seemed to appreciate it. According to Scholem, Horkheimer's text shows that he has no interest in the Jewish question and that his model was still Marx's text, *On the Jewish Question*. The author does not ask what will be Europe's fate once the Jews have been completely driven away or annihilated, and he verges on the grotesque when he writes that "the pogroms are aimed politically more at the spectators"¹² and that anti-Semitism is a question of propaganda particularly addressed to people abroad. Scholem is very severe, insisting that "dialectics is prostituted" through Horkheimer's shameless instrumentalization of the question, and "this *Jew*" is therefore the last person that one could ask for an analysis of the situation, and whose final words of encouragement, addressed specifically to the Jews facing the Second World War, make one feel, as a Jew, "*ratlos wie Geisterrede* [disconsolate like spectral speech]."¹³ However, Scholem did

---

9   *Ibid.*, 90.

10 *Ibid.*

11 Gershom Scholem, *Walter Benjamin: Story of a Friendship*, trans. Harry Zohn (New York: New York Review Books, 2003), 278-280.

12 Horkheimer, "The Jews and Europe," 92.

13 Scholem, *op. cit.*, 279-280.

recognize that *after* the massacre perpetrated against millions of Jews, *after* the Annihilation, Horkheimer clearly changed his position with regards to the question.

Alongside this criticism by Scholem — with whom I agree, though I do not share his severity — we can add that a similar limit consists of making anti-Semitism a historical phase which will have a natural end and thinking that in Germany it is only "a valve" for the young people in the SA. However, it seems to me that Horkheimer demonstrates a certain concern, or even intuition, almost imperceptible in its clumsy blindness due to certain ideological simplifications, when he speaks of the "reproduction of inhumanity."[14] This "reproduction of inhumanity" confirms that old humanity, religion and all liberal ideology have no value; that all their values, including the concept of humanity, are nothing but a false ideology where "the individual is ruthlessly sacrificed." In this state of "confusion," of disillusion and of "defeat," Horkheimer finally appeals to intellectuals, to the demands of their theoretical reflection, to resistance, to the necessity of thought and its dissemination. At the same time, in this appeal, he takes the Jewish faith as a model, in the sense of the age-old rejection of idols, which now obliges them not to give in to the Idol or the Beast, and to dedicate themselves — as intellectuals or as Jews? — "to something better." "The Jews were once proud of abstract monotheism, their rejection of idolatry, their refusal to make something finite an absolute. Their distress today points them back. Disrespect for anything mortal that puffs itself up as a god is the religion of those who cannot resist devoting their life to something better, even in the Europe of the Iron Heel."[15]

But was this appeal, dependent on resisting Behemoth, sufficient to give hope to the Jews already persecuted, hunted down, exiled and soon to be exposed to the Annihilation?

This interpretation of anti-Semitism is continued, but also exceeded, in another essay, "*The Authoritarian State*," written in 1940 and circulated among the members of the Institute in 1942 in a thin publication in homage to Walter Benjamin. In this, Horkheimer speaks explicitly of "state capitalism" as a successive phase to monopoly capitalism, which led to a new order: "the authoritarian state of the present," that is, "a

---

[14] Horkheimer, "The Jews and Europe," 92.

[15] *Ibid.*, 94.

new breathing space for domination." His analysis of fascism moves a little away from the orthodox Marxism still present in "*The Jews and Europe*," as here the idea of fascism as "state capitalism" is coupled with a criticism of the technological and bureaucratic rationality that can be applied to "socialism" just as much as "fascism." "State capitalism is the authoritarian state of the present,"[16] writes the author, because it emerges as the most consistent expression of what bourgeois society can offer, i.e. the appropriation of production bodies and control of the economic mechanism by the State. And yet, the most consistent form of the authoritarian State, according to Horkheimer, is "full government control or state socialism," as embodied by the Soviet Union. But "state socialism," or bolshevism, and "fascism" are only two different forms of "state capitalism" in its new form as the "authoritarian state." The first is "the most consistent form" and the second, specific to fascist countries, is a "mixed form." In these two cases, the authoritarian structure of society based on monopolies is accentuated and produces characteristics of the totalitarian system. "State socialism" and "fascism" are in fact based on the bureaucratization of power, on mass parties, on rigidity of thought, on technical rationalization and on the domination of consciousnesses exercised by the leader's charisma, the police system, terror and purges. What makes the authoritarian state so powerful is not only the psychological submission implied by the authoritarian personality, although this plays an essential role, but primarily the permanent use of terror and coercion. "The authoritarian state" is repressive in all its forms, as humanity "is thoroughly educated and mutilated" by it. At first its victims are targeted and selected, then later "the selection for the concentration camps becomes more and more arbitrary. […] In principle anyone could be there."[17]

Beyond the fact that the most radical expression of what might be called "a 'Luxemburgist' or syndicalist strain in Critical Theory"[18] can be found in this text, and beyond its catastrophic utopian tone that is very close to Benjamin's — for social revolution can be achieved not

---

[16] Max Horkheimer, "The Authoritarian State," in *The Essential Frankfurt School Reader*, trans. The People's Translation Service, Berkeley (New York: Continuum International, 1982), 95-117. Here 96.

[17] *Ibid.*, 103.

[18] Jay, *Dialectical Imagination*, 158.

by an acceleration of progress but by a leap beyond all progress[19] — there remains the question of what place should be granted by the author to the "victims" of the authoritarian state, and especially to the victims of German fascism. Indeed, if on the one hand we understand that the question of racial persecution, of violence and of internment in concentration camps is once again not tackled explicitly or in depth since the selection of victims is considered to be arbitrary, on the other hand it can be noted that the question is paid more specific attention towards the end of the essay, although the reader is still left wanting. Horkheimer seems to have changed his stance compared to the 1939 article. Here, in fact, he distances himself from views which support "state capitalism" as the only solution possible for the historic present and maintains that "it would be sentimental to remain opposed to state capitalism merely because of those who have been slain. One could say that the Jews were for the most part capitalists."[20] Horkheimer seems to accept this rejection of state capitalism "because of its victims," and here they are at least recognized, albeit obliquely and negatively, in their singularity as Jewish victims. The Marxist idea previously held, relegating the Jews to the sphere of monetary circulation, no longer seems to apply, at least not as the sole means of interpretation. On the other hand, he recognizes that such arguments rest on the polarized schema according to which the course of history is decided between progress and regression, and where the victims — all the victims of history, this time — are always considered as "social magnitudes" or as "commodities." And, he concludes: "as long as world history follows its logical course, it fails to fulfill its human destiny."[21] Here there is a progression in the interpretation of historical events and the specificity of the Jewish question, at the same time as affirmation of an anti-Hegelian philosophy of history. But the distinctive and interesting feature in this text is the fact that it shows a tension, particularly at the end — the author's vacillation between considering the singularity and specificity of the persecution of the Jews and, at the same time, the universality of the suffering of victims in history. It reveals a tension, a difficult duality to which the author finds no solution, swinging between considering the Jews as the main victims

---

[19] Cf. *infra* Chapter II, I, 1.

[20] Horkheimer, "The Authoritarian State," 117.

[21] *Ibid.*

of national socialism and as victims in their singularity and collective particularity as Jews, on the one hand, and on the other, considering them as victims as part of the universality of the victims of history, even if they are victims of social injustice. It is as if Horkheimer, vacillating in this tension between a singularist and universalist position, was not yet able to really grasp the term "Jews." It was only *afterwards, after* the "real" destruction of the Jews of Europe that Horkheimer eliminated the conceptual-metaphorical sense of "Jews" from his analysis and saw them as singular persons, singularly stigmatized.

II. ANTI-SEMITISM: A PRODUCT OF CIVILIZATION, ACCORDING TO HORKHEIMER AND ADORNO

Horkheimer and Adorno achieve a more profound analysis of anti-Semitism in *Dialectic of Enlightenment*, written between 1944 and 1945, and published in 1947. In particular, the chapter dedicated to anti-Semitism[22] shows that the authors are not interested in the reactions of anti-Semites, but — as the introduction points out and I have already highlighted — in considering "the reversion of enlightened civilization to barbarism."[23] They confront and encounter the difficulty of understanding the link between this aptitude for the domination of reason and anti-Semitism as the "limits of Enlightenment." In the days of triumphant anti-Semitism, during the great persecutions that devastated Europe, these authors attempted to identify, perhaps without completely succeeding, the complicity whereby "anti-Semitism and totality have always been profoundly connected"[24] and a "tendency toward self-destruction has been inherent in rationality from the first."[25] This tendency is visibly and concretely present in the midst of the period's darkness.

The authors speak explicitly of "extermination," of the desire to "exterminate them like vermin," of "persecution of the Jews," of "mass murder," of "universal murder," of "gas factories," of the "gas

---

[22] Horkheimer and Adorno, *Dialectic of Enlightenment*, 137-172.

[23] *Ibid.*, xix.

[24] *Ibid.*, 140-141.

[25] *Ibid.*, xix.

chambers,"[26] to the extent that it could even be said that the discovery of the death camps was what gave impetus to the whole book and to this chapter in particular. But their style is bereft of pathos. There is only a troubled clarity, an unsatisfied desire to make sense of events, a philosophical and rational exploration appealing to reason and to the necessity of understanding that "the Jewish question" is the "turning-point of history."[27]

Straight away, the title of the chapter "Elements of Anti-Semitism: Limits of Enlightenment," indicates that the interpretation will be non-exhaustive. The authors do not aim to offer a complete panorama, nor to write a history of anti-Semitism, but more simply, or perhaps more difficultly, to outline a "philosophical prehistory of anti-Semitism" — in other words, to highlight some of the elements and features that played a fundamental role in its birth, its reiteration and its growth. It is entirely possible that this is an attempt at comprehension using the means that these philosophers had at their disposal or that they were most familiar with, thanks to empirical research and theoretical work by others associated with the Institute. Their attempt is desperate and lucid at the same time, stemming from the urgent need to interpret historical events, to see the irrationalism of anti-Semitism as directly derived from "the nature of the dominant reason and of the world corresponding to its image,"[28] to consider "universal murder"[29] as being "already latent" in the history of civilization and also to recognize present or future versions in certain ways of thinking, such as "ticket thinking."[30]

Made up of analytical elements and propositions, this long chapter is daunting in its complexity and obscurity. Although the structure appears simple, as each paragraph corresponds to one interpretation of anti-Semitism, the reasoning is sometimes tangled. The questions raised in each section are often resolved in the following section or left open. There is therefore no shortage of contradictions, and the internal logic is difficult to identify. However, its difficulty, not to mention opacity, its limitations, are a strong indication — a *testimony* — of the difficulty in

---

[26] *Ibid.*, 137, 137, 139, 160, 166, 171 and 167 respectively.

[27] *Ibid.*, 165.

[28] *Ibid.*, xix.

[29] *Ibid.*, 166.

[30] Cf. *infra*.

understanding the object of investigation by a single logic. Multiplicity, on the other hand, is expressly required.

After dealing with the two opposing theories of the time, fascist and liberal, on what "Jews" are, Horkheimer and Adorno move on to an interpretation of anti-Semitism as a national populist movement. Why does anti-Semitism affect the masses so easily? First, the authors reject the possibility that this is due to an economic reason; then they rely on the idea that economic marginalization makes anti-Semitism even more fascinating to the masses. A real benefit for the masses is that it "does not help men but assuages their urge to destroy," with the result that their "rage will be sanctioned by the collective."[31] There is something obscure in their destructive hate, a "primeval-historical entrapment" that remains impenetrable and is neither controllable nor neutralizable by means of knowledge or reason. Purely rational, economic or political arguments are insufficient to explain it because "rationality itself, through its link to power, is submerged in the same malady" and because anti-Semitism is truly a "ritual of civilization," and pogroms "ritual murders" where the victims are necessarily "unprotected," where hate cannot be relaxed because there is no "fulfillment," where the persecutors are moved by a sort of "dynamic idealism," and where the rational part is completely overwhelmed and blinded. The root of this destructive hate seems to be the idea of happiness. Hate is directed against those whom the masses perceive as enjoying a happiness of which they are deprived: "the banker and the intellectual, money and mind, the exponents of circulation, are the disowned wishful image of those mutilated by power, an image which power uses to perpetuate itself."[32]

This analysis cannot be understood unless we keep in mind the work's *leitmotif* about the process of civilization as the process of domination, where the necessity of dominating external nature requires the domination of internal nature. In other words, anti-Semitism is interpreted here as a violent and destructive form of resentment over the renunciations imposed by civilization, from which the Jews would have been exempt as they still enjoyed an absolute happiness associated with power and expressed by the possession of money or intelligence. The archaic and indistinct impulses that civilization has suppressed re-emerge in destructive hate, and they re-emerge through the ancestral *topoi*

---

[31] *Ibid.*, 139.

[32] *Ibid.*, 141.

of ritual sacrifice and conspiracy, or through the more "sophisticated" *topoi* of an innate Jewish disposition towards intellectual work and their exemption from physical productive work, allowing them to devote themselves to luxury, the pleasures of sensuality and gilded living, and the splendor of money. Anti-Semitism is thus interpreted and inserted into the logic of the domination-repression-domination process of enlightened western civilization.

Alongside more classical interpretations, such as those of religious anti-Semitism and bourgeois anti-Semitism — here the Jews are no longer the agents of the sphere of monetary circulation, but they are the symbols of it, the *"bête noire"* of the petty bourgeoisie downgraded by capitalism and "the bad conscience of the parasite"[33] — Adorno and Horkheimer introduce two concepts from Freudian psychology and psychoanalysis which give an original nuance to their interpretation: *mimesis* and projection. *Mimesis* is physical adaptation to the surrounding environment which, being unable to express itself as an uncontrolled biological stimulus, is transformed, in an era of civilization, into a principle of identification with the "outside" or the "enemy." During this transformation, the mimetic reflex is transmuted into controlled reflection, that is, into "recognition in a concept," into "the *subsuming of difference under sameness.*"[34] As to projection, or false projection, it "makes its surroundings resemble itself," and it is this mechanism that allows impulses or tendencies suppressed inside the individual to be attributed to the outside world and, once overthrown, to be finally attributed to the potential victim. Here, these philosophers attempt to show how much this behavior is made political in fascism, and above all that *"the mechanism which the totalitarian order takes into its service is as old as civilization."*[35]

Next there is paranoid projection, traces of which can be found not only in the taboo impulse converted into aggression, but also in the objectivizing cognitive process. Here the philosophers add an epistemological dimension (which I feel is more interesting) to a purely psycho-analytical interpretation. Wherever intellectual energies are concentrated on the external world, they explain, "wherever it is a matter of pursuing, ascertaining, grasping — of exerting those functions which

---

[33] *Ibid.*, 144.

[34] *Ibid.*, 148 [my emphasis].

[35] *Ibid.*, 154 [my emphasis].

have been sublimated [...] into the scientific methods of controlling nature," we inflict violence on it. Objectifying thought, which contains "the arbitrariness of a subjective purpose,"[36] exercises the subject's purpose on the object, on the external thing, and thus forgets the thing itself, committing violence against it in the act of knowledge[37] even before doing so in practice.

But where is anti-Semitism in this consideration? The authors seem to place it at the end of a process that is social, psychological and philosophical at the same time; a process that took shape in the dialectic of the Enlightenment itself and culminated in totalitarian order. And yet, in this process, the Jews seem "predestined" to attract projection: "no matter what the makeup of the Jews may be in reality, their image, that of the defeated, has characteristics which must make totalitarian rule their mortal enemy: happiness without power, reward without work, a homeland without frontiers, religion without myth."[38] Put another way, the characteristics that the Jews embody are rejected by totalitarian domination because, deep down, anti-Semites — dominated, manipulated and subjugated themselves, first by the domination of nature, then by the domination of civilization and finally by totalitarian terror — secretly aspire to them and "turn what they yearn for into an object of hate." Projection therefore plays a fundamental role in this metamorphosis from object of desire to object of hate, as the "ruled" achieve it thanks to this fusion: "hatred leads to union with the object — in destruction."[39] Anti-Semites therefore turn the world into the hell they have always suffered.

Without a doubt, these few reference points that I have tried to establish show a richness, albeit with limits, in this interpretation of anti-Semitism compared to the one previously proposed by Horkheimer, but above all they reveal a deep tension between two positions assumed by the authors: on the one hand, the interchangeability of the victims of destructive hate, and on the other, the specificity of the Jews as an incarnation of what is hated by the masses who cannot acquire it. Thus, when the philosophers speak of persecuting hatred mobilized by

---

[36] *Ibid.*, 159.
[37] Cf. *supra*, Prelude.
[38] *Ibid.*, 164-165.
[39] *Ibid.*, 165.

anti-Semitism, they draw attention to the fact that it is not specifically targeted at a single category of people, and that other victims[40] can also become the object of it or, even worse, be transformed into subjects of persecution. In this sense, anti-Semitism is a type of hatred directed against the weak and "defenseless" from which no one is excluded; a hate which can emerge from a particular constellation of circumstances. When the authors consider the deep impulses rallied by anti-Semitic practices, they assert that the Jews are not the only possible victims and, in addition, by introducing the psychological concepts of *mimesis*, projection and paranoia, they reduce the specificity of anti-Semitism as hate directed exclusively against the Jews.

Furthermore, they concentrate their reasoning on explaining this hate by referring to the characteristics considered to be typically Jewish, i.e. those which the Jews have always seemed to embody, or which anti-Semites have always wanted to attribute to them. Consequently there is a dual fluctuation in the text: one, already highlighted, between the interchangeability of victims and specificity of "Jewish" characteristics; the other, within this second aspect, between a certain correspondence between the "history" of the Jewish people and the way it is perceived by the anti-Semitic ideology on the one hand, and on the other, the fact that the elements considered to be "Jewish" are only the result of projection. In this sense, Horkheimer and Adorno seem to construct the hypothesis that the "history" of the Jewish people — their role in capitalism, monotheism, intellectual disciplines, their rejection of idolatry — forms the basis for the development of anti-Semitic ideology, and at the same time, they seem to attribute it to a false projection.

Although it is difficult to fully understand the reasons for these fluctuations other than the extreme difficulty of the subject, it is clear that they cannot be attributed to the absence of a historical or sociological interpretation of anti-Semitism. While it is true that the authors make the distinction, though allusively, between modern and contemporary anti-Semitism only at the start of the last paragraph, this partial historical perspective adds nothing to their aim: to analyze anti-Semitism as a structure within which the different elements belong to diverse constellations, yet share the fact that they are implications of, in being reactions to, the process of civilization.

---

[40] Cf. *ibid.*, 140, 157, 171.

These uncertainties also show that the authors face the requirement of maintaining the alternation between the singularist and universalist view of anti-Semitism. Indeed, though in a different form, a similar tension to that which already cropped up in Horkheimer's text is revealed here between a singularist interpretation of anti-Semitism (where the Jews would be victims par excellence in their singularity and collective particularity of being Jews, though without being reduced to a scapegoat theory) and a universalist interpretation which attempts to formulate a general — universal — theory of hatred mobilized by and in anti-Semitism. However, in this second interpretation, the very concept of anti-Semitism is at risk of becoming ambiguous and taking on the role of a signifier that can refer to all persecution of the weak and thus signify a decline in the domination exercised "on all the persecuted, whether animals or human beings."[41]

Nevertheless, without being a drawback, is this risk not also a challenge, an interpretative opportunity in the analysis of anti-Semitism proposed by Horkheimer and Adorno? An analysis which has the audacity to think that anti-Semitism has "ceased to be an independent impulse," that it has become a turn of thought, implicit in all "stereotyped thinking" and "ticket thinking"?[42] That all anti-Semitism is lying dormant in "the loss of subjective experience," in "the indifference to the individual," in forgetting "the human being as person" as a singular person?

In the last paragraph, added in 1947, they write: "If, even within the field of logic, the concept stands opposed to the particular as something merely external, anything which stands for *difference within society itself must indeed tremble.* Everyone is labeled friend or foe [....] Ethnic groups are transported to different latitudes; individuals labeled 'Jew' are dispatched to the gas chambers."[43] So at the end of this long chapter, the philosophers seem to want to emphasize that anti-Semitism is a product of the dialectic of Enlightenment (*Aufklärung*) in its compound movement (domination suffered–resentment–domination inflicted); a characteristic of reason itself that good logic can lead to in its predilection for the identical and the universal; and particularly in these pages, a product of "stereotyped" or "ticket" thinking characterized by the fact that the

---

[41] *Ibid.*, 165.
[42] *Ibid.*, 170.
[43] *Ibid.*, 167. [my emphasis]

singularity of the individual — every decision, awareness, experience, thought, in a word the subjective in each person — is lost in the jumble and density of "stereotypes" or "tickets."[44] In short, at the end of this long excursus on the "elements of anti-Semitism," the reader can conclude that anti-Semitism does not arise from a reaction to something specifically Jewish, nor is it a characteristic of just "the anti-Semitic ticket," but of "the ticket mentality itself. The rage against *difference* is teleologically inherent in that mentality,"[45] and in being expressed as the resentment of the subjects dominated and subjugated by the process of civilization, it prepares to attack every minority, whether natural or social.

Anti-Semitism is therefore a product of civilization that even "reason" (the Enlightenment) in full possession of itself could not break, and the contents of the fascist program are a "blatant but insistent lie" which continues to blind all "ability to exercise judgment"[46] today, in our industrialized, bureaucratized, technological, conformist and leveled modernity.

III. HITLERISM: PAGANISM ACCORDING TO LEVINAS

Levinas's reflections on Hitlerism and on anti-Semitism took on a very different tone to Horkheimer's reflections on "fascism" and the "authoritarian State" and to Horkheimer's reflections on anti-Semitism with Adorno. This different tone is due to the different source and school that these authors draw on, and highlights not only a thematic difference, but also a quite important temporal gap between the analyses developed by one as early as the 1930s, and by the others during the 1940s.

Written in 1933, almost at the same moment as Hitler took power, *"Reflections on the Philosophy of Hitlerism"* is the only text where Levinas explicitly tackles this event, and one of the first to respond — in a sort of "return-to-sender," to use the words of Miguel Abensour who

---

[44] The sense of the "ticket mentality" evokes the electoral voting system where a list is imposed on the names of the candidates and where the voters have only to choose between already established groupings.

[45] *Ibid.*, 172.

[46] *Ibid.*, 167.

commented on this essay[47] — to Heidegger and his discourse on "The Self Assertion of the German University" (27 May 1933). Far from being an analysis of the "philosophy" of the Nazis, and also far from the sociopsycho-political approach of the Frankfurt School, Levinas analyses the phenomenon of "Hitlerism" from a philosophical point of view and following a phenomenological technique where the use of this term indicates distancing from the political event, and where the "*ism*" does not constitute an ideologization of Hitler's thinking, but rather the collective dimension of the phenomenon.

Likewise, in the other texts, in the reports or opinion articles which appeared in the journal *Paix et Droit* (the voice of the *Alliance Israélite Universelle*), collected and introduced by Catherine Chalier under the title "Epreuves d'une pensée,"[48] Levinas's approach to Hitlerism and anti-Semitism, far from being a socio-political analysis, is absolutely philosophical as it aims to discover the deepest and most concrete roots of the phenomenon through the ideas for which it is a mouthpiece. Furthermore, these texts reveal, in Chalier's words, that "faced with the threat of a barbarity devoted to the cult of power and to the legitimacy of its development in the being, Levinas realized the urgent need to consider Judaism in its irreducible opposition to paganism, not in order to rebut Nazism — it is unworthy of that — but to remove some of its foundations."[49] In other words, in these texts, which sometimes are very short and do not directly deal with anti-Semitism, particular attention is placed on what is specific to Judaism in its opposition to Hitlerism and its derivatives, a specificity that appears in the "being-foreign-to-the-world" and goes against the "radical inability to escape from the world"[50] in Hitlerism, which coincides with paganism in this respect.

Based on the opposition between Judaism and paganism, I will attempt to compare these texts to show this philosopher's alarm at and

---

[47] Miguel Abensour, "Le Mal elemental," in *Quelques réflexions sur la philosophie de l'hitlérisme* (Paris: Payot et Rivages, 1997), 32.

[48] Emmanuel Levinas, "Epreuves d'une pensée (1935-1939)," in *Levinas, Cahier de l'Herne*, edited by Catherine Chalier and Miguel Abensour (Paris: L'Herne, 1991), 142-152 [these texts are cited as a whole].

[49] Catherine Chalier, *Introduction* to texts by Levinas (1935-1939), in *Levinas, op. cit.* 139.

[50] Levinas, "Epreuves d'une pensée," 144.

growing awareness of the constraints of Behemoth and the excitement of the "worshippers of Thor,"[51] along with his efforts to understand the role or the fate of Judaism challenged by Hitlerism. And while "the truly philosophical aspect of a philosophy is measured by its actuality" and consists of "merging with current preoccupations,"[52] as Levinas says, it is undeniable that this task is rightfully accomplished by his own philosophy, which was pitted against events while the threats towards German Jews were on the point of unfolding in all their violence.

"The philosophy of Hitler is simplistic [*primaire*]. But the primitive powers that burn within it burst open its wretched phraseology under the pressure of an elementary force. They awaken the secret nostalgia within the German soul. Hitlerism is more than a contagion or a madness; it is an awakening of elementary feelings."[53] Thus begins the article on Hitlerism. While attention to feelings by a good phenomenologist is justified because feelings hold intentionality and always reveal "something," here these feelings that are interpreted as "elementary" conceal "a philosophy." They reveal the primacy accorded by this "philosophy" to the body and to "bondage to the body," specifying a way of existence that is new to European culture; and in this way they reveal that Hitlerism weakens the principles on which Europe is built and which gave major orientations such as Judaism, Christianity, liberalism and Marxism to its culture.

What characterizes Hitlerism and makes it "frighteningly dangerous" is not the fact that it opposes one or other aspect of the main foundations of civilization, nor that it questions a particular political form, "a particular dogma concerning democracy, parliamentary government, dictatorial regime," nor even that it increases the definitive break with the "spirit of freedom"[54] that these principles created, but rather the fact that it questions a "conception of human destiny" based on the "spirit of freedom" and threatens "the very humanity of man"[55] that these principles have tried to develop and offer for centuries.

---

[51] *Ibid.*, 144.

[52] *Ibid.*, 142.

[53] Emmanuel Levinas, "Reflections on Hitlerism," trans. Seán Hand, *Critical Inquiry* 17, no. 1 (1990), 64.

[54] *Ibid.*

[55] *Ibid.*, 71.

Levinas seems to suggest that the innovation and danger of Hitlerism are not its threat to political freedoms, but more obliquely, its threat to the spiritual freedoms of Europe. This threat arose from a concept of man and his destiny that consisted of a new way (for man) to exist and to relate to the being: to no longer exist by striving to free oneself from the tyranny of time and the body, as civilization's features suggested, but to exist by accepting the condition of "being bound," i.e. by accepting what "forms the very foundation" of man's being and to do so based on the body's experience. Levinas writes, perhaps still too allusively: "a view that was truly opposed to the European notion of man would be possible only if the situation to which he was bound was not added to him but formed the very foundation of his being. This paradoxical requirement is one that the experience of our bodies seems to fulfill."[56] This condition of "being bound" to one's being,[57] "adherence" or "bondage" to the body, this state of servitude to one's being, in short, was at the heart of the new concept of man, the "essence" of his spirit. The concept is associated with a new idea of truth that no longer appeals to an external "world of ideas," is no longer devoted to "the contemplation of a foreign spectacle," but is instead based on the "sincerity" and "authenticity" of an anchoring "in [one's] flesh and blood"[58] where man does not have to be anything but his own master. The plunge towards a consanguineous and race-based society is therefore taken very quickly. But this new truth declared by Hitlerism and never before so close, so personal — because it pertains authentically to each person and is assured by his own flesh — must also become universal. And to become universal while being compatible with its implicit racism, it requires not propagation, like any idea or truth, but expansion by force. It is therefore not only the Nietzchian desire for power which brings German Hitlerism to life, but "an ideal that simultaneously brings with it its own form of universalization"[59] — hence the necessity for war and conquest.

It is clear here that Levinas has not yet developed the idea that Hitlerism's barbarity is in some way *complicit* with civilization, that

---

[56] *Ibid.*, 67.

[57] For references to Heidegger in the analysis of "the bound being" and its association to time, cf. Abensour, *op. cit.*, 45-54.

[58] *Ibid.*, 70. Cf. *infra*, Chap. IV, II.

[59] *Ibid.*, 71.

Hitlerism does not deepen a radical rupture with its foundations. However, Levinas seems to already have taken a certain responsibility for these principles inherited from classical philosophy, most particularly in the traditional interpretation of the body — as an obstacle to be overcome or a tomb from which to be liberated — in its eternal strangeness "that has nurtured Christianity as much as modern liberalism" and that has persisted through "every variation in ethics [...] since the Renaissance."[60] It is perhaps here, in this underestimation of the body, that civilization and its foundations have been blind and allowed a new "philosophy," based instead on the principle of the most aggressive and dangerous identification with the body, to gain a foothold at the heart of Europe.

But where are Judaism and paganism in this discourse?

Only a few lines in the essay are devoted to Judaism and to its place in that work of liberation from the irreversibility of time which is also due to other features of civilization. Judaism brings "a magnificent message" to European culture, heralding the "pardon" which "restores" time: "man finds something in the present with which he can modify or efface the past. Time loses its very irreversibility."[61] But Judaism is not alone in this. Christianity, with its "mystical drama" and through the grace, liberalism and autonomy of reason, shares it. However, although the truth of the philosophy of Hitlerism, that of being unable to "escape" from the "adherence" to the body and to the being, holds "the tragic character of finality,"[62] as Levinas writes, it is Judaism, in its singularity, that must offer its opposition, its alternative to the "finality" of the chains of the being and of time.

This article is no more explicit and leaves many questions open. However, the aforementioned texts from the years 1935-1939 may help us in developing this hypothesis of Hitlerism explicitly associated with paganism: "Judeo-Christian civilization," writes Levinas, "is challenged by an arrogant barbarity inhabiting the heart of Europe. With an unrivaled audacity, paganism rears its head, overthrowing values, confusing up elementary distinctions, erasing the boundaries between the sacred and the profane, and dissolving the very principles which hitherto allowed

---

[60] *Ibid.*, 68.
[61] *Ibid.*, 65.
[62] *Ibid.*, 68.

order to be re-established."[63] This is the same view, then, as in the 1933 essay: the foundations of civilization are shaken, and minds are led astray by the success of a demagogy that attempts to be both "a doctrine" and "an adventure" at the same time. But beyond these analogies and the image of the beast which "rears its head" at the heart of Europe, with what — more deeply — do Hitlerism and paganism identify? And in what way does Judaism oppose paganism?

In his text on Hitlerism, Levinas associates "bondage to the body" with "bondage" to the being, deciphering a "philosophy" from it. Here "escape from the being" — thus from the state of servitude and the realm of "finality" — is possible through Judaism: "paganism is neither negation of the spirit, nor ignorance of a single God. The mission of Judaism would only be a small thing if it contented itself with teaching monotheism to the world's nations. [...] *Paganism is a radical inability to escape from the world*. It does not consist of denying spirits and gods, but of situating them in the world."[64] The pagan meets the Hitlerian, and Hitlerism reveals a paganism, in the being firmly established in the world; the being bound to its body; the being that is comfortable in itself; the being confined in itself; the being "on an even footing with things"; and even the being anchored to the certainty of the past's irreversibility thanks to the heredity of blood; in short, the being embedded in these *"definitive positions."*

Likewise, but conversely, Judaism does not oppose paganism by its monotheism, or by a particular morality or metaphysics, but by a feeling — the phenomenologist is at work again — "Israel's feeling towards the world," the "immediate feeling of contingency and insecurity,"[65] in other words the anxiety of the stateless, the homeless, and the exiled, the alarm of the "temporary" and increasing awareness of "foreignness to the world." Put another way, Judaism — "anti-paganism par excellence"[66] — opposes it not by its "doctrines" but by its "way of living and feeling," by its way of relating "to the natural development of the being which takes pleasure in nature" — to Levinas, a way of saying *conatus essendi*. It opposes it by its way of being foreign to the myth of installation, foreign to the "cult of strength and worldly greatness,"

---

[63] Levinas, "Epreuves d'une pensée," 142.
[64] *Ibid.*, 144. [Levinas' emphasis].
[65] *Ibid.*, 150.
[66] *Ibid.*, 152.

foreign to "the legitimacy of strength asserting itself as strength," foreign to the cult of pursuit and war. Thus, Judaism is a "madness" to a world inhabited by warriors and demi-gods anchored to the chains of the being and its perseverance, fixed in the irreversibility of time. Judaism's "madness" is that it "separates human dignity from power and success" and above all, as Horkheimer would later say in a similar tone, "maintains a choice which manifests itself only through suffering."[67]

But the most original idea in this line of thinking, certainly meriting deeper analysis than is possible here, is that in Levinas's view Hiterlism, with its anti-Semitism and racism, becomes "the incomparable test"[68] for Judaism: "the moral and physical suffering which it values and which it signifies to German Israelites are no longer commensurate with their ancestral endurance. What gives a unique accent to Hitler's anti-Semitism [...] is the unprecedented situation in which it has placed the Jewish consciousness, because this is not only wounded by the offences inflicted on it. Insult, in its racist form, adds a poignant flavor of desperation to humiliation. The pathetic fate of being Jewish becomes an inevitability. [...] The Jew is inescapably tied to his Judaism."[69]

Beyond the fact that the author testifies to his preoccupation with the fate of German Jews after the promulgation of the Nuremberg Laws and demonstrates his anxiety over their destiny, in this text from 1935 he reveals the hard demand, imposed on the Jewish consciousness by Hitlerism, to submit to an examination of their essence and their role among nations — a demand that Levinas tried to consider in his work *after* the Catastrophe, in line with the spirit that animated the Jewish School of Paris and the Colloquia of Francophone Jewish Intellectuals, as testified by the Talmudic Lectures. But also, and perhaps more problematically, Hitlerism cruelly reveals the need to become aware of "the full seriousness" of being Jewish and of "the ineluctability of one's being."[70] Being unable to escape one's condition, "being inescapably *tied* to one's Judaism," is the staggering test that Hitlerism imposes on Judaism. And if *"one does not desert Judaism,"* according to the racist demand, it is not in order to

---

[67] *Ibid.*

[68] *Ibid.*, 144.

[69] *Ibid.*

[70] Emmanuel Levinas, "Etre juif" (1947), in *Cahiers d'Etudes Levinassiennes*, no. 1 (Paris: Verdier, 2002), 103.

submit to the "earthly fate" required by the philosophy of Hitlerism, but in order to resist in one's own "spiritual destiny": to raise awareness of the impossibility of a world without transcendence or an existence cut off and enclosed in itself, to raise awareness of an existence oriented towards a hereafter.

Over the course of this book, Horkheimer, Adorno and Levinas's reflections on fascism, anti-Semitism and Hitlerism, with their different perspectives and problems, aim to highlight the first stage of their *testimony*. It is the first stage of a testimony that I will attempt to explain, clarify and recognize as such, as a testimony, only to the extent that they existed in the period *afterwards*, once the Catastrophe was completed. But it is a testimony which, for these Jewish intellectuals, already took shape and was problematized during the alarm following Hitler's rise to power, the tragic hours of *crescendo* of the Nuremberg Laws, up to the invasion of Poland and the *final* setting up of the "final solution."

And it is precisely in this state of extreme alarm and tension, and on the temporal *threshold* between the disaster's *before* and *after*, that we will meet the first witness to the Disaster, and also the most anxious and elusive: Walter Benjamin.

Chapter II

On the Threshold: Walter Benjamin

Thought is obligated to weakness.
Auguste Blanqui

Walter Benjamin committed suicide on September 26, 1940, "in those early fall days,"[1] as Hannah Arendt writes, pursued by the *Gestapo* and while trying to cross the border between France and Spain to reach the United States, to cross the demarcation line between persecution on one hand and hope on the other. But the border at Port-Bou is not only a spatial allegory representing a *before* and a *beyond*: a horizon *before* and the end *beyond*. It is also a temporal allegory that marks out the caesura which divided history into a *before* and an *after*. The date of Benjamin's death can in fact be considered as the temporal *threshold* between a time *before* the "final solution" and a time *afterwards*.

This is because autumn 1940 is the exact temporal boundary after which mobile massacre operations were rallied to devastate Jewish families remaining in occupied territory in the Soviet Union in June 1941. Indeed, although the "final solution" had not yet been enacted in a systematic manner according to the terms and parameters established at the Wannsee Conference (January 1942), in 1941 mass murder had already started to strike Soviet Jews. Plans for the military and civilian campaign began to be prepared from July 1940. Around the end of 1940 and the start of 1941, then, the fate of the Jews was at stake.

After definition, expropriation of goods and concentration in ghettos, all that was left was for Nazi Germany to accomplish the last stage of the "final solution to the Jewish question" (*die Endlösung der Judenfrage*). But this stage contained something new. As Raul Hilberg writes, "the new 'solution' removed all uncertainties and answered all questions. The aim was finalized — it was to be death." Furthermore, the

---

[1] Hannah Arendt, *Men in Dark Times*, trans. Harry Zohn (New York: Harcourt, Brace & World, 1968), 151.

term "final solution" carried a deeper implication foreseen by Himmler himself: afterwards, "the Jewish problem would never have to be solved again." Indeed, until this moment, the evolution of the oppression and exploitation could have been stopped or redefined, but not *after* the decision to kill, because "killings are irreversible. Hence they gave to the destruction process its quality of historical finality. [...] The invasion of the Soviet Union and the mobile killings carried out in its wake mark a *break with history*."[2]

And yet to place Benjamin at the boundary of this bleak epoch, as a *witness* to the instigation of the worst, does not require us to strain historical events or play with the dates. Quite on the contrary, we simply have to view this author as one who, while remaining on the boundary, while being *on* the *threshold* of the caesura produced by the Extermination, knew how to see beyond it. Not only was he capable of seeing the complicity between modernity — especially the concepts of universal history and historic progress — and the idea of permanent catastrophe, but he also anticipated the affinity between modernity's successes — technological progress, industrialization — and the destructive systems of Hitler's Reich.

Furthermore, to place him *on* the *threshold* of the Catastrophe represented by the "final solution" involves restoring to his thoughts the degree of peril that flows through them and accentuates the very rhythm of his life. This peril is not only due to his Jewish origins, the suspension of his German citizenship, the *Gestapo*'s censorship of his clearly anti-fascist writing and his imprisonment,[3] but is also due to an attitude of the soul, experienced as a way of being-in-the-world. According to Benjamin, this precarious way of being, always in danger, is what the Jew and the proletarian share and have most deeply in common. For them, the state of exception is the rule. It is precisely in this sharing of the state of exception that Benjamin's two closely connected "souls," the "Jewish" and the "Marxist," can come together and each be translated into the other's

---

[2] Raul Hilberg, *The Destruction of the European Jews* (New York: Holmes & Meier, 1985), 99-100 [my emphasis].

[3] He was imprisoned while leaving German for France, then transferred to the Vernuche work camp in Haute Loire, which he left in November 1939 thanks to intervention from friends.

language. Consequently, the effort to consider Benjamin as being *on* the *threshold* of the Disaster acquires a legitimate sense because his entire life, and even his thoughts, were inhabited and almost haunted by the threats of Nazism and the black shadow of a constantly threatening danger.

Finally, to place him *on* the *threshold* above all allows us to approach his thoughts as a *threshold* — a *threshold* as Benjamin himself understands it, i.e. as a *passage*. Indeed, the philosopher's thinking, like every passage, serves "transitory purposes."[4] In its incompleteness and inexhaustible research, it shows his ability to dwell on the threshold or the features that can represent it, whether they are the glazed corridors of the Parisian arcades, or the passage from sleep to waking, or even the transition between two eras. And he does so not only to consider them as essential stages in a progressive movement whose purpose is to determine space, time and history, but to restore importance and dignity to each of these moments, pauses and passages. Through their implicit longing, Benjamin's passages, like the moments of the present, are opened up to a longing that they will always fulfil and satisfy. But in this longing, which almost becomes infinite dissatisfaction or a dream, the passages lead to the unpredictable, to the new, to what we could reservedly call hope.

Thus contemplated, i.e. as a *threshold* and *passage*, Benjamin's thinking lends itself to a different interpretation. It need not be reduced to an antecedent, to a reflection on the Catastrophe, anticipating the "final solution" in the form of a study of divine violence, as Jacques Derrida suggests;[5] it will not be considered in the single *sense* of *ante*, in other words as thinking inhabited by the presentiment of the Nazi horror, attributed with the clairvoyance of prophecy and with Benjamin becoming both "the herald" and "the first victim" of the Catastrophe, as in Enzo Traverso's interpretation.[6] However, his thinking also cannot be tackled in a retrospective approach aimed only at the *after*, because

---

[4] Walter Benjamin, *The Arcades Project*, edited by Rolf Tiedemann, trans. Howard Eiland and Kevin McLaughlin (Cambridge: Harvard University Press, 2002), 16.

[5] Jacques Derrida, "Force of Law: 'The Mystical Foundation of Authority'," trans. Mary Quaitance, *Cardozo Law Review* 11 (1990): 921-1045.

[6] Enzo Traverso, *L'Histoire déchirée. Essais sur Auschwitz et les intellectuels* (Paris: Cerf, 1997).

this position would freely allow interpretations of Benjamin that are conditioned by an *a posteriori* view that would be likely to strain or manipulate some of his ideas.

My aim is therefore to find the conjunction of a *double sense* of interpretation: on the one hand, to keep in mind the insights that Benjamin was able to have about catastrophe *before* the Catastrophe, thus considering the *sense* from the *ante* towards the *after*; and on the other, to consider his reflections *afterwards*, in our *present day*, to re-interpret them and see what they can tell the present about the recent past, through and by the idea of *remembrance* (*Eingedenken*). We should not only consider the potential that his thinking has been able to exert *afterwards*, for example on Adorno's philosophy and, in certain aspects, on that of Horkheimer, but also reflect on what his views on catastrophe on the one hand and remembrance on the other can say to *us after* the Event. Without opening the way to a *singular sense*, and thus following the same method as Benjamin in his work *The Arcades Project* (*Das Passagenwerk*), "we can speak of two directions in this work: one which goes from the past into the present and shows the arcades, and all the rest, as precursors, and one which goes from the present into the past so as to have the revolutionary potential of these 'precursors' explode in the present."[7] Consequently, my interpretation will attempt to keep this *double sense* in mind: the *sense* that goes from the past to the present — or, more precisely, from the *ante* to the *after*; this *sense*, rich in intuitions and premonitions that make Benjamin a "prophet" of the Disaster — should never come into play or be used without the other *sense*, a look backwards or *retrospectively* that makes the "revolutionary" impact of Benjamin's thinking explode in the present — the present of our coming *after*.

And this *double sense* can perhaps be maintained through the allegorical idea of the *threshold*.

Benjamin's thinking will therefore be interpreted without forgetting the place of passage represented by the border at Port-Bou, the real and allegorical *threshold* where Benjamin decided to stop by killing himself. Thus, the focus of my interpretation will be to reflect on his thinking while retaining the perspective of the *double sense* of the *threshold* increased by the historical caesura of the "final solution." And as each *passage* is filled with a longing, but at the same time contains something

---

[7] Benjamin, *The Arcades Project*, 862.

unexpected, this thinking, progressing along this narrow and immense boundary, crossing the *threshold* between the *ante* and the *after*, offers a glimpse of an unexpected and improbable flash of hope, even if it is the hope of someone who has nothing left to hope for. It is a flash that would probably be unbearable to eyes of those who, *afterwards*, saw the chimneys and ruins of Auschwitz.

This flash of hope which emerges from the *passage* or *threshold* of Benjamin's thinking, accidental and unhoped for as a dream,[8] unexpected as the illusion of the moment, is certainly what allows us to take a step forward which otherwise would be difficult to take. It is a step into the void, perhaps, yet one which leads to new ground, to a temporal or spatial "utopia," to the heart of all "utopia," i.e. to constantly re-emerging hope.

I. FROM THE *BEFORE* TO THE *AFTER*: CATASTROPHES

To give Benjamin this place as a *witness* on the *threshold* of the Disaster, or a "fire alarm,"[9] following the *sense* of a *passage* from a *before* to an *after*, first requires an investigation and clear examination of the idea of catastrophe, a notion that Benjamin endeavored to consider throughout his life. It is an idea that is difficult to trace in the fragments of his texts, and even more difficult to decipher due to the dual movement that it seems to take on. Indeed, though on the one hand it is linked to the Benjamin's criticism of modernity, in particular to the criticism of the progress and *continuum* that are supposed to determine universal history, on the other hand its very unusual nuances link it to the destructive character of a certain apocalyptic messianism which Benjamin was able to develop non-systematically due to his friendship with Scholem. So although, on the one hand, this idea runs in parallel to criticism of the constructive and productive structures of modernity, on the other hand, as these analyses will tend to show, it becomes one of the ideas that contains Benjamin's *asymptotic messianism*.

---

[8] *Ibid.*, 389.

[9] Traverso, *L'Histoire déchirée*, 13. Cf. Michael Lowy, *Fire Alarm: Reading Walter Benjamin's On the Concept of History* (London: Verso, 2005).

1. CATASTROPHE AND TECHNOLOGICAL PROGRESS

Benjamin could certainly not have foreseen the exact proportions of the Second World War's disasters, and yet even in 1930, before the rise of Nazism, he predicted the growth of "something" when, in memory of the First World War and long before the unleashing of the "final solution," he declared that "millions of human bodies will indeed inevitably be chopped to pieces and chewed up by iron and gas."[10]

Benjamin was clearly and tragically aware of the harmful nature of war, which allowed him to rebel indignantly against those like Ernst Jünger who extol, even post-war, the heroism and the intoxication that the forces of war can arouse in man. In this incandescent and cautionary text, *"Theories of German Fascism"* (1930) — his review of the collaborative work edited by Jünger[11] — he not only denounces the aesthetic, mystical and cultural origins of the glorification of war, but also analyzes the dangerous liaisons between technological development and war. Unlike the "bloody schemes conjured up"[12] by the book's authors, Benjamin shows the dangers hidden in the disparity between technology's gigantic resources and the "moral illumination it affords."[13] This imbalance between "moral illumination" and the power of technological means predicts a catastrophic situation where the "revolt of technology"[14] will take on the form of an atomic cataclysm or a hellish mechanism of destruction. If, indeed, the First World War revealed how human resources could be sacrificed as fodder for cannon and mines, "gas warfare [...] promises to give the war of the future a face which permanently displaces soldierly qualities by those of sports [...]. Gas warfare will rest on annihilation records, and will involve an absurd degree of risk. Whether its outbreak will occur within the bounds of

---

[10] Walter Benjamin, "Theories of German Fascism," trans. Jerolf Wikoff, *New German Critique* no. 17 (Spring 1979): 128.

[11] The work in question is *Krieg und Krieger*, edited by Ernst Jünger (Berlin: Junker & Dünnhaupt Verlag, 1930).

[12] Benjamin, "Theories of German Fascism," 122.

[13] *Ibid.*, 120.

[14] *Ibid.*

international law — after prior declarations of war — is questionable."[15] But does not this perceptiveness, that in 1930 was capable of anticipating the catastrophic proportions of a second war — a world war, a war beyond international law and human rights, an atomic war — and also capable of foreseeing a transformation of the nature of war into that of "record-setting," also call to mind the nature of the extermination camps' record-keeping; the Nazi nature that transformed military war into a war of annihilation; the catastrophic nature of the atomic bomb indiscriminately striking "civilian and military personnel"?[16]

While speaking of "gas warfare," despite his astounding prophecies, Benjamin certainly could not have foreseen either Auschwitz or Hiroshima.[17] However, his awareness that the catastrophic dimensions of the war to come would be due to the disparity between the potential of technological progress and the "moral illumination" that should guide it also allowed him, several years later, to see the harmful combination between technological progress and modern barbarity embodied in Nazi Germany. But in this text he was already trying to understand how and why this glorification of war by Jünger's circle is specifically German.

Benjamin attributes mystical concepts that aim to use technology as the "key" to "solve the mystery of an idealistically perceived nature" not only to the representatives of this "male thought,"[18] but also to the revival of German nationalism. In other words, "this new nationalism" calling for a new war and "eternal war" can be understood through the triptych of nature-technology-idealism: "the surroundings become a problem, every wire entanglement an antinomy, every barb a definition, every explosion a thesis; and by day the sky was the cosmic interior of the steel helmet and at night the moral law above. Etching the landscape with flaming banners and trenches, technology wanted to recreate the heroic features of German Idealism."[19] The three elements metamorphosed into one,

---

[15] *Ibid.*, 121.

[16] *Ibid.*

[17] Cf. The image of the solitary pilot according to Benjamin (*ibid.*, 128) and that of the Hiroshima pilot by Günther Anders, *Burning Conscience: Guilt of Hiroshima* (New York: Paragon House, 1989).

[18] Benjamin, "Theories of German Fascism," 121.

[19] *Ibid.*, 126.

a chaotic fusion between technology, nature and idealism, converging in the desolate landscape of the field of battle, strewn with weapons and bodies under a starless sky. Technology, first responsible for this chaos, while believing itself to be reproducing the traits of German heroism, namely idealism, conversely suffered its deadly, "Hippocratic" aspects, because what it believed to be heroic were in reality "the features of death." Thus, for the idealist school, instead of liberating nature and giving it a voice, technology gave it a deathly silence and forged for it a lethal "apocalyptic face."

Benjamin puts forward the hypothesis whereby idealism not only provoked this logic of death — though he does not explain how — and took on the "features of death," but was also a victim, though not the first, of technological revolt which seems to take on catastrophic proportions. The other side of what we are accustomed to call "progress" sometimes takes on aspects of "imperialist war"[20] (as in the First World War) or of imminent catastrophe (in the prediction of a Second World War) — an uncontrolled, dark catastrophe, destroying every last son of man.

His concept of technological progress and also his representation of Germany's "Medusa-like beliefs"[21] give Benjamin's reflections an apocalyptic tone. However, despite the extreme tension in his writing, his clarity allows him to put forward hypotheses ahead of his time. They should therefore not be interpreted as the last words of a nostalgic conservative rebelling at seeing the changing structure of the world. On the contrary, they should be read as attempts to penetrate the revival of German nationalism during the 1930s which would contribute to the rise to power of Nazism, and equally as "warnings" of the lethal implications of technological progress which, in the absence of ethical explanation, could be transformed into barbarity. Though on the one hand we must read in these pages a profound recognition of the dangers of the modern civilization of the "decline of the West,"[22] on the other hand we must see the *rational* effort to rob false discussions of war (particularly German ones) of their irrational and magical component. Indeed, he writes, "all the light that language and reason still afford should be focused upon that 'primal experience' from whose barren gloom this mysticism crawls

---

[20] *Ibid.*, 120.

[21] *Ibid.*, 128.

[22] *Ibid.*, 123.

forth on its thousand unsightly conceptual feet."[23] All rational powers should be mustered to denounce not the catastrophic dangers of a new war to come, but rather the ruses implicit in conceptual — typically German — discussions which aim to mystify nature and technology.

Admittedly, we cannot say that Benjamin presents an *ante litteram* analysis of Nazism, but his intuitions about German nationalism, particularly concentrating on the interconnections between technological progress and the mystical vision of nature, are also valid for National Socialism even if the degree to which idealism is involved is still unclear.

We can then ask ourselves whether this concept of technological progress with catastrophic nuances remains constant in Benjamin's thinking. Indeed, it is necessary to admit the presence of a dual vision of technology[24] which, instead of calling into question the relationship between disaster and technological progress, reveals nuances in it. Its shades are revealed and accentuated by showing the dialectic of the idea of disaster. On one hand, this idea underlines the blackness of destruction linked to a "first technology," and on the other hand reinforces the idea of revolution or of deliverance in messianic redemption or utopia (depending on interpretation) linked to a "second technology." As *The Work of Art in the Age of its Technological Reproducibility*[25] (1936) shows, we can effectively note a distinction and dialectic between two techniques of reproduction. On one hand, the first technology is linked to destructive catastrophe due to the domination of nature and the subjugation of man even as far as bodily sacrifice; on the other, the second technology is the cornerstone of a revolution delivering the individual from the mass condition and opening up new possibilities to him as an individual. The first technology causes disasters, while the second inspires revolutions

---

[23] *Ibid.*, 128.

[24] Cf. Miguel Abensour, *L'utopie de Thomas More à Walter Benjamin* (Paris: Sens & Tonka, 2000), 168-174.

[25] Walter Benjamin, "The Work of Art in the Age of its Technological Reproducibility," trans. J. A. Underwood, in *Selected Writings III* (Cambridge: Belknap Press, 2006), 251. Cf. also "The Storyteller: Observations on the Works of Nikolai Leskov," trans. Harry Zohn, *Selected Writings III, op. cit.*

and encourages utopia, or redemption, blurring "the boundary between the possible and impossible."[26]

If this is the case, we can consider these two technologies as two sides of the same concept. The destructive dimension related to the first technology and the revolutionary utopic dimension of the second simply reflect the two senses of Benjamin's vision of catastrophe — devastating *and* liberating, apocalyptic *and* redeeming at the same time. Thus, disaster is not opposed to redemption, but involves it: "the destructive powers contained in the idea of redemption must be brought to light."[27] There is a dialectic within disaster itself, moving between a time of destruction and a time of emancipation, a time of darkness and another of salvation. Without one or the other taking precedence, without there being continuity from one to the other, these two times, these two senses coexist dialectically in the idea of disaster. The question of how remains to be seen.

2. CATASTROPHE AND THE HISTORICAL CONTINUUM

"The concept of progress must be grounded in the idea of catastrophe. That things are 'status quo' *is* the catastrophe. It is not an ever-present possibility but what in each case is given. Thus Strindberg [...]: hell is not something that awaits us, but this life here and now."[28] This pithy phrase from the *Passagenwerk* once more confirms Benjamin's criticism of the idea of progress and highlights an important aspect: not only does technological progress bring catastrophes and cataclysms, as

---

[26] Abensour, *L'utopie de Thomas More à Walter Benjamin*, 173.

[27] Cf. the manuscripts and preparatory materials in "Über den Begriff der Geschichte," in Walter Benjamin, *Gesammelte Schriften* I, 3, edited by Rolf Tiedemann and Hermann Schweppenhäuser (Frankfurt-am-Main: Suhrkamp, 1972-82), 1229-1252. For the most part, I have translated from the original version of this text. Where a definitive translation is available, the version published in *Selected Writings* has been used. Here, "Über den Begriff der Geschichte," 1246 [my translation].

[28] Benjamin, *The Arcades Project*, 473.

has just been shown, but *catastrophe is implicit in a concept of history based on progressive continuity*. But why and how is catastrophe "the *continuum* of history"?[29] And above all, what relationship can be sketched between this historiographic catastrophe and the historical Catastrophe of 1941-1945?

One of the key points of Benjamin's theory of history, which would have influenced both Adorno and Horkheimer, revolves around the fact that "the *continuum* is that of the oppressors,"[30] whereas "the history of the oppressed is a *discontinuum*."[31] This demarcation, which may seem too facile or too easily manipulated for a simplistic approach capable at all times of distinguishing the side of the oppressors and that of the oppressed, nonetheless reveals the full sense of catastrophe in its link to history. For Benjamin, what is catastrophic in history is "the eternal repetition of the same"[32] — the repetition of the same story, the same violence, the same insignificance attributed to the victims; to those who have been subjugated, put down, exploited, defeated, destroyed, violated, annihilated; to those whose names are not found in the history books. The catastrophe is that "things are 'status quo,'" i.e. that they remain identical and loyal to the "current rulers,"[33] that they remain oblivious to those who are "lying on the ground," those who are dying on the ground, who fight and lose. And yet it is to the memory of these that Benjamin wants history to return: "The historical construction is dedicated to the memory of the *nameless*."[34] It should be reconstructed on another *tradition*, one that is absolutely *discontinuous*, opposed to that of the victors. It should make a *tradition* of the forgotten — a *tradition* of the *nameless* opposing "the *tradition* that is catastrophe,"[35] the *tradition* that celebrates great men and great nations, salutes the illustrious men of the Pantheons, and

---

[29] Benjamin, "Über den Begriff der Geschichte," 1244.

[30] *Ibid.*

[31] *Ibid.*, 1243.

[32] Cited in Löwy, *Fire Alarm*, 63.

[33] Walter Benjamin, "On the Concept of History," in *Walter Benjamin: Selected Writings* (Cambridge: Harvard University Press, 2003), 391.

[34] Benjamin, "Über den Begriff der Geschichte," 1241 [my emphasis].

[35] Benjamin, *The Arcades Project*, 473.

keeps events as a "heritage" or as the "spoils"[36] of honorable triumphs for which so many arches have been constructed and thousands of men destroyed.

The *tradition* of the *nameless* is opposed, without contradiction, to the catastrophic *tradition* that appeals to "great men" and "great nations," a *tradition* which, according to Hegel, has established history and historiography in the categories of universality, progress and evolution — or even in the different forms of the same type, the same *continuum*, as the identical return of the *same* — categories which, for at least two centuries, have done nothing but accompany an accumulation of ruins.

Hegel did, admittedly, observe that history is a heap of ruins, but differently from Benjamin. With Hegel, there is no lamenting or protest. For him, the necessity for impersonal and eternal reason justifies the unjustifiable and pardons the unforgivable. It is the logical necessity, or even the "ruse of Reason" which makes History "the Calvary of the Absolute," not to mention a progression which is both somber and triumphal and engulfs passions, individuals, nations and states, and all morality too in its sorrowful and grandiose cortege. If the question for Hegel is to know *"for whom, to what purpose"* we witness this "distant spectacle of wreckage and confusion" and bow down to this "altar on which the happiness of nations, the wisdom of states and the virtues of individuals are slaughtered,"[37] for Benjamin it is to understand how we can "make whole what has been smashed"[38] from out of these ruins, how we can gather up what has been lost, welcome what has been rejected, and "revive" those that are no more — how the "whole past" can be "gathered."[39] The important thing is therefore not to know the *purpose* of history, but to raise an interruption at all times — to say a name each time, to name someone.

---

[36] Benjamin, "On the Concept of History," 391.

[37] Georg W. F. Hegel, *Lectures on the Philosophy of World History*, trans. H. B. Nisbet (Cambridge: Cambridge University Press, 1975), 69.

[38] Benjamin, "On the Concept of History," 392.

[39] Irving Wohlfarth, "Et Cetera? The Historian as Chiffonnier," in *Walter Benjamin and the Arcades Project*, ed. Beatrice Hanssen (London: Continuum International, 2006), 24.

I. FROM THE *BEFORE* TO THE *AFTER*: CATASTROPHES 69

Not that Benjamin begins a moralizing approach to history. But for him, it is men's injuries, their failures, like their happiness, which give sense to history — a sense that can appear as a counter-sense. And while Hegel's history is already a final judgment "in and of itself," Benjamin sees history in this way only in the extent to which it becomes an *apocatastasis*[40] *of all* the lost moments of the "sacrificed" into history — an *apocatastasis* — a re-integration, a re-habilitation — of *all* of history's silences into history itself. In other words, history is only a daily final judgment if it is applied, instantly, to a displacement of the "angle of vision,"[41] bringing out "positive" and the "different" elements in what has previously been rejected. Thus, the different and the rejected, *all* of the forgotten, can find a place and a voice in the counter-history, or history going against the tide, represented by the *tradition* of the *nameless*, voicing itself in the "etcetera"[42] and opposing the "status quo" of catastrophe, the history taught by Hegel, and the *tradition* that is catastrophe.

And yet, the counter-history envisaged by Benjamin remains a *tradition*.

This poses a problem. Indeed, what difference is there between *continuum* and *tradition*? Is *tradition* not also based on a *continuous* vision of history and time? While history's object changes in Benjamin's historical vision, i.e. the triumphs of the "oppressors" give way to the injuries of the "oppressed," it seems that the temptation of *continuity* — or of *totality*? — remains present. Is there not in fact a risk, in this *other tradition,* or *tradition* of the *other*, of wanting to make up for the deficiencies of history, of wanting to fill in the blanks and thus to stifle these silences instead of listening to them and telling them? Is there not a risk, in short, of another *totality*, this time including the *nameless*?

The author is conscious of this. In the preparatory material for the theses *"On the Concept of History"* (1940), he writes: "fundamental

---

[40] *Apocatastasis* signifies the gathering of souls in Paradise, according to Origen, who considerably influenced Leskov. Cf. Benjamin, "The Storyteller," *op. cit.*, 158.

[41] Benjamin, *The Arcades Project*, 459.

[42] *Ibid.* Cf. Wohlfarth, "Et Cetera? The Historian as Chiffonnier," 32.

aporia: tradition as the *discontinuum* of the past in contrast to history as the *continuum* of events"; and at the same time: "the *continuum* of history is that of the oppressors. While the notion of a *continuum* destroys everything, the notion of a *discontinuum* is the basis of genuine tradition."[43] That is to say that, on the one hand, there is a *tradition* based on the temporal *discontinuum* — but how could this "tradition" continue to be one if not for the fact that it is linked to a certain *tradition*, in this case Jewish, of thinking about time?[44] — and on the other, there is history as a *continuum* and series of events, even as a tradition which is a heap or accumulation of ruins. On the one hand, the *discontinuum* and the *tradition* of the "oppressed," on the other, the *continuum* and the *tradition* of the "oppressors." Once again, there is a double sense of *tradition* — on one hand a constructive *tradition* (possibly) to be reconstructed, and on the other a destructive *tradition* (absolutely) to be destroyed — one *tradition* to be saved, another to be destroyed, one *tradition* redeeming and the other catastrophic.

But do we not find here, once again, the dual sense of Benjamin's idea of catastrophe? The same internal dialectic that we have seen in its relationship with technological progress? In other words, is not *tradition*, like technological progress, shaken by the dual rhythm of the winds of catastrophe, which destroys in one beat and redeems in the next? Catastrophe is thus precisely the dialectic within the idea of catastrophe which leaves its mark on everything it touches. One could even say that the tension between the destructive and constructive moments of catastrophe identifies with the sense of dialectical imagination, i.e. at the point where "the tension between dialectical opposites is greatest."[45]

There is a subsequent distinction to make. In a fragment very close to thesis XVII, Benjamin offers a key to understanding the difference between the two *traditions* and perhaps answering all these questions. He

---

[43] Benjamin, "Über den Begriff der Geschichte," 1236.

[44] Cf. Robert Alter, *Necessary Angels: tradition and modernity in Kafka, Benjamin and Scholem*, (Cambridge: Harvard University Press, 1991).

[45] Benjamin, *The Arcades Project*, 475.

makes the distinction between the "additive process" of the *continuum* of universal history, a process which accumulates the mass of events to fill in "homogeneous and empty time," and the "constructive principle" of the *discontinuum* (the other *tradition*), which is a "monadological principle." This principle, identical to the "messianic present"[46] that shatters the *continuum* of time and which historical materialism should appropriate, in fact explodes the homogeneous and progressive course of history, each time revealing within the crack a certain era, a particular life, a particular work, in other words, singularities.

The shattering of the *continuum* and stopping of its flow by this principle means that the small and the singular, what was invisible or inaudible, can emerge, appear and come to light, thus finding a place in what is *written* and words in what is *said*. But how can one write a *discontinuous* history while remaining in discontinuity, or express the *caesura* without betraying this history? Consequently, the structure of the monad in history corresponds to the *Jetzt-zeit* tearing up what is homogeneous and identical in time. It interrupts the *continuum* of history, cracks it with a "shock"[47] and fractures it by a short-circuit of tensions. However, something appears in this crack, in this miniature catastrophe, within the catastrophe of the *continuum*: a crystallized "constellation,"[48] a galaxy of little stars, of little histories, long ago frozen and fused in the *same*, takes shape and breaks free to become established in a *u-topos*, the messianic *u-topia*. In this explosion, a plurality of constellations or, to use a chemical image instead of an astronomical one, a network of molecules, has replaced the *continuum*. An order, or rather a molecular

---

[46] Benjamin, "Über den Begriff der Geschichte," 1251.

[47] Benjamin, "On the Concept of History," 396: "*Thinking involves not only the movement of thoughts, but their arrest as well.* Where thinking suddenly comes to a stop in a configuration saturated with tensions, it gives that configuration a shock, by which thinking is crystallized into a monad. [...] In this structure he recognizes the sign of a messianic arrest of happening, or (to put it differently), a revolutionary chance in the fight for the oppressed past" [my emphasis].

[48] *Ibid.*

non-order, where each particle has a sense and where each atom is a world, a microcosm, a grain,[49] "a precious [...] seed."[50]

It is here that the "constructive principle" of Benjaminian "monadology" takes effect by creating a *discontinuum* made of small, singular histories, composed of stops and pauses, and opening up "revolutionary chances" in and by interruption. It opens new possibilities for the "oppressed past,"[51] a past which is no longer told by "once upon a time,"[52] but by the "tiger's leap" or "dialectical leap"[53] of the *moment*, the *moment* of *remembrance*.[54]

History, therefore, takes on another aspect. It is a counter-history, or history brushed "against the grain,"[55] counter to Hegel and his ilk, a history that is allergic to the categories of the universal, the *continuum* and the progress which is supposed to determine history. It is a history of the small, of biographies, of daily lives, of chronicles. In short, it is a history at a standstill — a stopping of history and a history as a mosaic of halts. It is a history that is interrupted at each individual history, that takes time over each name and names each individual; a chronicle or final judgment.

The same applies to thought. It too becomes *discontinuous* and creative through this discontinuity because, as Benjamin writes, "where thinking comes to a standstill in a constellation saturated with tensions — there the dialectical image appears. It is the *caesura* in the movement of thought. Its position is naturally not an arbitrary one. It is to be found, in a word, where tension between dialectical opposites is greatest. Hence, the object constructed in the materialist presentation of history is itself the dialectical image. The latter is identical with the

---

[49] Like the two grains of wheat engraved with the *Shema Israël* exhibited at the Musée de Cluny in Paris and which fascinated Benjamin so much. Cf. Gershom Scholem, *Walter Benjamin und sein Engel: vierzehn Aufsätze und kleine Beiträge* (Frankfurt am Main: Suhrkamp, 1983).

[50] Benjamin, "On the Concept of History," 396.

[51] *Ibid.*

[52] *Ibid.*

[53] *Ibid.*, 395.

[54] Cf. *infra*.

[55] *Ibid.*, 392.

historical object; it justifies its violent expulsion from the continuum of historical process."⁵⁶ If the structure of the monad reverses the historical object by extrapolating it from and drawing it out of the *continuum*, the dialectical image is what produces a *caesura* in thought, or rather, is the *caesura* of thought. There is therefore an important relationship, a deep correspondence, between the monad and dialectical image. Both are the climax of accumulated tensions and the summit of dialectical oppositions. One acts in the *continuum* of history, and the other in the *continuum* of thought, tearing them. But when there is a "materialist presentation of history," i.e. when the historical hermeneutic follows the method proposed by Benjamin, namely the *science* of the *discontinuum*, there is no longer any difference and the dialectical image is identical to the historical object. It is not interpreted monadologically anywhere else but *in* the historical object. This, the dialectical image or "dialectic at a standstill," is ultimately part of its object, in the pinnacle of historical tensions that stop history itself, i.e. in the monad(s).⁵⁷ In this correspondence between dialectical image and monad, there is finally a supremacy of the latter over the former, i.e. a primacy of the historical *object* over the *subject* that interprets it, and *therefore* a precedence of history over thought.

But if this is the case, are we not therefore obliged to interpret the genitive of Benjamin's philosophy *of* history in an objective sense, aiming to testify to the object? Showing the stops, the "blockages" in history and *therefore* in thought? And would this "objectivity" not be one of the key points repeated by Adorno in *Negative Dialectics*? Because it is history — this history "against the grain" made up of many histories — which "approaches" thought. It is history that affects it and finally stops it. It is history's tears which tear it. It is these caesuras that open it by opening it to another image of itself (even if it is the dialectical image), to this *caesura* of thought and to this thought of the *caesura*.

To *think* of history with the *caesura* and *discontinuum* as a starting point is therefore the message that Benjamin leaves us as a legacy — a message that must be contemplated if one wants to think *after* the Catastrophe. The "category" of the *caesura* can in fact support the rift produced in history

---

56 Benjamin, *The Arcades Project*, 475.

57 Is the plural not in fact more appropriate, history being a beach of monads?

by the Extermination and restore the past's relevance to the present. The *caesura*, which moves intermittently and in leaps, with blockages and stops, is what can reveal and express the grinding up of personal histories and the crushing of private lives that took place during those terrible years. Through the perspective of discontinuity, as we have seen, history is no longer presented as the *continuum* of universal history, but takes on the appearance of a constantly new syncope, an unordered arrhythmia of histories that take shape, interlace, come together, unite, separate and interrupt each other. They live, too, but differently in relation to "what has been" for each one, differently in relation to their past, allowing a new possibility to be imagined in another present — ours. It is a chance for *redemption* in the moment of remembrance.

This is because the *caesura* disrupts not only historical continuity, but also its repetition, the catastrophe of the temporal *continuum* which fixes the past purely in what it was, in the repetition of itself. Thus, if we follow Benjamin up to this point, the event of Auschwitz becomes *one* monad of history and *therefore a caesura* of thought.

The Catastrophe produces a double *caesura*, one of history and of thought. More precisely, a *caesura* of thought because of the *caesura* of history. So, a *caesura* of history. If we retain the historiographic interpretation proposed by Benjamin and apply it to the Extermination, we can say that the latter, like every historical event, is a monad of history. It is not only an event that interrupts the progressive or evolutive course, but also the condensed representation of all that preceded it, in other words the *catastrophic tradition*'s accumulation of ruins.

But how can Benjamin's idea, whereby each historical event is a unique monad, be reconciled with my conviction as to the uniqueness of this particular event? In wishing to interpret it according to Benjamin's "category" of the *caesura*, do we not risk falling victim to a contradiction and opening the way to a counter-sense — that of wanting to show the *caesura* produced by the Catastrophe while maintaining that *all* historical events are monads requiring caesuras?

Taking on this risk in the first person nevertheless remains the aporia; an aporia that is perhaps due to the difficulty of *thinking* of the *caesura*, of thoroughly *thinking* about it in history and in thought itself, right to the center of our thought. But it is only if this effort is pushed to the maximum, at the risk of disappointing linear logic, that we will perhaps be able to *think* of the Catastrophe as a *caesura* of history and of thought, as if the wind of this storm shook and tore thought, interrupted it, suspended it and took it by surprise — even the thought in the process of thinking of and writing this book.

And if it is the Catastrophe that broke through the tight mesh of logic and variations of thought, it is necessary to ask ourselves *where* this jolt comes about, *who* generates this shock. What happens to it? Who is strong enough to block thought? Who is weak enough to weaken it?

Like a barricade, the suffering of those who died in the camps and the gas chambers "blocks" the flow of thought. It is the extremism, singularity and scandal of this suffering that beg for a halt.

Their nakedness, impotence and weakness. *Their* naked hands.

They create an obstacle to the flow of thought and its discourse. They build a dyke against it. They resist it.

And thus they open it up to thinking *differently*, to *other words*. They open it up to *words* that are a struggle *for* speech and a disruption *of* speech, a necessity of expressing the silence of these sufferings and, at the same time, an impossibility of doing so with existing words and rules.

But in this interruption, which is also a stop and blockage, a horizon brightens.

There, on this horizon, a star marks the sky — a "shooting star," a star that burns for one single moment and speaks of "the hope of *redemption* that we nourish for all the dead" because "only for the sake of the hopeless ones have we been given hope"[58] — this weak little star of *redemption*.

3. CATASTROPHE AND REDEMPTION

We have already seen during these reflections that the idea of *redemption* is one of the concepts that props up Benjamin's theological thinking. But as always with this sometimes "impossible" author, beyond all the patterns and all the approximations, the unique sense and the univocity of sense, this idea runs through his thinking without having been explained or clarified. Moreover, if on one hand the idea of *redemption* is inseparable from the "image of happiness,"[59] as supported by the second thesis, on

---

[58] Walter Benjamin, "Goethe's Elective Affinities," trans. Stanley Corngold, *Selected Writings I*, *op. cit.*, 355-356.

[59] Benjamin, "On the Concept of History," 389.

the other hand it constantly reflects catastrophe. And not by contrast, but by analogy: indeed, not only is redemption opposed to catastrophe, even in the brief *moment* of interruption of the *continuum* or in that of *remembrance*, but it also corresponds to it, or rather, redemption forms part of its internal dialectic. Put another way, redemption emerges from catastrophe while being its opposite, or is contained, even implicit, in its internal "logic." Are we encountering a paradox here?

In order to understand this paradox, it is necessary to look at and tackle in greater depth the question of the ambiguity of the idea of catastrophe as understood by Benjamin, which we have seen repeated in its relationship to technological progress and to the historical *continuum*. Consequently, it is useful to listen to those who, like Scholem, knew his friend's research at close hand, while also having a certain familiarity with the ideas involved in the discourse. "An apocalyptic element of destructiveness," writes Scholem, referring to his friend, "is preserved in the metamorphosis undergone in his writing by the messianic idea, which continues to play a potent part in his thought. The noble and positive power of destruction [...] now becomes an aspect of redemption, related to the immanence of the world, acted out in the history of human labor."[60] Furthermore, according to Scholem, Benjamin's destructive messianism corresponds to a "secularization of Jewish apocalyptic doctrine."[61]

It is difficult to determine which of these two close friends influenced the other over the apocalyptic tone relating in Scholem's case to messianic Judaism and in Benjamin's to the idea of redemption. I like to think that both shared it, and that it was passed from one to the other over years of a deep and sincere friendship to which a rich correspondence[62] testifies. If indeed Scholem's contribution

---

[60] Gershom Scholem, *On Jews and Judaism in Crisis. Selected Essays* (New York: Schocken Books, 1976), 194.

[61] *Ibid.*, 195.

[62] Gershom Scholem, *Walter Benjamin: the Story of a Friendship*, trans. Harry Zohn (Philadelphia: Jewish Publication Society of America, 1981) and *The Correspondence of Walter Benjamin 1910-1940*, ed. Gershom Scholem and Theodor Adorno, trans. Manfred and Evelyn Jacobson (Chicago: University of Chicago Press, 1994).

is the rediscovery of the historical role of the apocalyptic spirit in Judaism, showing the permanence of a "dialectic between restorative and apocalyptic messianism,"[63] Benjamin's is the accentuation of its dialectical attitude applicable to this entirely Jewish idea of redemption and moving among the specifically apocalyptic suggestions of Jewish messianism. In any event, it is not useless to mention the idea of redemption, following the avenue that Scholem opens up in his famous article *"The Idea of Redemption in the Kabbalah,"*[64] as it reveals milestones and in particular, inasmuch as it concerns us here, demonstrates once and for all its implicit, even inherent relationship with the idea of catastrophe.

Indeed, if we have become unaccustomed to thinking of redemption in relation to the catastrophic dimension that is "part and parcel" of messianism[65] this is due to the legacy of the nineteenth century and the idea of continuous progression and infinite perfectibility in history, which made redemption the symbol of the final fulfillment of a path of liberation. On the other hand, old classical sources speak of redemption (*Geoulah*) as a "new state of the world"[66] occurring following upheavals, catastrophes and calamities, and fulfilled by the establishment of an absolutely new situation. Redemption, according to Scholem, is therefore "a colossal uprooting, destruction, revolution, disaster, with nothing of development or progress about it."[67] Redemption is therefore the second movement of a dialectic that aims to end history through apocalyptic destruction and establish a state of emancipation and deliverance.

Benjaminin's concept of redemption established in the exploding of the moment is effectively connected to these two elements combined in a single construction. On the one hand, it involves a dialectic, albeit within history, between a destructive and apocalyptic moment — the

---

[63] David Biale, *Gershom Scholem. Kabbalah and Counter-History* (Cambridge: Harvard University Press, 1982), 76.

[64] Gershom Scholem, *The Messianic Idea in Judaism, and Other Essays on Jewish Spirituality*, trans. Michael A. Mayer and Hillel Halkin (New York: Schocken Books, 1971), 37-48.

[65] *Ibid.*, 37.

[66] *Ibid.*, 38.

[67] *Ibid.*

discontinnum, wrenching catastrophe from the *continuum* and interrupting its homogeneous course, is in fact a micro-catastrophe — and the creative moment of deliverance from political oppression and the slavery of the repetition of the *same* through the uniqueness and non-recursiveness of the moment. On the other hand, redemption is condensed into a restoration of history within history itself, occurring in the act of repair that is the moment of remembrance. It is thanks to the remembrance of man rising up and fulfilled in the moment that history can be repaired. But is it not, at heart, the redemption of historical time? Indeed, in Benjamin's words, *"our life* [...] is a muscle strong enough to contract the whole of historical time. Or the genuine conception of historical time rests entirely upon the image of redemption."[68]

Redemption thus takes on the appearance of the *"weak* messianic power"[69] mentioned in the second thesis, a power which, though "weak," has been entrusted to *us*, given in the precious and fleeting tension of the moment, perhaps by the moment itself. Redemption needs a destructive moment, because only in the ashes of things built, the ruins of creation, the silence of desolation can we manage, beyond any control and any mastery, to hear the "evanescent voice"[70] of the moment, the grace of the cry that comes from elsewhere.

Like the constantly new angels spoken of in the Talmud and mentioned by Benjamin, angels that "are at each moment created anew in countless throngs, and who, once they have raised their voices before God, cease and pass into nothingness,"[71] *moments* also emerge suddenly to make us hear their cry, to be received, revived, and then disappear in their fleetingness. These *moments*, like the *new angels* — we do not know whether their songs are to complain to, denounce or exalt God — arise and disappear in their flight. Nor do we know if they exist to lament or praise in their cry. Furthermore, these angels, as Scholem adds, are "the angels of judgment as well as destruction. Their *'quickly fading voice'*

---

[68] Benjamin, *The Arcades Project*, 479. Cf. "Franz Kafka," *op. cit.*, 447: "no-one says that the distortions that the Messiah will one day come to put right are only spatial; surely they also concern the *time* in which we live."

[69] Benjamin, "On the Concept of History," 390.

[70] Walter Benjamin, "Karl Kraus," trans. Edmund Jephcott, in *Selected Writings II, op. cit.*, 457.

[71] *Ibid.*

proclaims the anticipation of the apocalypse in history."[72] Each angel, like each *moment*, heralds the final judgment with its "immediately fading" voice, its breath that dies away. It heralds the destruction and redemption that it brings. The final judgment, in Benjamin's words (echoing those of Kafka), becomes "a court-martial" that is held every day because "each moment is the moment of judgment over the moments that preceded it."[73] The final judgment, as redemption, is fixed in the hollowness of the *moment*, in the rich emptiness of its arrival and its destruction.

This is because the *moment* is born to immediately die; to spring, like Baroque allegory, from the realm of salvation to "that grim store which signifies death and damnation,"[74] or to make the opposite leap. Nevertheless, it expects to be gathered in the fall or parabola it shares with the angels; it expects to be received, saved and judged by another moment that forms a constellation with it, the messianic moment of *remembrance,* the moment that is perhaps capable of reversing "the bleak confusion of skeletons" into a non-order of "resurrection[s],"[75] though not without dizziness.

But is it not indecent to put forward such a hypothesis based on the redeeming power of the moment and hoping for the "resurrection" of the dead, of whom no-one has the right to speak unless they are *He who judges the living and the dead*? Is it not obscene to turn our eyes towards that horizon of redemption and resurrection while being attached to the *here* and *now* of this moment of writing, the moment of remembrance produced by writing itself taking shape? Is it not unbearable to think of redemption when everything has been achieved, accomplished? Intolerable to imagine the valley of bones from *Ezekiel* (37: 1-14) reembodied in Polish graves?

And yet, once again, Benjamin's previously quoted phrase intrudes: "only for the desperate were we given hope" — for those abandoned to

---

[72] Scholem, *On Jews and Judaism in Crisis*, 195.

[73] Benjamin, "Über den Begriff der Geschichte," 1245.

[74] Walter Benjamin, *The Origin of German Tragic Drama*, trans. John Osborne (London: Verso, 2003), 232.

[75] *Ibid.*, 232 [translation revised].

the solitude of the night in the "bowels of the sky" at Treblinka or in the *Lagerstrasse* at Birkenau.

The thinking of this philosopher who was not present for the end of the Catastrophe, but who was haunted by its start,[76] and who wanted to point his "telescope *through the bloody mist*"[77] which rose on the horizon, therefore marks a fundamental stage in considering, as we have seen, that catastrophe can be linked to technological progress, the historical *continuum* and *redemption* in their various aspects. And it is not unimportant that the sense of the relationship between catastrophe and redemption is concentrated on the moment, and most particularly that of remembrance, because the moment, too, is also tension condensed to the maximum degree, the "dialectical image,"[78] or the passage or *threshold* between an/its end and a/its salvation, a/its destruction and a/its redemption. Because the very dialectic between catastrophe and redemption is part of the moment, and perhaps also the subject of the Lohenstein verses quoted by Benjamin at the end of his unique work: "Yea, when the Highest comes to reap the harvest from the graveyard, then I, a death's head, will be an angel's countenance."[79]

---

[76] To the extent that, in a letter to Werner Kraft, dating from 1935, he writes: "I hardly feel constrained to try to make head or tail of this condition of the world. On this planet a great number of civilizations have perished in blood and horror. Naturally, one must wish for the planet that one day it will experience a civilization that has abandoned blood and horror [...] I am inclined to assume that our planet is waiting for this," in Benjamin, *Illuminations*, trans. Harry Zohn (New York: Schocken Books, 2007) 37-38.

[77] *Ibid*. [my emphasis]

[78] "This 'here-and-now'," writes Benjamin, "is distilled into images that we can call dialectical images. They represent a 'saving invention' for humanity": cf. "Über den Begriff der Geschichte," 1248.

[79] Benjamin, *The Origin of German Tragic Drama*, 232.

II. FROM THE *AFTER* TO THE *BEFORE*: FLASHES OF REMEMBRANCE

The theme of memory and *remembrance* (*Eingedenken*), which allows me to reinterpret Benjamin's work from the perspective of *afterwards* and to consider the recent past of the Catastrophe using his telescope technique, discreetly open to hope — the hope of being able to gather up the past, even imperceptibly, to hold its moments and thus perhaps to save them in the present moment of *today* and this writing — is the common thread that runs through the philosopher's writing in the 1930s and the crossroads, even the spiral, where purely theological themes relevant to the Jewish tradition come together and interweave. *Eingedenken* is indeed, according to Benjamin, "the quintessence of Judaism's theological concept of history."[80] And Benjamin seems to want to stress this precise point.

The importance of this almost inextricable theological interweaving is not due to Benjamin's "mystical" nature, according to his friend Bertolt Brecht's interpretation, but rather his attempt to rethink history theologically, yet without being able to rewrite it in the terms of a theology of history. It is as if a filter and another language were necessary for his thinking to not be completely absorbed into theology. In short, as mentioned in the first of his theses, he had to translate it into the more audible and presentable language of historical materialism. Benjamin's theological spirit needed a gap, a distance, a translation, in order to be spoken and have an chance of being heard — and also to be heard where Adorno was trying, despite his indecisions and ambiguities, to prepare a place for it among the members of the Institute and particularly its Director. Adorno recognized the importance of Benjamin's theological dimension applied to history or, which interested him more, to art; and he believed that Benjamin's subjects and method, while remaining theological, could provoke a real revolution in social theory, but he was not certain of how the much more materialist and Schopenhauerian Horkheimer would react to and tolerate it.

And there was no shortage of criticism. Replying to a letter dated March 16, 1937 from Horkheimer, who, on the subject of the theme of remembrance, believed that his colleague was tempted by theology in having to resort to an idea such as that of the final judgment, Benjamin

---

[80] Benjamin, "Über den Begriff der Geschichte," 1252.

answers: "the corrective to this line of thinking may be found in the consideration that history is not simply a science but also and not least a form of remembrance. *What science has determined, remembrance can modify. Such mindfulness can make the incomplete (happiness) into something complete, and the complete (suffering) into something incomplete.* That is theology; but in remembrance we have an experience that forbids us to conceive of history as fundamentally atheological, little as it may be granted us to try to write it with immediately theological concepts."[81] This passage shows that reflections on this subject were essential, and asserts the necessity of remembrance in history that is to be rewritten or retold by the materialist historiographer, while emphasizing the "weak messianic power" that is part of remembrance. This is a power capable of redeeming the victims' pain, in the past, of fulfilling the lost hopes of the oppressed, in short, of *retroactively* vanquishing the power of "the Antichrist,"[82] the tentacles and the ever new disguises of fascism. And if this also involves the necessity of believing in the final judgment,[83] for which Horkheimer criticizes him, Benjamin is ready to accept it: "*nothing that has ever happened should be regarded as lost to history.* Of course only a redeemed mankind is granted the fullness of its past — which is to say, only for a redeemed mankind has its past become citable in all its moments. Each moment it has lived becomes a *citation à l'ordre du jour*. And that day is Judgment Day."[84] In Benjamin's vision of history, therefore, mid-way between historical materialism and theology, the events of the past and also its moments are entirely retained, saved and redeemed on Judgment Day, which does not occur at the end of time, but is, as we have seen, part of every moment of every day, "here and now."

Paradoxically, almost thirty years later, it is on the subject of remembrance, this completely theological and Judaism-related idea, an idea that is also a *knowledge of memory*,[85] that Horkheimer would eventually agree in the 1960s with Benjamin's stance in the 1930s.

Thus, it seems to me to be essential to the perspective of this work, which recognizes the power of that idea, that we pause to further clarify

---

[81] Benjamin, *The Arcades Project*, 471 [my emphasis].

[82] Benjamin "On the Concept of History," 391.

[83] Benjamin, *The Arcades Project*, 471.

[84] Benjamin, "On the Concept of History," 390.

[85] Cf. *infra*, III, II. 3.

it rather than to revive the interpretative argument about Benjamin's two souls or to develop the issues of Benjamin's relationship with Adorno[86] or even to show the latter's mediation with the Director of the Institute of Social Sciences. However, the influence that Benjamin had on the thinking of the Frankfurt School, and in particular on that of Adorno, remains unquestionable, to the extent that we can say, along with Frankfurt School specialist Rolf Wiggershaus, that no one was able to understand it or make it their own as Adorno did.[87]

1. DIALECTIC OF REMEMBRANCE

Conscious of the impact of his discovery, that is to say the application of the theological idea of *Eingedenken* to history, Benjamin believed he had found the key point, the pivot, the axis around which "an attempt to become aware of the dialectical — the Copernican — turn of remembrance"[88] is possible. Sometimes humbly considered as the "wisp of straw clung to by something drowning,"[89] sometimes thought of as a "pivot"[90] where universal history can be broken, remembrance indeed moves between the personal and collective spheres, i.e. between a biography that must be rewritten and a history woven from chronicles that must be narrated. Therefore *Eingedenken* appears in Benjamin's writing not only to save history and rethink historiography, although this is one of the *leitmotifs* of his thinking, but also to give time *another* chance: the chance to not yield to forgetting, to not be reduced to a continuous and identical flow that, in its homogeneity, can melt and merge everything. In short, the chance to open up to it the possibility of *another* way of being time, of being on time for the end of time, of being a time of messianic times.[91]

---

[86] Cf. on this subject, Theodor Adorno, *Über Walter Benjamin: Aufsätze, Artikel, Briefe* (Frankfurt am Main: Suhrkamp, 1990).

[87] Cf. Rolf Wiggershaus, *The Frankfurt School*.

[88] Benjamin, *The Arcades Project*, 388.

[89] Benjamin, "Über den Begriff der Geschichte," 1243 and 1244.

[90] *Ibid.*, 1252.

[91] Cf. Gérard Bensussan, *Le temps messianique. Temps historique et temps vécu* (Paris: Vrin, 2001).

We can put forward the hypothesis whereby the "Copernican revolution" which Benjamin speaks of concerning his work is a revolution that specifically concerns time — not only by providing a vision of time applied to history and a revision of historiography, but also a concept of time that is developed thanks to his use of texts from the Jewish tradition (on the one hand) and the writings of Marcel Proust (on the other). Indeed, he writes in an authoritative fragment that I will quote in full: "The Copernican revolution in historical perception is as follows. Formerly it was thought that a fixed point had been found in 'what has been', and one saw the present engaged in tentatively concentrating the forces of knowledge on this ground. Now this relation is to be overturned, and what has been is to become the dialectical reversal — the flash of awakened consciousness. Politics attains primacy over history. The facts become something that just now first happened to us, first struck us; to establish them is the affair of memory. Indeed, awakening is the great exemplar of memory: the occasion on which it is given us to remember what is closest, tritest, most obvious. What Proust intends [...] is nothing other than what here is to be secured on the level of the historical, and collectively. There is a not-yet-conscious knowledge of what has been: its advancement has the structure of awakening."[92]

This complex fragment must be contemplated, as it offers various avenues of research not only for a new concept of history, but also suggestions to be applied to a new interpretation of the Catastrophe. First, Benjamin tries to define his "Copernican revolution" in "historical perception." Instead of considering "what has been" in the past as a fixed point towards which the present is turned, it is — according to him — necessary to think of it the other way around, i.e. as a movement and the interruption of a movement. In other words, the fixity of a point on the line that is supposed to represent time must be transformed into an intermittent dynamic that shakes the present. Furthermore, in parallel to this reversal of a fixed point into a movement, the direction itself must change. It is also not a question of a knowledge that the present should have of the past, in a groping attempt to approach it and master it, but the past's "not-yet-conscious knowledge" of the present. The past must therefore turn and gravitate towards the present, and burst into it. Thus, the past-present relationship is doubly inverted. A point is transformed

---

[92] Benjamin, *The Arcades Project*, 388-389.

into a dynamic, and a tension towards what is behind is changed into a "secret index"[93] extended towards what is ahead, as if, as far as the subject of this book is concerned, the recent past of the Extermination were still tacitly, secretly waiting for its future in *this* present, *our* present. It is clear that the present and other points in time have completely changed status in Benjamin's vision.

Later, Benjamin compares the "dialectical reversal" of the historiographic vision to an "awakening." What applies to collectivity, i.e. to knowledge in/of history, also applies to the individual. Or rather, it is the individual experience of awakening that can serve as a model for historiography. Indeed, the "awakening" represents the "paradigm" of remembering, because in the moment of awakening, remembering — of the dream in this case — intrudes suddenly, bursts in unexpectedly. According to this paradigm, the past, "what has been," takes the form of a dream that, remembered at the moment of awakening, is linked to the previous day's world. The past intrudes into the present, just as the dream makes its appearance at the moment of awakening. There is, in short, a passage from a "not-yet-conscious knowledge" (of the present by the past) to an "awakened consciousness" (of the past by the present). This passage from one state to another, awakening or "dialectical reversal," is consequently what allows the dream or the past — the past as a dream — to be extracted, to brought to the surface and to our consciousness. Benjamin draws a genuine parallel: "To pass through and carry out what has been in remembering the dream! — Therefore: remembering (*Erinnerung*) and awakening are most intimately related. Awakening is namely the dialectical, Copernican turn of remembrance (*Eingedenken*)."[94] If the parallel between remembering and awakening indicates the "new method" for historical science and the "Copernican revolution" attempted by Benjamin, it also highlights the "dialectic of remembrance" that is crucial for individual life.

The philosopher's alternation between these terms is revealing. Both words, remembering (*Erinnerung*) and remembrance (*Eingedenken*), appear in this last passage. We have already said that the act of awakening corresponds with that of remembering. But how does remembrance differ from this? Remembrance, it seems to me, is the *fulfillment* of the past

---

[93] Benjamin, "On the Concept of History," 390.

[94] Benjamin, *The Arcades Project*, 389.

in the present — "to *fulfill* the past in remembering the dream" — while remembering is an involuntary consciousness of "what has been." In the same way that awakening is the dream emerging and reaching the consciousness, remembering is the moment where the past "comes to mind." Remembrance, by contrast, is the *act* of *fulfilling* the past in the present, which presupposes the moment of remembering. There is a distinction between the *passivity* of remembering, where the past appears suddenly and unexpectedly, like a dream, occurring in the present, and a sort of *activity* of remembrance which acknowledges this coming and transforms it into an action, acting on the occurred past in and by way of the present. Once it has occurred, and reached our consciousness, this past must be transformed, and to do so requires the actuality of the present. If not, the past will not only remain past, but it cannot even be restored, i.e. it cannot be different from what it was, be transformed and actualized. The present of remembrance not only acts retroactively, restoring the past, but it transforms it by actualizing its unexpressed future promises. It gives the past a "higher grade of actuality than it had in the moment of its existing"[95] because it gives vent to what was tacit, secret, implicit, to what was only a promise at that moment. The present is consequently actualized itself by actualizing the intrinsic potential of the past. It is modified and invigorated in its turn.

We can say, in short, that Benjamin is led to speak of a "dialectic" by, on the one hand, the movement between the recovery of the past by remembering, and, on the other hand, its actualization by remembrance, i.e. its enactment, coming to be an act *in* the present and *of* the present itself. Indeed, why would there be a "dialectic" if there were no *double sense* in the movement of remembrance: the *sense* of remembering (the past towards the present) *and* the *sense* of remembrance proper (the present towards the past and towards the past's future)? "The dialectic of remembrance" is therefore a method of approaching time by transforming the present — the "here-and-now" (*Jetztzeit*) of the moment — into a *threshold*.

---

[95] *Ibid.*, 392.

2. DIALECTIC OF MEMORY AND FORGETTING

Although Benjamin does not always make the distinction between remembering and remembrance, it is extremely important to highlight it, as it is crucial to understanding the issue of "the dialectic" of remembrance. Indeed, this "dialectic" creates — or presupposes? — another, that of forgetting and memory. Is there not, ultimately, a "dialectic" between the forgotten that comes to mind, and the memory of the forgotten? This movement, this tension, but also this halt, which brings the forgotten to consciousness and brings memory to this "not-yet-conscious knowledge" of the forgotten?

The long, difficult but rich passage quoted above to explain the "dialectic of remembrance" also shows the influence of Proust on Benjamin's development of *Eingedenken*.

However, Benjamin goes further than Proust. The German philosopher, a passionate reader and the translator of two books of *À la Recherche du temps perdu*,[96] often cites the author in *Passagenwerk*, frequently coming back to the classic extract which describes *involuntary memory*.[97] He also dedicates the wonderful essay *"On the Image of Proust"*[98] (1934) — which is important for understanding this dialectic — to him, noting that Proust's work is not the narration of a life described as it was, but the "weaving of his memory, the Penelope work of recollection [*Eingedenken*]."[99]

Proust's research work, in the method and practice of its production, is a work of remembrance, a woven work that gathers up the threads of memories, instead of weaving/narrating experienced events. Remembrance, a weaving crowded with memories, opens up the dizzying heights of the "infinite"[100] dimension, whereas experiences are restricted to the finite, the limits of what we have experienced in our lives. Experiences are a limit, an end; remembered memories, however, are

---

[96] He translated *À l'ombre de jeunes filles en fleur* in 1927 and *Le côté de Guermantes* in 1930.

[97] Cf. *The Arcades Project*, fragment K 8,3-K 9,2; N 3a,3 and N 4,3.

[98] Walter Benjamin, "On the Image of Proust," trans. Harry Zohn, *Selected Writings II, op. cit.*, 237-247.

[99] *Ibid.*, 238.

[100] *Ibid.*

a *threshold*, a *passage*. "An experienced event is finite," writes Benjamin, "at any rate confined to one sphere of experience; a remembered event is infinite, because it is merely a key to everything that happened before it and after it."[101] Remembrance is the key, the *passe-partout* allowing memory to come and go, allowing *passage* from "everything" behind to "everything" ahead and vice-versa, allowing it to *pass through everything* in the memory. Memory's *pass* or *passe-partout*, remembrance is the act that unifies the text in Proust's weaving. Indeed, in the working of this cloth, it is remembrance that weaves, while memory dictates the "method of weaving." Fundamentally, remembrance is what makes the cloth, "the continuum of *memory*"[102] of weaving, and at the same time the result of this *act*, the right side of tapestry whose reverse side is made up of the intrigue of history.

However, although the work of this weaving is comparable to the saga of Penelope, we must consider that the moment of weaving is succeeded by the act of unpicking. She weaves during the day what she unraveled the night before. Thus, Benjamin wonders, as do I, whether Penelope's work, the act of remembrance, is closer to forgetting or memory: "is not the involuntary recollection, Proust's *mémoire involontaire*, much closer to forgetting than what is usually called memory? And is not this work of spontaneous recollection, in which remembrance is the woof and forgetting the warp, a counterpart to Penelope's work rather than its likeness? For here the day unravels what the night has woven."[103] In short, should we read remembrance, which seems to save the past and forgetting, as being in fact the sister to forgetting? Or more subtly, must we, with Benjamin and by way of Proust, recognize in remembrance a dialectic between forgetting and memory?

Benjamin's suggestion leads in this direction. Proust, Benjamin seems to tell us, weaves memories not because he remembers, but because he forgets them and rediscovers them in the depths of forgetting. It is forgetting that makes memories emerge, in some way. Proust's work, like the work of remembrance, is not only a search for recollections in

---

[101] *Ibid.*

[102] "Memory issues strict regulations for weaving. Only the *actus purus* of remembrance itself [...] constitutes the unity of the text."

[103] *Ibid.*

the memory, but an excavation in the hidden, buried ruins of forgetting, and thus the result woven by the dual movement of memory and forgetting — as if the horizontality of forgetting gave its sense to the stratum of memory, thus growing by way of and through forgetting.

And yet through the weaving metaphor, Benjamin fixes his attention on the "awakening" which, going beyond Proust and what he says at the end of his work, is what reveals the dialectic between memory and forgetting. Benjamin seems to reverse it, however, and give it a new sense, because he gives a double stratum to forgetting.

According to Benjamin's interpretation, the moment of "awakening," comparable to the highest degree with the moment of involuntary memory, in fact involves *both* memory *and* forgetting. More precisely, it involves the *passage* from one *to* the other and the *meshing* of one *with* the other. But the dialectical intrigue is complicated when Benjamin asserts that: "when we awake each morning, we hold in our hands, usually weakly and loosely, but a few fringes of the carpet of lived existence, as woven into us by forgetting. However, with our purposeful activity and, even more, our purposive remembering, each day unravels the web, the ornaments of forgetting."[104] In this passage, which immediately follows the metaphor of Penelope's tapestry, the terms are reversed. It is forgetting that weaves, and not memory[105]; forgetting weaves experiences while memory, prisoner to the awareness of ends, unweaves them. It is forgetting that allows its "ornaments" to decorate the "carpet of lived experience" during the night's sleep, in the state of unconsciousness or, as Benjamin prefers, in a "not-yet-conscious knowledge." By contrast, memory, prisoner to its aims and intentions, only undoes and unweaves during the day and by conscious activities what forgetting has created during the night. Forgetting therefore possesses a double stratum or a dual aspect. Although on the one hand, negatively, forgetting erases, destroys, undoes, and submerges everything in the indistinct, on the other hand, positively, it creates the dreams, the phantasmagoria, the arabesques. In undoing the conscious subject, it opens the door not to the unconscious or the irrational, but to a not-yet-conscious "knowledge" containing signs and promises, a knowledge to be deciphered and

---

[104] *Ibid.*

[105] However, there is a difference: forgetting weaves experiences; memory weaves recollections.

fulfilled. Paradoxically, forgetting allows the emergence of something longed for, of a longing.

The reversal that Benjamin carries out is not only with regards to Proust. Along with Proust, but going in a different direction than him, Benjamin changes the temporal structure that forms the basis of the classic relationship between memory and forgetting.

The issue in this line of thinking from Proust about remembrance and the memory-forgetting dialectic, which seems to distract us from our subject, also engages Adorno. Indeed, his criticism of Benjamin rests on the fact that the latter neglects one of the two elements of the dialectic, namely forgetting. "The great difficulty of the problem," he writes, "concerns the question of the background impression's unconscious character, which must be necessary if this impression is to fall to involuntary memory and not to the consciousness. But can we really talk of this unconsciousness? Is the moment when the madeleine is tasted, the source of Proust's involuntary memory, really unconscious? It seems to me that this theory is missing a dialectical link, that of forgetting."[106] Despite this criticism by his friend, Benjamin, on the contrary, seems quite aware of the role of forgetting in his analysis of involuntary memory and remembrance in his letter of February 29, 1940. He replies, stressing that "to give a true account of forgetting, one need not call into question the notion of *mémoire involontaire*,"[107] nor, above all, its *unconscious* character. Indeed, the experience of involuntary memory, in the famous passage about the madeleine, shows that it is doubly unconscious — in the moment where memory comes to mind, and in the moment when the child experiences the taste of the madeleine for a second time.

Contrary to what Adorno believes, Benjamin's emphasis on the involuntary, even unconscious, aspect of involuntary memory shows the central role of forgetting in remembrance. It is thanks to forgetting that the influences or dominations of the subject decrease their power, because forgetting is primarily a *forgetting of self*. It is forgetting applied by the conscious subject to itself, and therefore *forgetting of the consciousness,*

---

[106] Adorno, *Über Walter Benjamin, op. cit.*, 175.

[107] Walter Benjamin, *Selected Writings IV* (Cambridge: Belknap Press, 2006), 413. [translation modified]

forgetting of its intentions, its goals, its aims. And consequently, it is forgetting of the temporality managed by and based on consciousness. In this *forgetting of the subject, of self* and *of the consciousness*, even time is forgotten — the time of repetition, the identical and the same. This forgetting therefore allows time to be another time, to open itself up to the call of the new and the unseen, to the time of the other. It allows it to open itself to the unseen of the moment, which is always new and always other, even though it may already be past. It is forgetting, in short, that enables and elicits a longing for the present by the past moment. It is forgetting which transforms the temporal distance which separates them into a productive longing for one (the present moment) by the other (the past moment), and which creates this longing. Indeed, forgetting tears the temporal chain that makes two moments identical in the memory, one the repetition of the other. When everything seems to be already established, when the die is cast, forgetting — by forgetting *itself*, the *subject* and the *consciousness* — creates things that are original, new, and unseen. It interrupts a certain time and gives free rein to another time, a time when the past is free to be different than it was, free to be other. Free to be.

However, in order to fully become "knowledge," this "not-yet-conscious knowledge" (to use Benjamin's expression) — "knowledge" *without consciousness* that is brought by forgetting, half-knowledge that springs from the night and that speaks of another time and of time as other — needs the light of day. It needs to be explained by consciousness and deciphered by memory. It needs realization, the moment of awakening and searching of the memory. It needs a searching memory, a memory that sifts through forgetting, a memory that is vigilant towards the knowledge of the night. But most of all, it needs to be *active*, to search for what is supposed to be lost and actualize what is neither lost nor found but only waiting to be fulfilled, because it is memory, and not forgetting, that can *activate* a past that has not yet happened and *actualize* it in the present. It is memory that can give it a present, the possibility of happening, the possibility of being — even if only in the present moment of the *act* of realization, in the moment when the "lost future" of the past *passes* and is *actualized* in realization.

It is only in this way, thanks to this *passage* from a "not-yet-conscious knowledge" of forgetting to the conscious "knowledge" of active or activating memory, that remembrance — or involuntary memory, if we retain Proust's terminology — becomes a *"knowledge" of memory* for

Benjamin; a *knowledge of how to remember* a past that has never been, a past that has never taken place and yet that happens in the very moment when it is remembered. It becomes a paradoxical *knowledge*, then, that teaches the *memory* something *new*, something original, in the form of remembrance: according to the dialectic of forgetting and of memory, *knowledge of how to remember* the promises and yearnings of the past — a past that does not belong to us — that are once again claiming their future today. It becomes a *knowledge of how to remember* not the lost past but its future that is still waiting for its present, and waiting for it in *our* present, because, in the words of Benjamin, "there is a secret agreement between past generations and the present one. Then *our* coming was expected on earth."[108] This *knowledge of how to remember* is therefore a *knowledge* of how to listen to the tacit cries that link *us* to the past, and, at the same time, thanks to the activating and living power of the dialectic of remembrance, a *knowledge* of how to respond to this "secret agreement" with the past in the flash of a moment — in the moment that is a *passage*, a *passage* from the "not-yet-conscious knowledge" of forgetting to the conscious "knowledge" of memory; in the moment of remembrance "flashing up in the now of its recognizability (*Jetzt der Erkennbarkeit*),"[109] shining like a flash of lightning in order to finally be saved, or more imperceptibly, shining like a teardrop that is lost and unknown yet demands to be caught.

---

[108] Benjamin, "On the Concept of History," 390 [my emphasis].

[109] Benjamin, *The Arcades Project*, 473.

Interlude

A Philosophy of Testimony

No one testifies for the witness.
Paul Celan

"Open thy mouth for the dumb in the cause of all such as are appointed to destruction." This verse from the book of *Proverbs* (31:8) is in the epigraph of the testimony of Filip Müller,[1] one of the survivors of the *Sonderkommando* that opened and closed the gates of death at Auschwitz-Birkenau. Those who, like this man, saw the face of death, who saw the faces of the living become the faces of the dead, were supposed to be swallowed up by the storm like all the others. *None* of those who saw the laboratories where murder was committed or worked in the gas chambers, *none* of them were supposed to survive or tell the tale.

This man survived, however. This man, however — and despite himself — accepted the imperative of the biblical verse, the imperative of testimony: he opened his mouth. "So," he recounts, "I went into the gas chamber with them, and I was resolved to die. With them. [...] Suddenly, some people who recognized me came up to me. [...] A small group of women approached. They looked at me and said [...] One of them said: 'So you want to die. But that's senseless. Your death won't give us back our lives. It's not an act. You must get out of here alive, *you must bear witness to our suffering* and to the injustice done to us.'"[2]

---

[1] Filip Müller, *Eyewitness Auschwitz: Three Years in the Gas Chambers*, trans. Susanne Flatauer (New York: Stein & Day, 1979) [my emphasis].

[2] Claude Lanzmann, *Shoah* (Paris: Gallimard, 1985), 235 [my emphasis]. The episode is related in more detail in Müller's testimony, cf. Müller, *op. cit.*, 113-114.

Filip Müller wanted to die and accept the same fate as them. But the women, already stripped, already on the threshold, pushed him out by force. Seized by the arms and legs, he was returned to life so that he could *tell*, so that he could *testify*. And the imperative of the Word resounded — and still resounds today in the ears of those who listen and read — on the lips of one of these women: "Open thy mouth for the dumb in the cause of all such as are appointed to destruction." It is an imperative to speak; an imperative to bear witness when speech and words have lost the right to say anything; an imperative to speak when not only history, but also language, have been torn up and broken.

It is in listening to the account of this *Sonderkommando*, who saw death without facing it head on, that we can attempt to consider the testimony of the Extermination. He is, indeed, the closest to those swallowed up and the last to have heard their voices, their songs, their silence, and despite himself, he can communicate the "sense" of testimony.

The act of testimony by this man, returned from among the dead, and returning because he was forced by dead witnesses to testify to their death, thus reveals the paradox of testimony: telling the interruption of telling. Though in this account Müller's living voice speaks for the dead, it should nonetheless express the interruption of their voices. It should communicate the incommunicable and speak the unspeakable. It should tell of the voices that were raised inside the gas chamber. But as Shoshana Felman very accurately says about this account that is also featured in Claude Lanzmann's film *Shoah*, "the inside is *incommunicable* […]. Inside the crematorium, 'on the other side of the door, where everything had disappeared and everything had become silent,' there is loss: loss of voice, of life, of knowledge, of awareness, of truth, of the capacity to feel, of the capacity to speak."[3]

Inside.

Outside, on this side of the door where all sound has died away, stands this man with his story. He stands on the threshold of the crematorium, between death and life, and he stays there as a witness.

---

[3] Shoshana Felman, "A l'âge du témoignage," in *Au sujet de Shoah, le film de C. Lanzmann*, edited by Michel Deguy (Paris: Belin, 1990), 88.

So can we not venture the idea that his testimony, on the threshold of the gas chamber, is a passage? A passage that separates the inside and the outside? A passage that holds the silence of the inside, but also carries a message to and for the outside? In other words, can we not think of testimony as this crossing from the inside to the outside, a crossing that requires an outside? That demands to be listened to, and thus communicated? That requires a *through* and calls for an *other* to communicate to?

In the following pages, I aim to establish whether a philosophy of testimony, particularly testimony of the Extermination, is possible, and under what conditions.

These reflections will, therefore, open up questions on the paradox of testimony and will merge with and problematize Jean-François Lyotard's discourse on the silences of witnesses as tackled in *The Differend*. What does the silence of the absent tell us? How should we interpret it? Can there be a testimony of the silences of the annihilated? Furthermore, what does this testimony contribute to philosophical discourse? Afterwards, another survivor, whose testimony is more familiar to me, will be allowed to speak: Primo Levi. From him we will learn the distinction between "the drowned" (*i sommersi*) and "the saved" (*i salvati*), that is to say between the real witnesses, all swallowed up, and the survivors whom it is problematic to speak of as witnesses. By paying attention to this other voice, we will discover, as Müller's testimony indicated, that the saved bear witness *in primis* for the absent, but also so that someone else receives their testimony, i.e. so that their testimony is called for by another and addressed to an *other*, to *us*. Finally, with Paul Ricœur we will approach the question of the possibility of a philosophy of testimony in order to outline a philosophy of testimony of the catastrophe.

In this book, a philosophy of testimony will bear witness to the Holocaust, drawing together authors and making them witnesses. And it calls for them, in their testimonies, to address their testimony to an *us* capable in our turn of becoming witnesses to the communication of testimony.

SILENCES OF THE WITNESSES

The problem of bearing witness to the death camps is confronted in a direct way by Lyotard, the "courageous author of an enduring *meditation* on the destruction of European Jews,"[4] in the words of Elisabeth de Fontenay who dedicated a good book to him. In *The Differend: Phrases in Dispute* (1983), on the basis of the only unquestionable object — "the phrase" — and raising a problem of logical order, Lyotard admits that what is at stake in his thinking is to "save the honor of thinking."[5] The book thus begins with the description of a particular *case* where a *differend* arises: "You are informed that human beings endowed with language were placed in a situation such that none of them is now able to tell about it. Most of them disappeared then, and the survivors rarely speak about it. When they do speak about it, their testimony bears only upon a minute part of this situation. How can you know that the situation itself existed? That it is not the fruit of your informant's imagination? Either the situation did not exist as such. Or else it did exist, in which case your informant's testimony is false, either because he or she should have disappeared, or else he should remain silent, or else because, if he or she does speak, he or she can bear witness only to the particular experience he had, it remaining to be established whether this experience was a component of the situation in question."[6] We can see where the irony is leading: the absurdity of the gas chambers' reality becomes clear in the arguments and theories of negationists who apply a very specific logical device to a certain type of argument to conclude that the gas chambers did not exist. This logical device is not often distinguished by historians, hence the necessity to know how to recognize it and, if necessary, to make a correct argument using valid inferences.[7] Lyotard makes much of the logical basis on which the impossibility of survivors'

---

[4] Elisabeth de Fontenay, *Une tout autre histoire. Questions à J.-F. Lyotard* (Paris: Fayard, 2006).

[5] Jean-François Lyotard, *The Differend: Phrases in Dispute*, trans. Georges Van Den Abbeele (Minneapolis: University of Minnesota Press, 1988), xii.

[6] *Ibid.*, 3.

[7] Lyotard questions the attitude of the historian, in this case Pierre Vidal-Naquet who tries to respond to Mr. Faurisson's denial. Cf. *Assassins of Memory: Essays on the Denial of the*

testimony is formulated. As the quoted passage shows, the device on which this position is constructed includes the simultaneous use of two logical operators: exclusion (either, or) and implication (if... then). Either such an extreme situation did not exist, or it did. If it did, then *no-one* should bear testify to it. Hence the *differend*. And, if there are some witnesses, their testimony can only bear witness to a singular experience, too singular to truly relate to the situation in question, or so personal — an "account," as Hilberg says[8] — that it reveals only what the witness has decided to say.

The *differend*, the impossibility of pressing charges to obtain reparation for a wrong or of presenting proof of damages suffered, particularly relates to the testimony of extermination camps because those who would have been able to bear witness directly — those who died in the gas chambers — are all dead, and those who survived cannot take the place of the dead. Nor do they have the right to testify, because their testimony is considered as false, given that they are still here, still alive. As Lyotard firmly states, "the only witnesses are the victims, and [...] there are no victims but dead ones."[9] In other words, the fact of *bearing witness* runs up against the impossibility of *being* a witness, or rather, testimony revokes and invalidates the witness because the true witness has died, has been annihilated, and with him his possibility of speech, including the speech to provide testimony. Thus, a *differend* is established when speech is interrupted; when something that should be able to be put into speech, "into phrases,"[10] is not; and when, for those who remain, the "feeling" arises of not having the words — when there is something to say and yet this thing remains unsaid. One *cannot*.

And yet silence, several silences even, have been caused which require interpreting — silences which call for speech. But these silences, which according to Lyotard are betrayed by the survivor's "feeling" of

---

Holocaust, trans. Jeffrey Mehlman (New York: Columbia University Press, 1992).

[8] Raul Hilberg, *Sources of Holocaust Research* (Chicago: Ivan R. Dee, 2001), 49. Cf. also *Perpetrators, Victims, Bystanders: The Jewish Catastrophe 1933-1945* (New York: Harper Collins, 1992).

[9] Lyotard, *The Differend*, 5.

[10] *Ibid.*, 13.

not having the words, are precisely the indication of the *differend*. In these silences, the *differend(s)* are revealed and ask to be heard as such. But in this path from *differend* to silence and from silence to *differend*, we must know how to decipher the silences, and how to recognize them. There is the silence — or silences — of those who are dead. This silence is unutterable, with no possibility of being told, final. Another silence separates the living and the dead, the dead and the survivors. It is a silence of separation, the silence of impossible communication, impossible communion — those who are alive cannot speak for those who those who are no more. Finally, there is the silence of the survivors, which on the contrary can say something, testify *to* (or *against*) something, and which can be arranged in different categories. Lyotard distinguishes four of them in this case: the silence of survivors who say that the extermination camps and the existence of gas chambers are not the addressee's business; the silence that gives credit to the arguments of Holocaust deniers; the silence that is a sign of the insane and the inexpressible; and the silence that denies survivors any authority as witnesses.

But does the silence of the survivors, though eloquent, or the reticence of the saved to tell the tale, as Lyotard imagines, correspond to the reality of the facts? Was there not already a "mass of testimonies," to use historian Annette Wieviorka's[11] expression, in 1983 when his book was published? Furthermore, can we not criticize Lyotard, despite his good intentions, for a misinterpretation of the facts, and particularly the testimonies of the *Sonderkommando*, those who were next to the death chambers, such as that of Filip Müller (1980) and the manuscripts buried and discovered in the ground at Birkenau (1982)?[12] Can we not say, like de Fontenay, and while recognizing that Lyotard "refuses to plug this hole in the world that has been called *anus mundi*," that he forbids himself from filling in this hole by forbidding the saved to do so, and that he does this "by virtue of an excessive deference towards the drowned"?[13]

---

[11] Cf. Annette Wieviorka, *Déportation et génocide. Entre la mémoire et l'oubli* (Paris: Plon, 1992), 167-190 and *L'ère du témoin* (Paris: Plon, 1998).

[12] Ber Mark, *Des voix dans la nuits* (Paris: Plon, 1982), resumed in *Des voix sous la cendre. Manuscrits des Sonderkommandos d'Auschwitz-Birkenau* (Paris: Calmann-Levy/FMS, 2005).

[13] de Fontenay, *Une tout autre histoire*, 140.

These silences of which Lyotard speaks testify *against* something: against the authority of the addressee, against that of the witness, against language's capacity to signify the absurdity of the gas chambers' existence. But they also testify *to* something; they testify to something absolutely new, to the interruption of language: "With 'Auschwitz,' something new has happened in history (which can only be a sign and not a fact), which is that the facts, the testimonies that bear the traces of a *here* and *now*, the documents which indicated the sense or senses of the facts, and the names, finally, the possibility of various kinds of phrases whose conjunction makes reality, all this has been destroyed as much as possible."[14] Auschwitz becomes a sign of the sign's erosion; not only the facts and the documents relating to these facts, but also the testimonies, the names, the phrases in which reality is inscribed in its entirety, and by which all testimony can be expressed and all language uttered — all this was destroyed at Auschwitz. Thus, Lyotard does not want to reconcile or stitch up this absolute fracture in history, which is also a fracture in thought, and, primarily, a destruction of language. He wants us to watch over "a modality of nothing: what has happened is nothing that can be set out in language, none of it can be told."[15]

Lyotard speaks of the "destruction of language." I prefer the term "interruption." And this very preference highlights a different attitude, a less radical one perhaps, that something exists *afterwards* instead of an absolute nothing. And it exists not for a reconstruction at any cost, but rather as the price of a fidelity and of a testimony to these silences.

It is true that the "caesura of Auschwitz" not only interrupted history, but also language, and did so in two dimensions: interruption *in* language and, at the same time, interruption *of* language. At Auschwitz, and outside it, the impossibility of telling or finding the words to recount it becomes the rule. It is a rule that has been sealed by the survivors' fear of not being heard or believed, but an absurd rule, because a demand to tell of the event is added to the impossibility of speaking about it.

But the injury that kept the survivors silent for years was followed by the obligation to reveal it, and in the revelation is an obligation to tell of this absurdity. A caesura, an interruption, is therefore curled up within language, within its semiotic function, the communication of

---

[14] Lyotard, *The Differend*, 57.

[15] de Fontenay, *Une tout autre histoire*, 140.

meaning — a caesura that Filip Müller, like so many others who survived the massacres, experienced in the first person, as a *witness*.

On the other hand, the speech and voices of millions of men were suffocated at Auschwitz. Speech was violently transformed into its opposite. It was punctuated by silences. And *afterwards*, the speech and voices — are they similar? — of those who could attest to what had happened took a long time to make themselves heard and welcomed, admittedly for various reasons. However, was not this delay also a delay of language? The delay of a language not yet ready to find correspondence between words and events? Between the words and the "unreal" — beyond the imaginable — facts that were proven?

Language, indeed, was not — and still is not — prepared or willing to record and translate the interruption that it suffered. But to be precise, such research work on a new language would be a matter for a literature and philosophy of *afterwards*: "to bear witness to differends by finding idioms for them,"[16] says Lyotard, by finding words, names, phrases and a syntax capable of telling.

How to tell, in fact? How to tell, here, in this book, of the interruption of language and at the same time the weak power of testimony? How to express the caesura of language while listening to the words of the survivor-witnesses? While interpreting philosophers from the perspective of testimony and considering them as witnesses?

The difficulty of such a task is manifested above all in the confusion, difficulty and shifting, which also apply to me, over the term used to designate the event; Holocaust, *Shoah*, *Churban*, Catastrophe, Genocide, Extermination and Auschwitz are only terms — sometimes more appropriate, sometimes less — that partially designate the event or throw light on a single aspect of it, but which, all together, demonstrate the inability of language to translate in a single word — in a concept? — the fracture that took place. As to the metonymy of Auschwitz, which makes a whole — all of the extermination camps — from a part — a single place of torture — and which, at a pinch, should be replaced with Birkenau or Treblinka — we can say that it also bears witness to some difficulty regarding its usage. Sometimes used in italics, sometimes in inverted commas as Lyotard does and sometimes not, as I do here when I cannot avoid resorting to the word or if I want to best designate the event itself,

---

[16] Lyotard, *The Differend*, 13.

it must be recognized that it becomes a powerful model — although sometimes suffering from rhetorical redundancy — that tacitly establishes and condenses into a name what actually took place, as if this horror was impossible to express except through the name developed by those who transformed Oswiecim into Auschwitz, those who invented the structures and conditions of that abyss. This place name, Auschwitz — written without inverted commas because it then becomes a relevant abstraction of the concept — can now say the unspeakable about what happened there and, at the same time, the difficulty of saying it. "A name without a 'speculative name,' irrecuperable in terms of a concept,"[17] as Lyotard writes, it is however a *non-witness* that can *testify* to both the event itself and the fracture of language which occurred there, as if this name were of the same order, or rather dis-order, as the fracture: a name as a fracture and as a caesura.

For Lyotard, another example of the interruption *of* language is the loss of the subject of the phrase, the loss of subjects in phrases relating to the Extermination, a loss due to the absence of witnesses: "In the concentration camps," he writes, "there would have been no subject in the first-person plural. [...] no *Selbst* which could prevail upon itself to name itself in naming 'Auschwitz.' No phrase inflected in this person [we] would be possible. [...] There would be no collective witness."[18] No one can bear witness to Auschwitz using the first-person plural — no *"we."* No plural subject, I can agree; no "adding up" of *I, you* and *they*. But is testimony not characterized precisely by the fact that the person testifying uses the first person, albeit in the singular? Is what he says not valid precisely because the *I* implies the *here* and *now* of a singular history? But why, then, can that history not bear witness to anything or anyone? It would at least testify to what says "I," even if it cannot in any circumstances say "we"?

While sharing the philosopher's line of thought on the paradox (for him, an aporia) of testimony, and even on the impossibility of collective testimony, on the impossibility of a plural subject of witnesses — the engulfed — I do not yet understand (or rather, I understand but do not agree with) why Lyotard does not afford any importance to the *singularity* of testimony, even that of a single survivor. It is as if the subject itself,

---

[17] *Ibid.*, 88.
[18] *Ibid.*, 97-98.

whether in the singular or plural, had no possibility of surviving either; as if the subject as such, the *Selbst*, was annihilated and along with it the plural subject of the saved *we* and of the *we after* Auschwitz.

And yet Lyotard's issue with regards to the *we* is not unimportant to my discourse. Indeed, the logical impossibility of a "we" at Auschwitz — an impossibility due primarily to the absence of an *I-you* relationship between the SS and the deportees, and even to the absence of a relationship between individuals, because there no longer were any individuals; and due secondly to the powerlessness or incapacity of new arrivals to identify with any community — according to Lyotard, this impossibility also determines the impossibility of a *we afterwards*. The annihilation of a given "we," the Jewish "we," implies the elimination of *we* who come *afterwards*: "Delegitimation is complete [...]. Were this *we* called humanity (but then it wouldn't have been a collective proper name), then 'Auschwitz' is indeed the name for the extinction of that name. That is why the question 'Auschwitz?' is also the question 'after Auschwitz?'. The unchaining of death, the utmost obligation, from what legitimates it is perpetuated 'after' the crime."[19]

Must we therefore construe that the murder of the individual is accomplished not through the murder of the singular individual, but through the suppression of the plural individual, namely the elimination of the *we*? Thus, with and through the death of the "we," are *we* also dead? Does the *afterwards*, which I have spoken of from the outset and which will be crucial in the following pages, therefore have no right to be? Is the memory of this annihilated "we" therefore not held by any *we*? Is it, as Lyotard says, "nobody's memory, about nothing and no one"?[20]

Lyotard is drastic. With death at Auschwitz, the possibility of an *afterwards*, of a logical *we* "bearing this name," a *we* that holds the memory of the impossible "we" of the engulfed, also died. For this philosopher, death at Auschwitz ordains the absolute end, the final solution to thought. And the question of knowing what the "spirit has gained at 'Auschwitz'"[21] or what we can reconstruct from its ashes and its ruins seems to him to be indecent, superfluous: "As for 'us,' 'afterward,'"

---

[19] *Ibid.*, 101. [my emphasis]
[20] *Ibid.*
[21] *Ibid.*, 104.

he writes, "we receive these two phrases as two silences [...] 'we' deem it more dangerous to make them speak than to respect them. It is not a concept that results from 'Auschwitz,' but a feeling, an impossible phrase."[22] A *feeling*, mixed with silences: for us, this is *what remains of Auschwitz*.[23]

Nevertheless, despite the "dispersion without witnesses," a third person — another witness — makes their appearance in Lyotard's line of thinking. Paradoxically, another *we* appears, this *we* consisting of he or she who is in the process of reading and understanding. In order to express the "extinction of the third," as the author does throughout his book, a third was needed — a *we* consisting of a person who writes and a person who reads, a *we* consisting "at least of *I* who write and *you* who read."[24] But this second degree testimony, this testimony that makes *us* witnesses in some way, is not a "reflective movement"[25] of the impossibility of testimony, as suggested by Lyotard. Rather, its very intrigue, its paradox, asserts the possibility of testimony even while denying it, and asserts it through this external *we*, even if this is only *witness* to the "extinction" of the witness, and notes "that something remains to be phrased,"[26] still according to Lyotard. Here, thanks to the idea that passes through this *we* — through the author of *The Differend* and its reader, but also through the author of this book and its reader, and so forth — it becomes, paradoxically, possible to tell, to testify to the impossible testimony.

And yet, is it not going too far to say that *they*, the saved, are not witnesses, and that *we*, by contrast, are? That *we* are witnesses in the testimony of the impossibility of testimony?

This discourse, what is said, will remain decent only if this second degree testimony bears witness to *what is left of testimony*, only if it is a discourse that bears witness above all to the silences of the witnesses.

---

[22] *Ibid.*

[23] This expression indirectly echoes Giorgio Agamben, *Remnants of Auschwitz: the Witness and the Archive*, trans. Daniel Heller-Roazen (New York: Zone Books, 2000). Cf. also the critique of this book by Philippe Mesnard and Claire Kahane, in *Giorgio Agamben à l'épreuve d'Auschwitz* (Paris: Kimé, 2001).

[24] Lyotard, *The Differend*, 103

[25] *Ibid.*

[26] *Ibid.*, 57.

It must be a discourse, but also a knowledge, that lends "an ear to what is not presentable under the rules of knowledge,"[27] discourse and knowledge that are torn and interrupted like language, and even in language. This knowledge and what is said can thus only be prevented, in their shamelessness, from repeating murder if they fulfill the sad task of giving a voice to the silences — the silences caused by murder — despite everything. For, according to Lyotard, it is up to the historian — but why not also the philosopher? — to "take into account not only the damages, but also the wrong. Not only the reality, but also the meta-reality that is the destruction of reality. Not only the testimony, but also *what is left of the testimony* when it is destroyed (by dilemma), namely, the feeling. Not only the litigation, but also the differend."[28]

Nonetheless, I believe it is up to the philosopher to take into account above all the silences that indicate human suffering and not only, as Lyotard suggests (too concerned here about sophistication), the silences indicating that phrases are "in abeyance of their becoming event."[29] Indeed, these silences first reveal someone's suffering, and only then the suffering of language, a suffering that emerges from the fracture between language and event. In any case, to take into account these silences, the historian — but also the philosopher — must break with the "monopoly [...] granted to the cognitive regimen" and venture forth to "lend an ear" to what is not found in the rules of knowledge, i.e. to what exceeds, eludes and escapes, like these silences, this suffering.

But to "lend an ear" to what is at the limits of the knowable and speakable does not necessarily imply giving in to the temptations of the irrational or the insane, or even the absurd. On the contrary, it suggests venturing into a new typology of sense, towards a utopia of sense which at least has the sense of forbidding us to ignore the silences of history.

"The silence imposed on knowledge does not impose the silence of forgetting," writes Lyotard again.[30] And I agree. The silences of witnesses, these silences that we have said are impossible to bear witness to, do not require *us* to intensify our forgetting. On the contrary, and despite the problems raised by Lyotard's study, they call on *us* to testify, even

---

[27] *Ibid.*

[28] *Ibid.* [my emphasis].

[29] *Ibid.*

[30] *Ibid.*, 56.

if it is to testify to the impossibility of testimony that is imposed on knowledge. This address to *us* tells us something. Despite the silence, it tells something to us — *we* who are writing this book. *We* who want to let these silences *speak* in what philosophical thought *says*. *We* who want to "lend an ear" to them. *We*, in short, who allow ourselves to be affected by these silences and by the "alarm"[31] sounded by feeling, which is the sign of "the wrong done to the victims,"[32] so that these silences can come to our knowledge. So that they make *us* know. So that they say something to our way of knowing.

But what the words of those who bear a testimony despite everything — those who make a counter-melody to these silences with their words — tell *us* remains to be shown. It is left to *us*, in short, to "lend an ear" to the words of those who survived, to these witnesses — even if it is just one — on whom testimony is imposed.

WORDS OF THE SAVED

Despite the Nazi project to eliminate all witnesses — to the point of forcing the detainees, the secret holders (*Geheimnisträger*), to undertake death marches at the beginning of 1945; despite the Nazi project to erase any trace — to the point of attempting to remove all trace of the bodies, which would have been able to testify physically to their own murder; despite the attempt to make any witness accounts inaudible due to the enormity of the facts to be related; despite all of this, some came back, and some have spoken of it. And one among them had the power to speak and write, to tell *us*, of the impossibility of testimony.

Although he dedicated his life *afterwards* to testifying to what he experienced at Auschwitz III-Buna-Monovitz — by writing, by interviews with journalists, friends or elementary school children — Primo Levi also tells *us* at the same time of the *necessity* of testimony and its *impossibility*. A witness testifies to the death of the witness, to the death of the "complete witnesses" who were engulfed by the storm. *They* all died. Thus, forty years later, Levi gives a revealing title to his final book: *The Drowned and the Saved* (*I sommersi e i salvati*). This title clearly makes the distinction

---

[31] *Ibid.*, 13.
[32] *Ibid.*, 56.

between those who were engulfed and those who — by chance? luck? ability? — remained alive. These are the saved, they are the "*salvati.*" Nevertheless, for Levi just as for Lyotard, these are not true witnesses. In one remarkable page, a page that should be reflected on and quoted in its entirety, Levi writes: "I must repeat: we, the survivors, are not the true witnesses. This is an uncomfortable notion of which I have become conscious little by little, reading the memoirs of others and reading mine at a distance of years. We survivors are not only an exiguous but also an anomalous minority: we are those who by their prevarications or abilities or good luck did not touch bottom. Those who did so, those who saw the Gorgon, have not returned to tell about it or have returned mute, but they are the '*Muselmänner,*' the submerged, the complete witnesses, the ones whose deposition would have a general significance. They are the rule, we are the exception. [...] We who were favored by fate tried, with more or less wisdom, to recount not only our fate but also that of the others, indeed of the drowned; but this was a discourse 'on behalf of third parties,' the story of things seen at close hand, not experienced personally. The destruction brought to an end, the job completed, was not told by anyone, just as no one ever returned to recount his own death."[33]

Levi's voice is thus raised among this anomalous "minority," by the exception that of being the saved, to say that the complete witnesses are all dead and that they could not bear witness in any way because no one has ever returned to tell of their own death. This voice is raised to tell of the historical impossibility of being a witness, and, *at the same time*, the historical impossibility of escaping the obligation to be or become a witness. Thus, testimony is thwarted by the impossibility of recounting, and at the same time *tells us* of this impossibility. The paradox of testimony produced by the Extermination is also an obstacle for Levi: he must testify to the murder of millions of human beings, and, *at the same time*, the death of the witness; the death of the complete witnesses, the "drowned" — of whom there is nothing left but ashes and silence — and *at the same time*, the death of his own testimony, i.e. the autobiographical moment of his own death as a witness. All that is left is for him to admit to the death of the subject of testimony, and *at the same time*, to express in *his* words the

---

[33] Primo Levi, *The Drowned and the Saved*, trans. Raymond Rosenthal (New York: Vintage International, 1989), 83-84.

first steps that allow him to formulate this line of thinking. In short, he must express a sequence of three paradoxes: firstly, testifying to the death of the witness, i.e. to death of those who were engulfed and the subject of testimony; secondly, testifying to the murder of the witnesses and his own death as a witness; and finally, while admitting this death of the testifying subject, by *his* words he *says* "I," first-person singular, which in some way restores life to the subject.

Of course, this radical line of thinking, which admits the impossibility of testimony and *at the same time* its necessity, and which is articulated in three paradoxes, took years for Levi to develop. At the start, in 1946, when he wrote *If This Is A Man*, Levi believed he was performing a work of testimony, but in another sense: he is an eyewitness, so his account must meet the requirement of a legal statement. His readers must judge; they must pass judgment on related things. Next, he understood that his testimony cannot remain solely at this first stage. He gradually understood that his life was heavily influenced by his testimony, and that writing and speech were, perhaps, the only way of living *afterwards*. Finally, in his last book, he admits his inability to decipher the reasons that drove him to persevere in his testimony: "I could not say," he confesses, "whether we did or do so out of a kind of moral obligation toward those who were silenced or in order to free ourselves of their memory; certainly we do it because of a strong and durable impulse."[34] This impulse, recognizable to psychoanalysts, is a "strong" impulse which allows the voice to speak, to resonate in the depth of the silences that accompany it and that — knowing that it cannot by any means take the place of these silences — it tries in some way to make into something, even if only a breath. It is a strong impulse for a voice which already knows it is so weak and fragile that it cannot really know for what or whom it is breathing or speaking, despite everything. But where does this impulse come from?

I do not know whether this impulse to testify, which Levi felt so deeply and which changed shape over the course of the years, is external or internal to him. One point seems clear, however: what opens Levi's mouth and drives his pen is not under his control. He testifies "because of" an impulse that perhaps has the force of a *plea*. Which perhaps is a *plea*. A *decree*.

---

[34] *Ibid.*, 84.

First, it is to *them* (as he constantly refers to them in this page) — to *them*, the drowned, the engulfed, the complete witnesses — that he responds. He responds to the plea of their silence. He responds to *them* by order, by warrant, because their summons is precisely their silence. And he, the proxy, the one who returned, can only accomplish his duty in the one way possible for him: to recount the things seen "at close hand," to write about what he experienced himself, without being able to tell what it is to "touch bottom" because he "never set foot in Birkenau."[35] Thus, he, Primo Levi, can only bear witness, by his breath, to the silent plea of the true witnesses.

Next — but this is perhaps the start — he responds to another silence, perhaps also to another silent plea. He responds to a silence that is worrying even for Levi, the atheist. By his testimony, he perhaps responds to the anguish created by the silence of abandonment, abandonment by God in the absence of man. He responds to the atavistic anguish whose "echo one hears" — he writes — "in the second verse of Genesis: the anguish inscribed in everyone of the 'tohu-bohu,' of a deserted and empty universe crushed under the spirit of God but from which the spirit of man is absent: not yet born or already extinguished"[36] — as if testimony was a response and a resistance to the anguish of God's silence already inscribed in the absence of man, a resistance that can only act by keeping alive the spirit of man through speech. In short, a resistance whose only modality is to reanimate in man the "divine spark"[37] that was extinguished in the death camps and in the gas chambers.

Finally, Levi responds to the plea that comes from *us*, from *our* request, *our* longing for knowledge, without knowing it. From *our* silent longing for learning — within the limits imposed by such knowledge — what happened. He responds to *our* longing, which, to his ears, remains silent, like a silence, because it has not yet taken shape, not yet happened in speech. It is a longing revealed in a great future silence. It is the plea of the *we* to come — *we*, the generations that have come after; *we*, the children who asked him questions from school desks; *we*, the philosophers

---

[35] Primo Levi, *Le devoir de mémoire*, French trans. Anna Bravo and Federico Cereja (Paris: Les Mille et une Nuit, 1994), 27.

[36] Levi, *The Drowned and the Saved*, 85.

[37] Levi, *If This Is A Man*, 96.

who wonder about the Catastrophe; *we*, the logical subject of this line of thinking; *we*... It is perhaps for *us* and to *us*, to *our* fertile silence, that Levi, like Filip Müller, has already responded.

THE *HERE* AND THE *NOW* OF TESTIMONY

After all this, after these reflections, is there any "sense" in speaking of a philosophy of testimony? Furthermore, is a philosophy of testimony possible? What can testimony contribute to philosophical discourse? What can these reflections on the testimony of the Catastrophe contribute to philosophy, to our philosophical discourse, which is being woven in this book?

If we follow Paul Ricœur's line of thinking in *"The Hermeneutics of Testimony,"*[38] if we take a few steps with him and immediately go further than him (ignoring what is marginal to this topic), a philosophy of testimony is possible only if it is a philosophy of *interpretation*. Testimony is indeed hermeneutic and involves hermeneutics. But the concept of testimony, as it emerges from the biblical exegesis on which Ricœur largely depends in his text, is a hermeneutic in a double sense: on the one hand, testimony *gives* content to be interpreted; on the other, it *calls* for an interpretation. On one hand, then, by offering itself as the "manifestation of the absolute" in a "*here* and *now*" and, consequently, by offering something to interpret, testimony becomes a "short circuit," a "halt" to the "infinite regress of reflection"[39]; an "alienation of sense" for classical logic; a suspension, something "external" to philosophy itself. On the other, testimony *calls* for and demands interpretation, and does so from "somewhere else," for three reasons. First, because of an internal "dialectic," or rather dialectics: on the one hand, a dialectic between narration and confession which immediately connects one to the other; and on the other hand, a dialectic between sense and event which, by contrast, expects an interpretation

---

[38] Paul Ricœur, "The Hermeneutics of Testimony," in *Essays on Biblical Interpretation*, edited & introduction by Lewis Mudge (Philadelphia: Fortress Press, 1980), 119-154. Cf. also "Devant l'inacceptable: le juge, l'historien, l'écrivain," in *Philosophie* 67 (Paris: Minuit, 2000), 3-18. Cf. the edition of *Philosophie* dedicated to testimony, No. 88 (2005).

[39] Ricœur, "The Hermeneutics of Testimony," 144.

from outside, an interpretation capable of publicizing them with another sense, a sense that "plays the role of interpretation with regard to their very relation."[40] Furthermore, and this is the second reason, testimony demands to be interpreted by the critical activity that it creates: indeed, it implies passage from things "seen" to things "said," the translation of one account into another. And it is precisely in this interpretation or transformation of the account of something "seen" into an account of something "said," in this other "dialectic," that testimony takes on its judiciary aspect, that it establishes the inevitability of judgment. Finally, and this is the third reason, testimony offers itself to interpretation due to the dialectic between witness and testimony, between "the *other*"[41] from whom "testimony proceeds" and the witness himself, for whom testimony is *his* own testimony anyway. Therefore, the dialectic between sense and event, between "seen" and "said," between the witness and the intermediary of testimony — "the *other*" — is what demands to be interpreted in testimony. Thus, the hermeneutic of testimony must be understood in the objective and subjective sense of the term — it is not only something that is external to testimony and applies to its contents. Much more difficultly, more subtly, the hermeneutic is called from within by the internal dialectic(s) harbored by testimony itself, as if testimony demanded this passage from an external to an internal hermeneutic.

Furthermore, according to this analysis, which might appear dry but which allows me to take a further step in my thinking, all testimony as such, as a *hermeneutic movement, is irreducible to the concept*. It is irreducible to the concept not, as Ricœur suggests, because it is a "manifestation of the absolute," but because it offers a precise and singular given to interpret, a given that appears in a specific place and at a specific time, in the *here* of a history and in the *now* of a time, someone's *here* and *now*. And it is precisely this singular given, this singularity, which makes — which is — the "short circuit" within the conceptual logic of philosophical reflection.

A philosophy of testimony is therefore possible, following Ricœur, as a hermeneutic of testimony. A philosophy of testimony is possible if it allows itself to be touched and affected by testimony, if testimony, precisely as a "short circuit," "halt," "suspension" and as a *hermeneutic*

---

[40] *Ibid.*, 145.
[41] *Ibid.*, 146.

movement, breaks the joints in conceptual logic and interrupts the fluidity of philosophical discourse based on this latter in order to dismantle and then reassemble them but in another way. Indeed, as Ricœur suggests — although for him it is thanks to the "absoluteness" of testimony — it is the immediacy, the instantaneousness, the uniqueness, the *here* and the *now* of testimony that make(s) an opening to an "alienation of meaning" for a logic built on the concept, but without opening a path for the illogical or the irrational. On the other hand, and more closely concerning the singular testimony of the Extermination, it is the *here* of Auschwitz and the *now* of the tragic hours of selections, to which many testimonies singularly bear witness and yet to which no witness can testify, that intrude(s) violently on philosophical reflection, on what is in the process of being said — my reflection — and disrupts it. It is Müller's testimony, and that of others, on the threshold of the death chambers, which shatters the conceptual logic and fluidity of my discourse. For, in the words of Alain Finkielkraut, it is "impossible to look with the concept's eye at the gas chambers, the final dissolution of the most basic links into a vast mêlée where the strong crush the weak and parents their children to find a little air near the ceiling [...]. No reconciliation occurs here, but a schism between the tragic and the logical. An irreversible divorce, a definitive caesura."[42]

It is impossible, in this philosophical discourse on the testimony of the Extermination, to maintain the secure logic of the concept, without any disruption. Hence the necessity of interrupting it by testimonies, even if they are told only through the silences of the witnesses or the words of the saved. Hence the necessity for an interruption to be imposed by this *interlude* which cuts and suspends the flow of philosophical argument in this book — suspends it by shattering it, only to then revive it.

This interpretation of testimony is intended to show that the interruption of the "logic of the concept,"[43] encountered (not by chance) by all the philosophers interpreted here, is possible precisely thanks to this singularity of testimony. It is the uniqueness of *this here* and *this now* — the *here* and the *now* of the testimonies mentioned, the *here*

---

[42] Alain Finkielkraut, *Une voix qui vient de l'autre rive* (Paris: Gallimard, 2000), 15.

[43] Ricœur, "The Hermeneutics of Testimony," 135.

and the *now* of the philosophers gathered as witnesses and called to testify, the *here* and the *now* of what interprets and follows in the wake of testimony — that suspends the magic circle of conceptual logic and the fluidity of philosophical reflection. It can even be said that it is the "humility," the smallness, the singularity of testimony, even its relativity, which tears up conceptual logic based on the universal that directs all philosophical discourse.

And it is specifically due to this fracture, this weakening, that a philosophy of testimony is possible here, in this discourse and in this book. It is a philosophy of testimony as a hermeneutic of testimony which comes from the outside, i.e. as something *given* to be interpreted — the given in Levi and Müller's accounts, but especially the given in the texts by the selected philosophers — and a hermeneutic which comes from within, as a *call* for an interpretation — here the call of the "other" from whom testimony proceeds and who is part of the other-*us* implicit in these texts, as I will show. The *here* and the *now* of a history and a singular time, the *here* and the *now* of a face, thus gives testimony this singularity that is irreducible to universality, and therefore offers an opportunity to the philosophy of testimony. It is the opportunity to be made, to be told in this book and in the hermeneutic movement's passage from the outside — facts to be interpreted — to the inside — the plea implicit in all these testimonies.

Appearing in the *here* and *now* of this book are in particular the faces of Benjamin, Adorno, Horkheimer and Levinas, who, perhaps despite themselves, left the reader signs for a hermeneutic of their works' testimony, and also the tools to be interpreted as thinkers of testimony. More specifically, they offered the reader hints to decipher their texts relating to testimonies of the Extermination.

To say that the thoughts of these philosophers are part of the testimony of the Catastrophe might be surprising, especially if we consider that one of them, Benjamin, only experienced the start of the disaster. But to say that the lives of these men, and perhaps also their deaths — as in the case of the latter — were disrupted by the horror of Nazism and by the hell that it created, this at least seems justifiable. However, in the interpretation that I propose, instead of placing these thoughts in the period when they came to light and were spoken, it must be shown how within them, in the rifts and links of their paths and movements, by the interruptions of what they say and by certain decisive ideas, the *here* and *now* of their testimony is revealed — not in the form of theories *on* testimony,[44] but that of the interruption, or the caesura, of testimony. Their philosophical reflections, as well as their main ideas, are themselves fractured, suspended and interrupted by the event and by the "short circuit" that testimony of this singular event causes. Put another way, they are testimonies fractured by testimony. They are injured by the testimony of tragic hours, certainly, but above all by the given that is suffering — so fragile, so difficult to say, so agonizing, so singular.

Thus the caesura of testimony, expressed through the arguments and also the interruptions of their work, through their fragmentary or hyperbolic texts, through the suspension and criticism of conceptual logic shared by all, is finally revealed, deep down, as the caesura or the interruption imposed by the *here* and the *now* of suffering — the suffering of bearing witness, expressed first through the suffering of telling and the impossibility of doing so, and then through suffering as a philosophical problem or question *par excellence*. These philosophers had to face not only the personal afflictions caused by historical circumstances and the very personal suffering of this testimony, but also the suffering that intrudes on thought like an obstacle or roadblock — like a caesura, to be precise. In short, their testimony consisted of confronting thought, their own thoughts, with reality, materiality, the singularity of suffering and most specifically the singular pain gnawing at and destroying the victims of the Extermination.

Thoughts as testimonies, then: testimony of the caesura, certainly; testimony or testimonies of the suffering that the event imposed; but also testimony or testimonies of a still-awakening *resistance* to the re-emergence of the catastrophe. Testimony that does not become bewitched by temptations or caught under the influence of revived evil and that does not give way to the attractions and dominations of its repetition. Testimony that is also a *resistance*, even if only a *resistance of thought*.

Whether it is in the hypothesis of a past which is not completely over and lost, according to the previously considered idea of *remembrance* put forward by Benjamin, or according to the *new categorical imperative* in Adorno's proposal, or even in the overtures towards the theological by the *knowledge of how to remember* in Horkheimer's final critical theory,

---

[44] Although Levinas's writing on prophecy in *Otherwise than Being* may be read as explicitly dealing with testimony.

or in Levinas' suggestion of an *ethical resistance* touching on subjectivity, these philosophers' thoughts certainly *bear witness* to a difficult and bare *resistance* against the repetition of evil. They bear witness to a *resistance* which, moreover, as in all testimony called for by another, by a "somewhere else," is also addressed to *another*, to the *other* that *we* are — to *us* — so that *we* interpret it and take it on in our turn; so that *we* continue, in our way, to *testify* to this *testimony*.

It is only in this way that the too-indiscrete presence of the *we* can be justified in this book, the *we* that very often says "I," the *we* that is too present, too audible. Shameless. It is in this way that it can be allowed — not to express the ideas and reflections of its author, but more modestly, to make it part of the filiation or fidelity of testimony which, despite the paradox brought to light by Lyotard's reflections or by Levi and Müller's accounts, can only be written in the first person, even if it is the plural. It becomes a fidelity of and in testimony, a fidelity in and through a philosophy of testimony that cannot respond personally — in the first person, in person and by personal work, by the *here* and *now* of my breath and writing — to the silent plea of those who are still waiting to be buried.

Chapter III

Thoughts of Exile: Theodor W. Adorno and Max Horkheimer

How goes the night?
William Shakespeare

Thoughts, or thinkers, of *exile*: this is the place, or non-place, towards which Adorno's and Horkheimer's line of thinking is directed, yet without being established in a definition or frozen in a classification. The fact of having been forced to leave due to anti-Semitic persecution and having reached America as a land of asylum and exile certainly contributed to this uprooting, this eradication of any place, whether real or metaphorical, physical or metaphysical. Exiled in the United States, the only[1] country that was ready to receive fleeing Judeo-German intellectuals, they experienced the difficulties that are encountered by every immigrant: the language barrier, cultural adaptation, isolation, the pain of separation. They particularly learned to avoid the temptation to return to their homeland, their base, their foundation. Not on a practical level, but from a philosophical perspective, they learned the mirage of home and the illusion of tranquility. They practiced non-resolution, *"unresumability,"* vigilance, concern. As Miguel Abensour maintains, "the thinkers in this group are thinkers of *exile*, Adorno most of all it seems, and their relationship to Judaism must be investigated. A thought of exile all the more radical as it does not at any moment contain the illusion of a return to a homeland (national state), or to a birthplace [...]. Only affirmation throughout this exile — making an abode in this nowhere place — can preserve the unguaranteed possibility of the other, of a transformed life, of a just society."[2] The suspension of settlement, being unattached to anything, even one's own luggage, acceptance of the open and the "nowhere," in a word the exile's approach, can in fact

---

[1] Jay, *Dialectical Imagination*, 38-40.

[2] Miguel Abensour, "La Théorie Critique: une pensée de l'exil?," *Postface* to Jay, *L'imagination dialectique* (Paris: Payot, 1977), 435.

protect the *other* — whether this is the different or the possible, another man or another world — from being imprisoned in some kind of "home," some kind of identity or system. Only the approach of someone who does not know the ground where his next step will fall and yet who is not lost in a horizonless desert can discover the following step, this *no man's land* of the possible, this *u-topos*, and allow the *other*, the "non-identical" or the "completely other," to come and to happen.

However, although in the outside of *exile*, which is above all an exile of thought, this process is freed from the enchantments of the circle of return, of the mirage of the place in the sun, of the "dumbfounding"[3] reduction of identity and totality; although, in other words, it is freed from the bewitchment of the sirens of the oceans' depths or buried in the ground, nonetheless this process requires an extreme vigilance and lucidity, an attention, a warning with regards to itself and the development in progress: "it thus encounters its own uncertainty, its own destitution, the mutilation that deforms or disfigures it, that stems from its venturing, as it were, out of the existing world into the unknown lands on which it has no hold."[4]

This *exile* or investigation of the interior, i.e. the self-criticism of reason, which may seem classic in the history of philosophy, being self-criticism, is thus carried out by Adorno and Horkheimer starting with the necessity of uncovering the chimeras that inhabit thought itself and its mythological terms — a necessity all the more urgent as humanity was "sinking into a new kind of barbarism"[5] and perishing under Behemoth's blows. It is a necessity, however, that they continued to state even *after* the Disaster. Indeed, as we have seen, although at the time when anti-Semitism triumphed they were faced with the difficult question of the complicity established between reason as domination and certain forms of anti-Semitism,[6] in the ravaged post-war landscape, in the devastation

---

[3] Daniel Payot, "Messianisme et utopie: la philosophie et le 'possible' selon T. W. Adorno," in *L'Ecole de Francfort: la Théorie Critique entre philosophie et sociologie*, edited by Miguel Abensour and Géraldine Muhlmann, *Tumultes* 17-18 (Paris: Kimé, 2002), 179-205; here, 184.

[4] *Ibid.*, 185.

[5] Horkheimer and Adorno, *Dialectic of Enlightenment*, xiv.

[6] Cf. *supra*, Prelude and Chap. I, II and III.

of *afterwards*, and in the prospect of re-emergent life, they persisted in showing that the task of thinking remained crucial to them, even though thought remained exiled.

Then comes the trial by fire of this exile of thought that Adorno and Horkheimer make their own: in the extreme vigilance of non-return, exiled thought — but also its means, reason — must move away and exile itself from itself. It is therefore not only forced into an exile of the exterior, but also an exile of the interior, of its own interior. It must face its own negativity, learn to hide nothing from itself, and therefore also to move away from its own devastation. Furthermore, despite and because of this desolation, and particularly *after* the devastations of the Catastrophe, it must persevere in seeking its horizon, which is that of thinking and finding solutions for philosophical thought. And it must do so, like always, through the concept. Hence the singular rift that can be found in these authors' writing between criticism and distancing of the concept, and at the same time the assertion of its necessity; a rift relating to the internal logic of critical theory and particularly to the negative dialectic whereby "the concept can transcend the concept,"[7] according to Adorno. In other words, these philosophers find themselves faced with a "singular work, not only *of* the concept, but *about* the concept," with a logic that aims to invent "another thought, another method of knowledge and another way of practicing philosophy,"[8] based on and while also criticizing its nucleus, the concept.

It aims, then, to invent another thought and another idea of reason, "another method of knowledge and another way of practicing philosophy," on the condition that these do not avoid the trial of the Catastrophe. It does so on the condition that they know how to search within themselves for complicity with the disaster outside, that they know how to become aware of it and, at the same time, to leave this state of desolation to regain their dignity — in short, on the condition that they *bear witness* to it.

On the subject of this testimony, looking to find signs of it in the thoughts and writing of these philosophers, attempting to re-travel the essential stages of it, I would like to show here that the Disaster touched the deepest part of their thinking, and went so far as to give rise to crucial ideas (especially in the texts from the 1950s and 1960s), leaving indelible signs that allow us to interpret them as testimonies. They are testimonies

---

[7] Adorno, *Negative Dialectics*, 9.

[8] Payot, "Messianisme et utopie," 193.

as to the facts of the past, certainly, but also proof of their effort to find a solution to the devastation by appealing specifically to other witnesses.

These conditions and challenges accepted, I would therefore like to receive the S.O.S that Horkheimer and Adorno send out to an imaginary *witness* at the end of their joint work: "if that invitation can be addressed to anyone today, [...it is] rather to an imaginary *witness*, to whom we bequeath it so that it is not entirely lost with us."[9]

I. ADORNO: A "SAD KNOWLEDGE"

"Sad knowledge" is the opening, or even the synthesis, of the disjointed reflections on mutilated life that make up the body of *Minima Moralia*, a text written in fragments between the years 1944-1947, at the time of the great liquidations, when the death factories were devouring the sons of Israel, and *afterwards*, when despair darkened everyone's hearts. The temptation of disillusion and resignation was difficult to banish. Yet Adorno, like others of the Frankfurt School, did not hesitate to believe that, despite this sadness, the pain, the mutilation inflicted on men and on thought, it was necessary not to give into this temptation. He believed that it was necessary to resist, and to do so using the methods that were the most familiar to him — reason and thought. Thought was precisely this *"force of resistance."*[10]

Between criticism of the events and the lucid awareness of their implications, including philosophical ones, Adorno's "sad knowledge" could be woven and expressed only through this sadness, in the form of a "lament." "Subjective reflection," writes Adorno, "even if critically alerted to itself, has something sentimental and anachronistic about it: something of a lament over the course of the world."[11] It is a "lament" that

---

[9] Horkheimer and Adorno, *Dialectic of Enlightenment*, 213.

[10] Theodor Adorno, "Resignation," in *Critical Models. Interventions and Catchwords*, trans. Henry W. Pickford (New York: Columbia University Press, 2005), 293.

[11] Theodor Adorno, *Minima Moralia. Reflections on a damaged life* (1951), trans. Edmund Jephcott (London: Verso, 2005), 16. [my emphasis].

mourns the historical and meta-historical "disaster"[12] of the destruction of European Jews and nevertheless turns, in its sadness, to the "sake of the possible"[13] that, at heart, is the very sense of redemption. It is a lament that turns, over the course of a philosophical and professorial work, towards the requirement of a concrete truth, such as the mutilated life of the oppressed, in order to restore all dignity to thought itself and to reason. And it does so not to save them, but to compensate for the forgetting on which they were erected and to open up to them another possibility.

1. PHILOSOPHICAL THOUGHT *AFTER AUSCHWITZ*: A TRUTH OF FEELING

The sadness of this knowledge whose nuances spread throughout the extraordinary book *Minima Moralia* is condensed in a more fastidious manner, perhaps less intimate but no less tense, in the "Meditations on Metaphysics" contained in *Negative Dialectics* (1966), an *impossible* work for several reasons, which echoes the themes and fragmentation of the preceding work. These "Meditations" — which to be better understood must be re-read in counterpoint to the pages on metaphysics after Auschwitz,[14] drawn from Adorno's seminars held in Frankfurt in July 1965, and to be considered as the testing grounds for *Negative Dialectics* — represent the third moment of the negative dialectic procedure, and can be interpreted as a condensation of the whole book. They are the end and substance of it. Opening with the paragraph entitled "After Auschwitz," they give this apocalypse a central place in Adorno's *magnum opus*.

So well-known that it is almost considered a *summa* of Adorno's thinking, this oft-quoted, criticized or praised paragraph will once again be analyzed here, as it touches the heart of Adorno's study, although its revival may seem banal: knowing in his sad *knowledge,* in his lucid and at the same time resistant *knowledge,* whether it is still possible to talk of metaphysics and, in this case, to *know* if it still has a *sense*. More precisely, to know if there is still any sense in speaking of *sense*.

---

[12] *Ibid.*, 55.

[13] *Ibid.*, 247.

[14] Theodor Adorno, *Metaphysics: Concept and Problems*, trans. Edmund Jephcott (Stanford: Stanford University Press, 2002), 93-103.

Can metaphysics and its questions survive *after* Auschwitz?

The start of the aforementioned paragraph shows that "we cannot say any more," that the immutable or eternal qualities of transcendence are truth and that the ephemeral or the "mobile"[15] qualities of immanence are appearance, as suggested by a certain tradition. Metaphysics has no possibility of surviving if it does not change its position; *now*, that is *after* the Catastrophe, it must turn towards transitory and material things. Truth must be guaranteed not by the transcendence of the eternal, but by the immanence of the ephemeral, the elusive and the fragile in human existence, because it is precisely this materiality, the concrete and the transitory elements of human life, which suffered violence at Auschwitz, including the very expropriation of its end, death.

And yet this indisputable truth, almost shouted by Adorno, this truth of the impossibility of a truth detached from all immanence and ephemerality, finds its justification in *feeling*.[16] It is *feeling*, i.e. the thing that is the most relative, subjective, sensitive and precarious, but also the most singular, which entitles this truth. It is in the *futility* of *feeling* that truth *after* Auschwitz, including the truth stated here by Adorno, will find its "foundation." "After Auschwitz," he writes, "our *feelings* resist any claim of the positivity of existence as sanctimonious, as wronging the victims; they balk at squeezing any kind of *sense*, however bleached, out of the victims' fate. And these *feelings* do not have an objective side *after* events that make a mockery of the construction of immanence as endowed with a meaning radiated by an affirmatively posited transcendence."[17] Consequently, for Adorno, *feeling afterwards* — the manifestation of an assertion without judgment, of an irrecusable repugnance, of an indignation at and revolt against the crimes of Auschwitz — is the first "point" of resistance, the "objective" moment that prevents *sense* from being attributed to the immanence of destroyed existences, starting with a transcendence. This *feeling* — felt by whom, if not by those who come *after*? — establishes the Adornian truth of the impossibility of a transcendent truth absolutely separated from the relationship with

---

[15] Adorno, *Negative Dialectics*, 361.

[16] In *Minima Moralia*, Adorno says that "it is rather for philosophy to seek, in the opposition of *feeling* and *understanding*, their—precisely *moral*—unity," 198 [my emphasis].

[17] Adorno, *Negative Dialectics*, 361[my emphasis]. The German term is *Gefühl*.

human existence. This *feeling* first clashes with the idea of the positivity of all transcendence, then with the possibility of giving a *sense* to the immanence of the "victims" existence — or rather, of their death — on the basis of some kind of transcendence. This is because Auschwitz destroyed and burned, with its victims, the possibility of a reconciliation between the "speculative metaphysical faculty"[18] surrounding transcendent truth and the concrete experience of the destruction of millions of human beings. In short, Auschwitz drives a chasm between a transcendent truth and the concrete reality of the annihilation of human beings from whom both life and death were torn.

However, Adorno proclaims *his* truth over this chasm. It is a different truth, certainly; a truth of the ephemeral and the concrete with its starting point in the most ephemeral of all: *feelings*. It is a truth that nonetheless remains such and that, despite disaster, seems to continue to look for a *sense* and to find it elsewhere, in the *sense* of *feelings*.

Indeed, this *feeling* that expresses revolt and denunciation reveals something more: its finding a place, emerging, revealing itself as a *feeling*, suggests that there is a possibility of a layer of *sense* spared by events — rationally intolerable because they are emotionally intolerable — a layer of *sense* where what is not rationally tolerable is set in motion, changing its *sense* under the weight of this emotional intolerability. Consequently, the rationally intolerable, emerging from the emotionally intolerable, indirectly expresses a *sense*, a layer of *sense* precisely where there is an interruption of a certain *sense*, of rational *sense* and the sensible. It is as if this *feeling* revealed to (theoretical) reason — considering the possibility of metaphysics and its own possibilities — that it too can be affected, touched and disturbed by the intolerable and the emotional reaction it causes. It is as if this emotional *feeling* of intolerability was not deprived of *sense*, and its profound *sense* was transmitted or "transferred" to what is not supposed to become entangled in the emotional — reason. Adorno thus makes *sense*, or the *sensing* of *feelings*, underpin the *sense* — in another sense — of reason; he makes the *sense* of *sensing* underpin the *sense* of *sense*, and therefore of truth.

Although the Catastrophe on the one hand created a chasm between a transcendent truth and the concrete experience of human existence by annihilation, on the other hand, through the intolerable *feeling* that *we*, like Adorno, experience towards these events, it reveals that *sense* can no

---

[18] *Ibid.*, 362 [translation revised].

longer be sought in transcendence. There is therefore a *sense* in this *sense* of *feelings* and of *sensing*; an ephemeral *sense*, a *sense* of the ephemeral (of immanence), a *sense* of *sense* (or of *senses*). A *sense* persists.

Though on the one hand the Extermination suspends reconciliation between truth and experience, on the other hand it suggests the possibility of another *sense*, another intelligibility and thus another truth — an intelligibility and a truth "based" on the *sensing* of *feelings*, on the *sense* of *sensing*.

With Adorno, this *sense* is characterized immediately as a *feeling* of guilt, the distressing feeling of being spared and existing in the place of another, like a nightmare about "a man killed twenty years earlier."[19] In his own words, "the guilt of a life which purely as a *fact* will strangle other life, according to statistics that eke out an overwhelming number of killed with a minimal number of rescued [...] is irreconcilable with living. And the guilt does not cease to reproduce itself, because not for an instant can it be made fully, presently conscious. This, nothing else, is what compels us to *philosophize*. And in philosophy we experience a shock: the deeper, the more vigorous its penetration, the greater our suspicion that philosophy removes us from things as they are — that an unveiling of the essence might enable the most superficial and trivial views to prevail over the views that aim at the essence. This throws a glaring light on truth itself."[20] The *feeling* of guilt at having living breath when another no longer does, mixed with the instinct for self-preservation — always shameful — is what prevents any reconciliation with life. For Adorno, it is not wrong to wonder "whether after Auschwitz you can go on living."[21]

But this *feeling* of guilt, which cannot be constant nor continuously present in the consciousness — thereby increasing guilt — is also what "compels us to philosophize." It is the *feeling* of guilt, united with the

---

[19] *Ibid.*, 363.

[20] *Ibid.*, 364.

[21] *Ibid.*, 363. On the subject of the feeling of guilt that the philosopher is filled with, and which, in his words "reproduces itself in each of us," see also *Metaphysics, op. cit.*, 113.
It is not unimportant to note that the English anthology of Adorno's seminars bears the title *Can One Live after Auschwitz? A Philosophical Reader*, edited by Rolf Tideman, English translation by Rodney Livingstone *et al* (Stanford: Stanford University Press, 2003).

feeling of non-reconciliation and the *feeling* of intolerability, that drives a philosophy of *afterwards*. It is a philosophy certainly shocked by the Catastrophe, but above all scandalized by the fact that this event constantly pushes it to look in more depth, towards what is "down-to-earth" and "pedestrian," thus moving it away from the height of essence, from "things as they are." Furthermore, "the most superficial and trivial views," precisely those of *feelings*, can "prevail" against those that aim for the "elevation" of essences and transcendence.

And yet observing the "shock" to philosophy — this injury to philosophical thought, traumatized by the Catastrophe and by the change of direction that it involves, shocked by the change in its own view which moves from the heights of the transcendent to the lowliness of what lies on the ground — throws "a glaring light" on truth. According to Adorno, this disruption of philosophy (and thought) also reveals the possibility of another concept of truth. Not only did the Catastrophe disrupt reason, in its various senses and terms, affecting it by the *feeling* of guilt and of intolerability that it continues to cause; not only did it shock *philosophy* by the same *feeling* of guilt — although how philosophy is guilty or complicit in what happened is yet to be determined — by turning its perspective upside down, i.e. by moving it from the heights of transcendence to the depths of immanence; but the Catastrophe also threw a new light, dark and "glaring," on *truth* itself. Truth should thus leave its traditional form of *adaequatio rei atque cogitationis* to take on another form, another *sense*, to become *another* truth. Indeed, as Adorno writes, "life feeds the horror of a *premonition*: what must come to be known may resemble the down-to-earth more than it resembles the sublime [...]. If the pedestrian had the last word, if it were the truth, truth would be degraded [....] unless the formation of a truth concept other than that of *adaequatio* should succeed. The innervation that metaphysics might win only by discarding itself applies to such *other* truth, and it is not the last among the motivations for the passage to materialism."[22] Adorno seems to confirm that, although philosophical temptation is connected to the elevation of transcendence and of a truth concept of *adaequatio, premonition* — another way to say *feeling*? — it reveals and testifies that the "object" of knowledge ("what must come to be known") is what is "down-to-earth," immanent, on earth, on the ground. It is

---

[22] Adorno, *Negative Dialectics*, 364-365 [my emphasis].

what is the most fragile, the most "mobile,"[23] the weakest, I would even say the "defenseless," in the humiliated existence of those who were tortured, violated, annihilated, the bodies that cover the ground of the extermination camps.

Here Adorno is not pleading the case for a return to materialism, but challenging a certain concept of truth — and of metaphysics — in favor of *another* truth, a truth that surrenders its control of *adequacy* and considers the "extremity that eludes the concept."[24]

But is it possible to completely renounce the model of *adaequatio* if one remains faithful, as Adorno seems to be, to the distinction between object and subject? If truth must free itself from the model of *adequacy*, how can it effectively accomplish this when the distinction between the two terms remains implicit, though with its axis leaning more towards the object, even if it is the most *abiectum obiectum*? Furthermore, is it possible to deconstruct metaphysics from within to make it "succeed" *after* Auschwitz?

These questions sum up the effort and the issue of what is developed throughout *Negative Dialectics*: "if negative dialectics calls for the self-reflection of thinking, the tangible implication is that if thinking is to be *true* — if it is to be true *today*, in any case — it must also be a thinking against itself."[25] Without fearing contradictions or paradoxes, Adorno strives to think *differently* — differently and in relation to the caesura caused by the Extermination — not only about the terms of *reason*, not only about *philosophy* as such, but also about *metaphysics* with one of his key ideas, that of *truth*. And he does so in the name of truth.

Although his struggle is fought on several fronts at the same time, it has only a single aim: to show that "*after* Auschwitz," *reason, thought, philosophy, metaphysics* and *truth*, all closely connected, can no longer be what they were. In the "glaring" light of the concentration camps and gas chambers, thinking must rethink itself, think against itself, in order "*to be true.*" There is a requirement for truth, then, even if it is *another* truth (and one to which we must return), that requires confronting the *today, after* Auschwitz. And if thought does not put itself to the test via the Catastrope, if it does not meet this obstacle in history and the history of thought, if it does not throw itself into the challenge of self-reflection

---

[23] *Ibid.*, 361.
[24] *Ibid.*, 365.
[25] *Ibid.* [my emphasis]

I. ADORNO: A "SAD KNOWLEDGE" 129

and self-censure, it risks empathizing with a new murder, keeping silent about the suffering of those who were tortured and annihilated, and re-covering the *truth of this suffering* with its illusory veil or its own melodious sound.

And it is perhaps in the name of this truth of suffering by the engulfed that thinking necessitates and requires this test by self-caesura and self-censure. It is a trial by fire, I would say — passing through the fire of suffering via the chimneys of Birkenau and the other sites of the Extermination.

Because is not "the extremity that eludes the concept," according to Adorno, precisely this suffering? What else does this evasion of the concept and being completely external to it represent, except the singularity of Auschwitz victims' suffering? What is the logical subject of this phrase except the agony of those who suffered and died there, except the singularity of their agony? Why else would Adorno talk of the "screams of its victims"?

Thought must be measured against this trial, certainly, but most particularly against the singular suffering, or rather sufferings, that were inflicted. The barrier that Auschwitz imposes on thought is concentrated in and defined by the barricade that suffering erects against the concept, that *physical suffering* imposes on it, since "the physical moment tells our knowledge that suffering ought not to be, that things should be different."[26] Thought can therefore no longer overcome this barricade and escape the requirement of thinking about it. It is up to the thinker, and critical dialectical philosophical discourse, to express this suffering and these cries.

2. ETHICS OF PHYSICAL SUFFERING

It seems to me that this hypothesis, which leads this book's inquiry, is confirmed by the second paragraph of "Meditations on Metaphysics," which opens with the declaration of a new categorical imperative that is worth citing in its entirety: "A new categorical imperative has been imposed by Hitler upon unfree mankind: to arrange their thoughts and actions so that Auschwitz will not repeat itself, so that nothing similar will happen. When we want to find reasons for it, this imperative is

---
[26] *Ibid.*, 203.

as refractory as the given one of Kant was once upon a time. Dealing discursively with it would be an outrage, for the new imperative gives us a *bodily sensation* of the moral addendum — bodily, because it is now the practical abhorrence of the unbearable *physical agony* to which individuals are exposed even with individuality about to vanish as a form of mental reflection. It is in the unvarnished materialistic motive only that morality survives. The course of history forces materialism upon metaphysics, traditionally the direct antithesis of materialism. What the mind once boasted of defining or construing as its like moves in the direction of what is unlike the mind [....] The somatic, unmeaningful stratum of life is the stage of suffering, of the suffering which in the camps, without any consolation burned every soothing feature out of the mind, and out of culture, the mind's objectification."[27]

This long and remarkable extract goes to the core of my study. But first some clarifications. While the first paragraph ("After Auschwitz") shows the necessity of a radical transformation of metaphysics and of the concept of truth in light of the radicality of the Catastrophe, the second ("Metaphysics and Culture"), from which this quote is drawn, highlights the now compromised relationship between metaphysics and culture and explains the necessary "materialistic" conversion, in the sense explained above, that they should undergo *afterwards*. However, the starting point for this transformation is presented as a moral standard, a categorical imperative. This imperative is therefore the pivot around which the transformation of both metaphysics (with all its implications) and culture can take place at different levels.

It must also be noted that this paragraph is a response or "solution" to the first, albeit a negative one, and not vice versa as Jay M. Bernstein[28] suggests. Indeed, for him, the first paragraph, which synthesizes a negative theodicy of modernity, is necessary to the second as metaphysics is necessary to ethics. "Metaphysics," he writes, "is the necessary complement of a wholly negative moral norm since ethics without transcendence is necessarily incomplete."[29] But would it not be more

---

[27] *Ibid.*, 365 [my emphasis]. Cf. also *Metaphysics, op. cit.*, 116.

[28] Jay M. Bernstein, *Adorno. Disenchantment and Ethics* (New York: Cambridge University Press, 2001), 385. See the chapter. "After Auschwitz," 371-414.

[29] *Ibid.*, 385.

pertinent to say the opposite? Would it not be more true to maintain, like Levinas, that there is neither transcendence nor metaphysics without ethics, and that ethics is the central philosophy? And in my opinion this is not to favor Levinas, but rather to fundamentally understand Adorno's reasoning in the quoted passage, because the structure and expression of the categorical imperative aims at a possible "foundation" of another metaphysics, a metaphysics of *afterwards*. However, before all philosophy and metaphysics can be deconstructed or reconstructed, ethics must be reiterated and reformulated, because the subject always targeted by ethics is precisely that whose absence or inadequacy "allowed" Auschwitz. It is primarily ethics that failed, and so it is starting with ethics, and relying on this imperative, that Adorno seeks a "solution" for metaphysics — not for metaphysics at any cost, but for Auschwitz to *never again* happen.

To return to the text, "to arrange their thoughts and actions so that Auschwitz will not repeat itself, so that nothing similar will happen" is the imperative communicated by Adorno and imposed by Hitler. This imperative, however, can only have a limited value if it is understood purely as the expression of the pain and horror of those who, like Adorno, escaped the tragedy. As long as we do not understand *why* the disaster occurred and *what* in fact happened, while remaining on a threshold of this knowledge, the imperative will remain a wish. Thus, throughout *Negative Dialectics,* Adorno seeks to demonstrate *why*, explaining in different ways that if Auschwitz represents in some way a product of the *thought of identity*, then it is necessary to free this thinking from its interior. In other words, the book aims to show how to *think* so that Auschwitz never happens again and how to negate, in the sense of a negative dialectic, the thinking that would have contributed to its creation. In short, Adorno applies — applies to himself — the first part of the categorical imperative for which he is the spokesperson. Likewise, in the quoted passage, he puts into practice the second part of the imperative, conveying how to *act* so that Auschwitz never happens again, i.e. stipulating that we should *act* by orienting our actions according to this moral norm. But in its turn, this norm *acts*, or is valid, only if it "gives us a *bodily sensation* of the moral addendum"; only if it makes us *feel* the *sensation* of the *body*. Consequently, for this categorical imperative to be *active*, for it to have a sense or a tangible value and not only a "discursive" value, it is necessary for it to be "based" on a baseless foundation — being impervious to its own foundations — in other words, on the tangibility of sensitivity and the physicality of corporeality. The *sense* of the body and of *physical sensation* give a *sense*, a base and a *substratum*, and therefore a truth and authority, to this very imperative.

The fact that Adorno's justification of the categorical imperative is not "discursive," that it does not belong to the order of discourse because this latter — in which Adorno partially remains thinking and writing — would inflict a new insult, an "outrage," on those who are dead, does not mean that it prevents any comprehension of the imperative itself. On the contrary, this justification or "foundation" unites the sensitive and cognitive components: on one hand, by providing the material basis for the new imperative and of this "materialistic" moral, it guarantees their effectiveness; on the other, it enables us to understand the Catastrophe to some degree as an apogee of the principle of identity that goes to the extremes of agony and physical death. But why this emphasis on the body?

Adorno explains: "bodily, because it is now the practical abhorrence of the *unbearable physical agony* to which individuals are exposed even with individuality about to vanish as a form of mental reflection." Bodily, then, because the individuality of those who suffered in the camps was abused within their bodies. Bodily, because the "practice" of torture is applied to the body as the remnant or medium of an individuality from which all "spiritual form" has been removed, as with the *Muselmänner*. Bodily, in short, because our reaction to the physical pain of those we have never known, to the abuse that their bodies suffered, is physical; it belongs to our way of *feeling*, to the *feeling* of the *body*. As Bernstein strongly states, without any embarrassment: "the force of the not and the ever in 'Not that ever again!' [the new imperative] is transmitted by our 'practical abhorrence' at the 'unbearable physical agony' which the victims of Auschwitz suffered, and to which, in the light of Auschwitz as apotheosis of rationalized reason, each individual is now potentially exposed. Physical agony is the ground of the imperative; abhorrence the response to the ground. It is, again, a question of feeling."[30] The physical agony of those who died at Birkenau, Treblinka, Sobibor, Chelmno, Mauthausen, Belsec... is what forms the "foundation" of the new imperative.

It would be its "foundation" — I use the conditional tense deliberately — but without "grounding" it, because only an unsteady, weak, suffering "foundation" can be built on suffering. Indeed, the idea of "grounding" the categorical imperative, as Adorno does, in the abyss of

---

[30] Bernstein, *Adorno. Disenchantment and Ethics*, 386.

suffering is problematic in two ways. First, it is problematic for Adorno himself because, in the preface of his book, he writes: "what would be the foundation, according to the dominant view of philosophy, will here be developed long after the author has discussed things of which that view assumes that they grow out of a foundation. This implies a critique of the foundation concept as well as the primacy of substantive thought."[31] Does critique of the foundation concept therefore go hand in hand with the necessity of giving substantive content, such as physical suffering, to thought? It seems that critique and the re-establishment of the foundation are part of the same issue, the same movement of negative dialectics. Secondly, this idea remains problematic from my perspective because it requires at least caution and delicacy: how can something, even the new imperative, be founded on the abyss of suffering and the agony of those who died in the gas chambers? It is due to this discomfort, this delicacy, that I put the word "foundation" and its associated verb *in inverted commas*. Furthermore, I explicitly leave open the question of the possibility of weakening the very concept of "foundation" by the fragility of suffering, i.e. the possibility of finding *sense* in the physical suffering of the other, in this case those who died in the Extermination.

Likewise, but in a different way and perhaps more properly, the sense of our abhorrence, the *feeling* of horror that *we* feel in response to the pain inflicted — this abhorrence towards those sufferings would be a response "grounded" on the difficult-to-ground "foundation" that is suffering. What "foundation" can it offer, except erosion of the "foundation" and, with it, the weakening of *sense*? What basis except the crumbling of the ground, except the bottomless abyss that constitutes all suffering?

At least the very *sense* of "foundation" changes, losing its sense of fullness, of solidity and certainty, to take on the sense of fragility and injury.

But this *physical* abhorrence, or this *feeling* of intolerability, or even this aversion that *we* feel towards the suffering perpetrated in the camps, is not only the result of the fear of potentially being exposed to a similar torment, in other words another expression of self-preservation and the

---

[31] Adorno, *Negative Dialectics*, xix. Adorno also speaks of this problem of foundation in *Metaphysics*, 116, where he spells out: "[T]he true basis of morality is to be found in *bodily feeling, in identification with unbearable pain*" [my emphasis].

process of identification; above all, it is the expression of human sharing and of the "living,"[32] the experience of bodily suffering. Although on the one hand this sharing affects other "living" beings — animals? — in their common destiny[33] as suffering creatures, on the other hand it prevents other individuals from suffering and dying as the Jews and non-Jews killed like them at Auschwitz suffered by sticking to the categorical imperative.

This abhorrence is not inspired by all suffering, but emerges as outrage *particularly* in response to the bodies that suffered and were abused during the Extermination. However, this does not mean that some suffering is worse than others, but that the fate of the camp victims illuminates, with its dark light, the fact that the collapse of these bodies also represents the collapse of all individuality. By standardizing all the bodies, whether through shaved heads and striped uniforms, through the identity of the illnesses caused, or even through the handling of the corpses and through mass murder, the concentration camp system and the machinery of annihilation decimated difference, singularity and each person's individuality even in their suffering and death.[34] Thus, the aversion that our own bodies feel towards the collapse of the "stacks" of bodies at Auschwitz is a recognition of this individuality and singularity. And while it is true that individuality is more than integrity and physical singularity, it is even more true that it is *at least physical integrity*, the integrity of the singular living body and that of the corpse. And the *physical* abhorrence that *we* feel becomes in the end a recognition, *at least*, of individuality and of the *physical* singularity of the other. It is our body that *first* discovers the alterity and singularity of the other in these tormented and destroyed bodies, even if the other is only a suffering body or abused corpse.

Ethics thus seems to be part of a *physical reaction*, because the morality of this reaction to the collapse of individuality and the body, of individuality in the body, is the moment when the other's body, and

---

[32] *Ibid.*, 364 and 204.

[33] Cf. on this subject Béatrice Berlowitz, "Comme des moutons à l'abattoir," in *Le messager européen* 4 (Paris: Gallimard, 1990), 219-228 and Elisabeth de Fontenay, *Le silence des bêtes* (Paris: Fayard, 1998), chap. XIX, 741-748. See also Orietta Ombrosi, "Le miserere des bêtes. M. Horkheimer et T. W. Adorno face à l'animalité," in *Lignes* 28 (Paris: Editions Lignes, 2009), 146-160.

[34] I will return to this subject later, in chapter 4.

the other as a body, becomes morally visible. But while all this comes about in the context of "the eclipse of the moral,"[35] morality survives *at least* by allowing this *physical* motive to prevail and have value. It survives by allowing itself to materialize through this "materialistic motive": "morality survives only in the unvarnished materialistic motive," Adorno writes in our source text. *After* the eclipse of morality, the "eclipse of reason" that overshadowed our lives and our modernity, it (morality) can only survive by finding its "fragile foundation," its cracked and shaken "foundation" — I can find no other term — in the materiality and fragility of the body, and more precisely in *physical suffering*, because, according to Adorno, "*the somatic, unmeaningful stratum of life is the stage of suffering, of the suffering which in the camps, without any consolation, burned every soothing feature out of the mind.*"[36] Since the mind was burned in the death chambers, with its false products and legislation, including those of morality which did nothing to prevent the disaster, the body alone — at the *somatic, unmeaningful* level — i.e. without the mind's *meaning* — must become the material place for the "fragile foundation" of a new morality that remains without any consolation, like all of the burned-up suffering. It is a morality that has no soothing or spiritual features; a worried morality, imposed in a state of submission and understood in a state of urgency; a morality that has no presumption of having anything to do with freedom. It is a morality "without any consolation" — because, as it must be remembered, it was "imposed by Hitler" — and emerging only through *our physical* response to the horrific and intolerable.

3. THEORETICAL THOUGHT IN THE FACE OF PAIN AND DEATH

Once a survival of morality is justified, even in the *minimum* of the somatic level, we can ask ourselves — returning to the starting point and not following Adorno's path which focuses on acknowledging the wretchedness of culture — how this morality of a new categorical imperative can in its turn reorient metaphysics. In other words, how can the imperative *after* Auschwitz also shape "our metaphysical faculty" and

---

[35] Bernstein, *Adorno. Disenchantment and Ethics*, 387.

[36] Adorno, *Negative Dialectics*, 365 [my emphasis].

thought as such. In fact, if this imperative prescribes how to "*arrange [our] thoughts and actions*" so that Auschwitz is not repeated, its consequence is a possible transformation or change in direction of thought itself, certainly (but not only) in the sense of thought affected by *feeling*.

Indeed, as we have seen, the question of metaphysics *after* Auschwitz becomes that of whether it is possible to link it to the experience of the "mobile," of the weakest, the "meanest" and "shabbiest," but also, as another passage reveals, to the possibility of another "reason." In Adorno's words, "the question of metaphysics is sharpened into the question of whether [...] it] survives only in the meanest and shabbiest, whether a state of consummate insignificance will let it restore reason to the autocratic reason that performs its office without resistance or reflection."[37]

Furthermore, and more generally, if "the need to lend a voice to suffering is a condition of all truth,"[38] as he writes in the introduction; if "all *pain* and all *negativity*" are "the moving forces of dialectical thinking,"[39] according to another fragment; if, in short, "its [dialectics'] *agony* is the world's *agony* raised to a concept,"[40] then it is sufficiently clear that thought, but also reason, must be directed towards physical suffering, and that thought must become and give a voice to pain.

The new categorical imperative has already revealed how the physical suffering that *we* feel — *we* who live *afterwards* — in the form of an abhorrence or aversion towards the pain without consolation of those who died in the gas chambers, as a result of which we must reorient our actions, is the basis of a "practical reason" — even though this is not Adorno's language. But we must still ask ourselves how this "practical reason," "grounded" in or affected by physical suffering, is in turn sufficient reason for "pure reason," for a conceptual approach to theoretical reason. In other words, we must ask ourselves, following the new categorical imperative, how suffering not only affects "practical reason," in the form of *feeling*, but also how pain can reorient thinking, i.e. conceptual theoretical reason itself. And we must

---

[37] *Ibid.*, 402-403.

[38] *Ibid.*, 17-18: "for suffering is objectivity that weighs upon the subject; its most subjective experience, its expression, is objectively conveyed."

[39] *Ibid.*, 202 [my emphasis].

[40] *Ibid.*, 6 [my emphasis].

do so not to yield to the temptation of despair or of irrationality, but to thoroughly follow the *moral* norm of Adorno's imperative: "arrange [...] *thoughts* and *actions*...." Therefore theoretical reason must *also* respect the new imperative and validate it as far as it is concerned.

But in what way can suffering, in other words the ultimate singularity, direct and reorient theoretical thought? How can the plurality and singularity of suffering(s), which almost prevent us from speaking of them in the singular, be "raised to a concept" without once more being subjected to domination, and without once again being reduced to silence? And more precisely, how can the singular pain suffered at Auschwitz, these sufferings "without consolation," truly reorient theoretical thought?

This is exactly the challenge of all negative dialectics. Not that of dialectically negating thought on the forgetful identity of singularity — especially the singularity of suffering — and complicity with disaster, but of showing that Auschwitz is precisely the lynchpin for a reorientation of thought, a reorientation towards something *else*, towards the *alterity* of the suffering and physical agony of Auschwitz. Towards the *alterity* that, more than any other, "recoils against dominion"[41] by the mind and identity, because it is something that is "downright incommensurable with it"[42] — the downright singular, like suffering.

Besides, is this not fundamentally where we find the sense implicit in the expression "after Auschwitz"? That is to say, "Auschwitz" as the "place" of a reorientation of thought, of "practical reason" as much as of "theoretical reason," and therefore of metaphysics?

To outline answers to these questions, it seems to me that we must reflect further on the relationship between the thought of identity that Adorno wanted to negate by the negative dialectic, and the thinking that must be reoriented *after* Auschwitz, thinking that Adorno makes himself the spokesman for, and which aims to highlight "the world's agony" by raising it to a concept. It is imposed on him, from now on and imperatively, by the individual torments that were perpetrated at Auschwitz. But what is the link between the thought of identity and suffering at Auschwitz? What is the relationship between the evil of Auschwitz and the "absolute evil"[43] of dominion by the thought of identity according to Adorno?

---

[41] *Ibid.*, 221.
[42] *Ibid.*, 405.
[43] *Ibid.*, 365.

It is difficult to answer this without taking risks… But in a fragment of *Minima Moralia* significantly entitled "On the morality of thinking," anticipating the topics in *Negative Dialectics*, he suggests this: "[the] tacit assent to the primacy of the general over the particular, which constitutes not only the deception of idealism in hypostasizing concepts, but also *its inhumanity*, that has no sooner grasped the particular than it reduces it to a through-station, and finally comes all too quickly to terms with *suffering* and *death* for the sake of a reconciliation occurring merely in reflection — in the last analysis, the bourgeois *coldness* that is only too willing to underwrite the inevitable. Knowledge can only widen horizons by abiding so insistently with the *particular* that its isolation is dispelled."[44] The thought of identity, in this case idealism, proved *inhuman* in its "tacit" acknowledgement of the conceptual primacy of the universal that reduces the particular to a "through-station"; in its inability to deal with or concretely tackle the experience of *suffering* and *death*; and in the silent complicity of "bourgeois *coldness*" whose task is to underwrite "the inevitable," to allow things to follow their necessary course. These three elements, then — the destruction of the *particular* in the concept, in favor of the universal or general; the inability to think of the concrete in *suffering* and *death*; and the *coldness* of abstraction and of necessity that justifies all — the elements alleged to constitute the inhumanity of the thought of identity, still re-emerging, are perhaps also relevant to Auschwitz.

Therefore, it is clear that, for Adorno, turning and orienting his own philosophy and theoretical reason towards the individual, towards the *particular* or the "non-identical;" "choosing the small," to use Abensour's happy phrase, leaning towards "what has been abandoned, neglected, rejected," is a way of resisting *afterwards*, a way of "learning to rediscover singularity at the moment when it is denied 'on a large scale.'"[45] But if, for Adorno, thought *after* the Disaster must turn towards that which "fell by the wayside," or towards "the waste products and blind spots that have escaped the dialectic"[46] — according to the legacy of and in the same way as Benjamin, who felt that history should turn towards the defeated and be written from their point of view — how can this thought,

---

[44] Adorno, *Minima Moralia*, 74 [my emphasis].

[45] Miguel Abensour, "Le choix du petit," *Postface* to the French edition of *Minima Moralia* (Paris: Payot, 1980), 234.

[46] Adorno, *Minima Moralia*, 151.

while being a protest and resistance, "speak of individual matters at all" "in face of unspeakable collective events"?[47] How can it become the voice and protest of the individual, without in turn becoming a matter of identity — or even "authoritarian" or "totalitarian" — and all while knowing that this individual was annihilated in the collective murder of millions of individuals? That the individual perished with other individuals in the gas chambers?

4. A DEATH WORSE THAN DEATH

There is a knot to unravel in all these questions — a very tight knot, a knot tightened between the *inhumanity* of the thinking of identity that swallows up the particular, and the *inhumanity* of the *death* conceived by the Nazi Reich, indiscriminately destroying the singularity of each individual in mass murder. And destroying it, paradoxically, after having acknowledged and pursued it, by hunting down and trampling every Jew in even the most concealed hiding places in the ghettos or the furthest corners of occupied Europe and beyond, in an inhuman and intense Jew hunt.

Furthermore, it is a knot held and tightened on the one hand by the *coldness*[48] that is supposed to characterize the thought of identity, and on the other the *coldness* that conceived of this death or, more ordinarily, that which allowed it to be silently and methodically implemented.

Signs of this knot can be found, it seems to me, in one of the crucial arguments formulated by Adorno for the surrender of thought of identity: *"Auschwitz confirmed the philosopheme of pure identity as death."*[49] This famous phrase indeed reveals the relationship between "pure identity as death" and Auschwitz. It says that Auschwitz confirms the equation of the "philosopheme of pure identity" to the death that was instigated there.

This means that pure identity would be tantamount to the death administered at Auschwitz. Identity — the thought of identity? — decrees the death of the particular in and on behalf of the universal in the same way that the death of the individual in and on behalf of the "specimen" was ordered at Auschwitz. Indeed, after the annihilation of

---

[47] *Ibid.*, 18.
[48] Cf. *infra*.
[49] Adorno, *Negative Dialectics*, 362 [my emphasis].

the spiritual individual by terror and the concentration camp system, whatever remains individual — the body and death — are also forced into extinction through annihilation. In fact, in the language of the SS there are no men, women, children or elderly to be killed, only *Figuren* (silhouettes, shadows). What comes out of the death chambers no longer has anything to do with the individual, but corresponds perfectly with what it was supposed to be, a "specimen." "It was no longer an individual who died, but a specimen,"[50] adds Adorno, because the way of dying at Auschwitz, dying as it was administered and dealt out there, is precisely what allows leveling, indistinction, and identity among the "non-identical." It is what makes death itself an identity, an identical death, a serial death. By denying the individuality and singularity of death in the uniformity of dying, the SS applied the identification of the non-identical even in death. The experience of Auschwitz confirms that the "non-identical" of each internee's suffering and dying is leveled, equalized, flattened in the identical fate, the identicality of fate which awaited all the innumerable people who stepped out of the cattle trucks to be taken to the gas chambers. Subsequently, the individual is dispossessed of his last remaining and "the poorest possession"[51] — his death.

According to Adorno, "genocide," as collective and totalizing murder, is therefore "the absolute integration" already set when "men are leveled off"[52]; the integration of what differentiates them, of what is the "non-identical." Furthermore, this indifference and contempt towards the different and the individual are expressed plainly and crudely by the words that sadists liked to utter to their victims: "tomorrow you'll be wiggling skyward as smoke from this chimney." These words certainly demonstrate "the indifference of each individual life that is the direction of history."[53] But they say something more. Not only is the individual "fungible and replaceable" by the slavery of forced work and in the killing factory, but it has no chance of survival as such, as an individual, even after its death. This is because the murder of the individual in the

---

[50] *Ibid.* Cf. also Adorno, *Metaphysics, op. cit.*, 108 *sqq.*: Adorno writes here: "What meets its end in the camps, therefore, is [...] only the invidual entity reducible to the body or, as Brecht put it, the torturable entity."

[51] Adorno, *Negative Dialectics*, 362.

[52] *Ibid.*

[53] *Ibid.*

I. ADORNO: A "SAD KNOWLEDGE"

totality of death at Auschwitz is absolute — there should not even be any remaining traces of its corpse. No-one and nothing should have been. The corpse, the *remains* of the individual, must melt and merge into the air....

Thus, even "the last trace of it would be engulfed in death, the absolute."[54] And in being engulfed, a new abyss is opened, a new anguish occurs: "in the camps death has a novel horror; since Auschwitz, fearing death means fearing worse than death."[55]

But could this something "worse than death" not also evoke the new death inflicted on victims in the universalist interpretation of history, against which first Benjamin and then Adorno react? The phrase "Auschwitz confirmed the philosopheme of pure identity as death" perhaps also suggests moving away from the interpretation of Auschwitz as one historical event among others. This phrase, being a response to Hegel and probably to his philosophy of history that drowns the particular in the universal, thus suggests that the identification of particulars, in history too, is equivalent to death. Even historical events cannot any longer be identified and justified by the universal *saying* that "things are always the same," or the universal of history's "ordeal." Although the eternity of horror, or, in Benjamin's words, the eternal catastrophe, endures in the *saying* and the *fact* that "things are always the same," we cannot continue, *afterwards,* to identify events or tragedies by simply highlighting that each of their new forms "exceeds the last in horror." It is not only a question of horror's gradation, but also, for Adorno, an increase in the supremacy that ensures "quantity recoil[s] into quality." As he explains in the following passage, which allows me to put forward this hypothesis, "Auschwitz cannot be brought into analogy with the destruction of the Greek city-states as a mere gradual increase in horror, before which one can preserve tranquility of mind. Certainly, the unprecedented torture and humiliation of those abducted in cattle trucks does shed a deathly-livid light on the most distant past, in whose mindless, planless violence the scientifically confected was already teleologically latent. The identity lies in the non-identity, in what, not having yet come to pass, denounces what has. The statement that things are always the same is false in its immediateness, and true only when introduced into the dynamics of totality. He who

---

[54] *Ibid.*, 371.

[55] *Ibid.*, 375.Cf. Lyotard's analyses on the subject of "the forbiddance of the 'beautiful death'" and his criticism of Adorno, in *The Differend*, 99-104.

relinquishes awareness of the growth of horror not merely succumbs to cold-hearted contemplation, but fails to perceive, together with the specific difference between the newest and that preceding it, the *true identity of the whole, of terror without end.*"⁵⁶ Indeed, can this always re-emerging, always expectant "identity of the whole" not be associated with "terror without end," and (because it is of the same nature) with the "worse than death" of Auschwitz? Can it not be associated with this death of "pure identity" or "pure identity as death"?

5. EDUCATION *AFTER AUSCHWITZ*, OR AGAINST COLDNESS

As we have seen, the focus that Adorno places on the *sense* of *feeling*, this *sense* of guilt that he feels as a survivor and, above all, the *sense* of intolerability that *we* share *after* Auschwitz, is coupled with his more theoretical than rhetorical emphasis on *coldness* as a preliminary condition to the event of Auschwitz. In addition, one could say that his repeated reflections on coldness are the reverse of those outlined above on *feeling*. It therefore seems necessary to me to show now, and by contrast, the relationship between this *feeling* and *coldness*, because in emphasizing coldness Adorno uses a contrast to confirm the importance of *feeling* and of one of its declensions, *compassion*. This is not to suggest that Adorno is a sentimentalist, but on the one hand to underline the issue of the semantics of *feeling* in his philosophical thinking, and on the other to show the complicity between this deficit of *feeling*, or coldness, and the very event of Auschwitz. It is a complicity that Adorno first encounters, as has been stated, in *his feeling* of guilt at having escaped the Extermination. This *feeling* reveals to him the coldness implied by this same survival, and which is necessary to the life of one who should have been killed: "his mere survival calls for the coldness, the basic principle of bourgeois subjectivity, without which there could have been no Auschwitz."⁵⁷ But beyond the coldness of survival, which has always been "culpable,"⁵⁸ where is the complicity between coldness, even "bourgeois" coldness, and the Catastrophe?

The thematic subject of coldness is transversal in Adorno's writing, but nevertheless it can be considered as a *leitmotif* which appears at

---

⁵⁶ Adorno, *Minima Moralia*, 234-235 [my emphasis].

⁵⁷ Adorno, *Negative Dialectics*, 363.

⁵⁸ *Ibid.*, 364.

every crucial moment, as for example in the conference broadcast on German radio in 1966 entitled *"Education after Auschwitz,"* and revived in *Critical Models*,[59] where the philosopher pays particular attention to this subject as a possible direction for the education of young Germans. After repeating, with different wording, the categorical imperative that "Auschwitz should never happen again," and after referring to the Armenian genocide and the atomic bomb, and quoting Freud's *Civilization and its Discontents*, according to which civilization generates anti-civilization, he admits that to understand the specific barbarity bearing the name of Auschwitz, "the roots must be sought in the persecutors." In other words, we must highlight the mechanisms that make men capable of the most horrific actions as if they were the most normal, and capable of killing under the poorest pretexts.

And yet what characterizes these people is that they were "cold"[60]: "if people were not profoundly indifferent toward whatever happens to everyone else except for a few to whom they are closely bound and, if possible, by tangible interests, then Auschwitz would not have been possible, people would not have accepted it." And several lines further down, he adds that "the inability to identify with others was unquestionably the most important psychological condition for the fact that something like Auschwitz could have occurred in the midst of more or less civilized and innocent people."[61] But what is this incapacity to identify with others if not the incapacity to *feel* with and for others? A lack of *feeling*, physical *feeling*, when faced with the physical pain of the other? An *indifference* towards their suffering and death? What is this indifference if not an absolute lack of *compassion*?

The indifference Adorno speaks of is comparable to the attitude of the "spectator" who keeps his distance and watches another man or animal suffer and die, or be carried away in cattle trucks, without a tremble, without any emotion. Moreover, this attitude of the spectator who moves as far as possible away from the other man by making him as different as possible from himself — a beast, to be precise — is, for Adorno, the source of all the pogroms: "[their] possibility is decided in the moment

---

[59] Theodor Adorno, "Education after Auschwitz," in *Critical Models. Interventions and Catchwords*, op. cit., 191-204.

[60] *Ibid.*, 201.

[61] *Ibid.*

when the gaze of a fatally-wounded animal falls on a human being. The defiance with which he repels this gaze — 'after all, it's only an animal' — reappears irresistibly in cruelties done to human beings."[62]

All this would certainly merit being considered further, but the coldness of the spectator and detachment highlighted here by Adorno is the same that allowed mass murder to be committed under everyone's eyes and with the tacit collaboration of the self-righteous. It is the same distance that can be seen among the bureaucrats who never set foot in a camp yet who directed the Extermination, such as Eichmann and many others less well known; the same distance, in the camps, between the reign of the SS and the sub-world of the deportees; the same distance created by the anonymity of the executioners and anonymity of their victims; an absolute distance, sealed by the doors of the *Krematorium*. And so on. The distance implied and implicit in coldness, then, justifies everything and facilitates tasks which otherwise would have been impossible, by decreeing their necessity or subscribing them to the "inevitable."[63]

It is clear that, in this radio broadcast, Adorno is not aiming to expose the psychological attitude of the Germans who contributed to the massacre by their indifference or coldness, nor to "preach love,"[64] because for him the lack of love is now a matter that concerns all men and demonstrates, among other things, the great failure of Christianity. His intention, in the wake of critical theory, is instead to increase awareness of this coldness — to make us aware of it and to investigate its nature, and to do so not exclusively from a psychological point of view. It is necessary to use every weapon to fight "*against coldness as the condition for disaster*,"[65] and to recognize all that influences it, so that human beings will individually watch for its dangers and prevent themselves from causing other catastrophes. In short, it is necessary to understand all of its conditions in order to "attempt to combat these conditions, initially in the domain of the individual."

This coldness, this Janus's head that accumulates the dead and produces disasters, is the "basic principle of bourgeois subjectivity." Adorno had discussed this with Horkheimer in *Dialectic of Enlightenment*, to which he

---

[62] Adorno, *Minima Moralia*, 105.
[63] *Ibid.*, 74.
[64] Adorno, *Critical Models*, 202.
[65] *Ibid.* [my emphasis].

refers, where coldness was already envisaged as the state of the very soul of "bourgeois" virtue and as the exact "opposite" of "*commiseratio*."⁶⁶ In this text, coldness is always qualified with the term "bourgeois" — for us, this adjective belongs to a now obsolete vocabulary — because as we have seen with the subject of Odysseus, it corresponds to the attitude of "bourgeois subjectivity" that mutilates or dominates itself while dominating its passions in order to preserve itself against the forces of mythology and nature. In addition, coldness applies to the physical element; in other words, when the consciousness is mutilated, coldness falls back on the body and the physical sphere, taking on the alienated form of an act of violence that reappears at the moment when violence is supposed to be permitted. Moreover, if the principal aim of the "bourgeois subject" is self-preservation, coldness is the principle without which it cannot realize the *principium individuationis*, expressed in Spinoza's famous phrase, "the endeavor of preserving oneself is the first and only basis of virtue."⁶⁷ For coldness is precisely this domination of passions, this control of nature in the self so that the subject can be confirmed in its *conatus essendi*, a domination that also implies a hardness, often synonymous with "virility," and which its core signifies, purely and simply, as indifference towards suffering. However, in *Dialectic of Enlightenment*, Adorno and also Horkheimer seem to limit the effects of compassion as it is unable to break the evil circle of universal alienation. It is partial and insufficient. But this limitation is, I think, due to the fact that there are still aggressive overtones of the first critical theory in the book written between 1944 and 1945, whereas in the text from 1966, there is another attitude, certainly more controlled, but no less subtle. However, the criticism of coldness and rejection of the "imperative" of pity or love remains identical: "the exhortation to love — even in its imperative form, that one *should* do it — is itself part of the ideology that perpetuates coldness. It bears the compulsive, oppressive quality that counteracts the ability to love."⁶⁸

66　Cf. the analysis of pity in *Dialectic of Enlightenment*, 79-81.

67　Spinoza, *Ethica*, IV, XXII, cited in *Dialectic of Enlightenment*, 22. This is "the true maxim of all western civilization, in which the religious and philosophical differences of the bourgeoisie are laid to rest." The Frankfurt School and Levinas agree on this point.

68　Adorno, *Critical Models*, 202.

An education against coldness, then, is what Adorno attempts to imagine "after Auschwitz"; not one, however, which is not an empty, rhetorical and fundamentally repressive exhortation to love, but rather an education to become aware of the mechanisms and derivations of "universal coldness" and of the coldness in each person, and thus to find "concrete possibilities of resistance."[69]

And to find them, for example, in the small resistance of a singular and spontaneous gesture, a gesture beyond all gestures, emerging in the moment of compassion. It is not on a large scale that we can break oppression, find a foothold or hope for those that are oppressed and caught up in suffering, but in the modesty of these *minima moralia*, in the compassion that seeks in some way to ease the suffering of the other, the other man as well as the animal.

For Adorno, as for Schopenhauerian Horkheimer, compassion — far removed from and purged of its "narcissistic deformations,"[70] of its philanthropic temptations, the complacency of social assistance — can open up the possibility of a *minimal*, rather than minimalist, morality, and *at least* serve as an antidote to the coldness of the morality of self-preservation, but also — and I say this provocatively — to "cool and reflective"[71] philosophy.

In short, compassion is what can *minimally*, i.e. to the *minimal* degree, warm coldness in all the domains where it is found, by revealing a tremor, a murmur, a "no" to the suffering of the other. And though it is not able to achieve justice in this *smallness* or "micrology,"[72] it is nevertheless the first sign, perhaps the most primitive sign, of what still endures as morality; the sign of a *remnant of morality*, just like the aforementioned *feeling* of intolerability towards the sufferings endured during the Extermination.

Thus, compassion — already anxious, unsatisfied, unresolved — informs our consciousness that "suffering ought not to be, that things should be different,"[73] and the physical sensitivity implicit in it can affect the coldness that seems unshakeable in its solidity. Eternally stunned. Compassion can immediately and spontaneously move coldness by the

---

[69] *Ibid.*, 203.
[70] Horkheimer and Adorno, *Dialectic of Enlightenment*, 81.
[71] *Ibid.*
[72] Adorno, *Negative Dialectics*, 407.
[73] *Ibid.*, 203.

simple burning "truth" of this "no." And through the burning this "truth," compassion can touch it, melting the "frozen waste of abstraction"[74] or the glacial density of "bourgeois" morals into the dew of a tear.

And yet, not without effort and pain, Adorno admits all the difficulty of living and resisting through these *minima moralia*: "for the intellectual, inviolable isolation is now the only way of showing some measure of solidarity. All collaboration, all the human worth of social mixing and participation, merely masks a tacit acceptance of inhumanity. It is the sufferings of men that should be shared: the smallest step towards their pleasures is one towards the hardening of their pains."[75]

Both despite and thanks to this lucidity, Adorno tried with all his philosophical power and resources to give voice to this otherwise forgotten or neglected suffering, and specifically to the singular suffering stigmatized by the disaster, to the extent that he felt he was "just the emanation of a wish of some victim of Auschwitz" and felt the obligation of *philosophically testifying* to this wish, to this suffering. For "if one is not oneself capable at each moment of identification with the victims [...], philosophy, in the necessary forms of its own reification, is perhaps the only form of consciousness which, by seeing through these matters and making them conscious in a more objective form, *can at least do something*, a *small* part of that which we are unable to do."[76] Auschwitz is thus the pivot of a new era of thought, a new dawn.

II. HORKHEIMER: BETWEEN LUCID DESPAIR AND MUTE HOPE

While it is possible in Adorno's writing to make out glints of a dawn, barely hinted, barely grazing the ruins of the Catastrophe, the bluish tone of twilight reigns in Horkheimer's. It is a twilight of the gods, deposing the divinities of the west and its ideologies and mythology, a twilight that particularly obscured the divine sun of reason which dominated the centuries of civilization. It is a twilight that started long before the night

---

[74] *Ibid.*, xix.

[75] Adorno, *Minima Moralia*, 26.

[76] Adorno, *Metaphysics*, 110 and 113 [my emphasis].

and is the prelude to what the philosopher calls "the night of humanity": "the less stable necessary ideologies are, the more cruel the methods by which they are protected. The degree of zeal and terror with which tottering idols are defended shows how far dusk has already advanced,"[77] wrote Horkheimer before the rise of Nazism.

It is a twilight leaving few hopes, few openings, then; but this does not mean that it sinks into total obscurity, total blackness, even *after* the darkness of the night. This is because for the German philosopher, this twilight, coming before and after "the night of humanity," is the only visible sky, the only possible horizon. It is a horizon that, even *afterwards*, still signals not only the "eclipse of reason,"[78] the decline and fall of the god immortalized by the *Aufklärer*, but also, in the weak hope re-emerging in man, in his mute longing, in his nostalgia, and even in the awareness of his abandonment, signals the "absolute" of the "completely other," of which one can say nothing, think nothing, write nothing, and which cannot be named under any circumstances. It is other, absolutely other, but signals another horizon: "we must all be united by the longing that what happens in the world, the horror and the injustice, is not the last word, but that there is an Other; and we assure ourselves of this in what is called religion."[79]

The chromatic tone that emerges in Horkheimer's writing, moving between lucid despair and mute hope, and which towards the end of his life was able to be expressed through a theological tension (if this term was not already too compromised) drawing on Jewish sources, should not invite an interpretation that demonstrates the author's pessimism — a pessimism that in this case would be more theoretical than practical, according to the point of the last critical theory — or a change of direction from — not to mention betrayal of, as several

---

[77] Max Horkheimer, *Dawn & Decline. Notes 1926-1931 and 1950-1969*, trans. Michael Shaw (New York: Seabury Press, 1978), 17.

[78] Max Horkheimer, *Eclipse of Reason* (1947), follow up to "The End of Reason" (1941), trans. unknown (New York: Continuum International, 2004).

[79] Max Horkheimer, "Kritische Theorie gestern und heute (1970)," in *Gesellschaft im Übergang. Aufsätze, Reden und Vorträge 1942-1970* (Frankfurt am Main: Fischer Taschenbuch, 1981), 167-168.

critiques have accused — the first version of critical theory. Instead, more productively for the subject of this book, it should urge an understanding of the implicit and explicit sense linking this twilight to the night of the Catastrophe.

Although Adorno's reflections on the subject are more plentiful, more avowed, and perhaps more explicit than those of his colleague, and despite Horkheimer's difficulty in *keeping up* with the comprehension of "Fascism," as shown in the early pages, it is important to recall, and to consider, as I will do here, that he had written an anticipatory text in 1942 — "The End of Reason" (*Vernunft und Selbsterhaltung*).[80] Admittedly, at the time of writing this essay, which was to be part of a tribute publication to Benjamin also containing the article written in 1940 on the authoritarian State, Auschwitz was not yet an extermination camp and we cannot know precisely at what point the author was aware of the mass extermination that had already started, but the existence of concentration camps already put him on alert with regards to the phenomenon of Nazism and especially to the possibility of reason being inverted into its opposite.

Unlike *"The Jews and Europe"* analyzed above, which shows a certain difficulty in understanding "the Jewish question," the article I will analyze here can be considered as a turning point in Horkheimer's thinking, which reveals the increasingly radical positions in *Dialectic of Enlightenment* and still more so in *Eclipse of Reason* — positions relating to the idea of reason, to torture and to their correlation with "Fascism," and *testifying* once again to the urgency, the necessity for Horkheimer to investigate the issues of Nazism, its barbaric system and its involvement with reason. This turning point, which is certainly connected to the intensification of his work with Adorno and through this with his reception of Benjamin's writing, thus touches on an increasingly radical criticism of the idea of reason complicit with domination and based on the principle of self-preservation; a criticism that never achieves a negativist liquidation of reason and is instead oriented towards seeking a reason that does not betray and suppress itself, but that puts itself at the disposal of human beings, their emancipation, their solidarity. It is a criticism of

---

[80] First published in English (*The End of Reason*), and then in German, this text was republished in German only in 1970. It appears in English in *The Essential Frankfurt School Reader*, 26-48.

reason reduced to pure domination, as we will see, that accompanies the declaration of another idea of reason, an *other* reason, which is not morally neutral and learns to name things rather than dominate them.

First, I will examine this text to follow one of the threads running through Horkheimer's thinking, showing how criticism of instrumental reason is mixed with criticism of fascism or Nazi Fascism after a certain time. Only secondly will I move on to consider the impressions and ideas that Horkheimer was able to develop *after* the Extermination, collected during the last years of his life and published posthumously in the private journal *Notizen 1949-1969*. The author painfully and lucidly touches on the subject of the Disaster in several fragments of this journal, notably the one entitled "After Auschwitz," which is essential to my topic. My aim is not to verify who among the members of the Frankfurt School to tackled the subject the earliest and most directly, but to understand how these philosophers, each in his own way, were able to live and make sense of the injury inflicted by the Catastrophe in their personal lines of thought. And I do so not to offer an exhaustive perspective of its interpretation according to the Frankfurt School, but to show how the thinking of these philosophers — troubled and personally affected by this night of history — can be read as a *testimony* to the injury of these dark times. It is a singular *testimony* that can only be singular and that confirms the historical caesura of this event in different ways, even if sometimes by the obscurity, insufficiency, ambiguity and fragmentation of their writing. It is a philosophical *testimony* of the fact that Auschwitz, and what it produced, is and remains the "turning-point of history"[81] for Adorno and for Horkheimer.

1. REASON AND ITS SHADOW: SELF-DESTRUCTION

One of Horkheimer's first assertions in *"The End of Reason"* spells out the decline and fall of the concept of reason: "Skepticism purged the idea of reason of so much of its content that *today* scarcely anything is left of it. Reason, in destroying conceptual fetishes, ultimately destroyed itself. Formerly, it was the herald of eternal ideas which were only dimly shadowed in the material world. Later, it was supposed to recognize itself

---

[81] Horkheimer and Adorno, *Dialectic of Enlightenment*, 165.

in the order of natural things and to discover the immutable forms of reality in which eternal reason was expressed. Throughout the millennia philosophers believed that they possessed such knowledge. Now they have learned better. None of the categories of rationalism has survived. [...] Reason itself appears as a ghost that has emerged from linguistic usage."[82] If the philosophers have been set straight, reason has been "cancelled"[83] and is "in a process of rapid decay."[84] It has lost its sense, and with it the ideas and concepts that were the basis of western civilization. Reason has lost its way; it has been led astray. It is lost. Why?

More than ever *"today"* — Horkheimer emphasizes the actuality of this decline to the extent that this term appears in almost every paragraph throughout the essay — reason is manifested in its instrumental form, or as an instrument that reduces all means to a single end: "it is a pragmatic instrument oriented to expediency, cold and sober."[85] These are identical virtues to those of the dictator who, while appealing for reason, is thinking of the "tanks"[86] he is having built and to which his subordinates, like all the German people, must necessarily submit, always in the name of reason. Once again, then, reason is revealed in all its essence. It is the instrument that allows the individual, who would be lost on his own, to reconcile his personal interests with the interests of the community, and only in this way allows him to survive. Furthermore, the individual must restrain himself, mastering his feelings and even, if necessary, sacrificing the self so that other individuals respect him and leave his interests and goals in peace; so that they leave alone both his person and his primary interest, namely self-preservation or his perseverance in being — here, again, is the idea of "bourgeois" defining itself in relation to self-preservation that is crucial in *Dialectic of Enlightenment,* as we have seen. Consequently, reason above all serves the sole aim of the individual's self-preservation, not only in the face of other men's power — a power which would otherwise, without reason, be uncontrollable — but also in the face of the power of nature.

---

[82] Horkheimer, "The End of Reason," 27.

[83] *Ibid.*, 28.

[84] *Ibid.*, 26.

[85] *Ibid.*, 28. Here is coldness again: the reduction of the particular to the universal that Adorno speaks of, is for Horkheimer the reduction of particular goals into universal goals.

[86] *Ibid.*

For this purpose of self-preservation, the individual must forgo his own nature, his passions and impulses, and be willing to sacrifice himself and accept the supremacy of the community — which is supposed to embody the universal — instead of being directly dominated by other individuals or by nature. *Coldness*[87] is therefore indispensible and necessary to him. Up to this point there is nothing new to those accustomed to reading this representative of the Frankfurt School.

And yet what is revealed as original in this essay is not the fusion of the two sources at the basis of the "destruction" and "collapse"[88] of reason — namely the development of large-scale capitalism[89] on one hand and "fascism"'s total domination on the other — but the fact that reason itself dies with the individual. More precisely, that the "historical reality" welding the economic situation of the development of large-scale industry and monopolies to the political situation of fascism proves that the individual — the individual for whom the mythology of a reason finalized in self-preservation was constructed — no longer matters and that, consequently, this same reason is just the projection of a "false universality"[90] in which the individual believed he had found his particular interest. Instrumental reason thus becomes a pure illusion, the shadow of itself, even at the time when it seems to triumph.

According to Horkheimer, the fact that the individual no longer matters in mass society is something that has already been shown and revealed by the capitalist structure. But what "fascism" reveals as absolutely new is the negation of the basis of bourgeois instrumental reason, i.e. death. If death was indeed the foundation of self-preservation for the bourgeois individual — as an end to be avoided and a boundary controlling all his actions — with fascism, this "boundary" falls apart and is exceeded. In other words, fascism shakes the foundation of bourgeois subjectivity and invents something worse than death: "It [fascism] strikes down that which is tottering, the individual, by teaching him to fear something worse than death. Fear reaches farther than the identity

---

[87] The adjective *cold* always accompanies the noun "reason" or "rational individuality": for example 33, 45.

[88] *Ibid.*, 36.

[89] We have already seen that at this time capitalism remained a vital key to understanding fascism for Horkheimer. Cf. *supra*, Ch. I, 1.

[90] *Ibid.*

of his consciousness. The individual must abandon the ego and carry on somehow without it. Under fascism [...] they lose their identical character, and are simultaneously Nazi and anti-Nazi, convinced and skeptical, brave and cowardly, clever and stupid. They have renounced all consistency. This inconsistency into which the ego has been dissolved is the only attitude adequate to a reality which is not defined by so-called plans but by concentration camps. The method of this madness consists in demonstrating to men that they are just as shattered as those in the camps."[91] By setting up concentration camps, Nazi fascism not only disturbs the consciousness or identity of the ego, but also changes the fear of death into terror — for as we have already heard from Adorno, although he said it twenty-four years later than his colleague, there is something to be feared that is worse than death. Terror takes the place of the fear of death. The terror that is part of the totalitarian system, as his friend Leo Löwenthal said with similar overtones in 1946 in the important but little-known article *"Terror's Atomization of Man,"* and as did Hannah Arendt[92] in 1951, is coupled with individuals' terror of being nothing but "shattered" men,[93] exposed bodies, defenseless, exposed to torture and physical suffering.

It is precisely this fear of physical suffering that, according to Horkheimer, took the place of the fear of death — but is this fear not already and primarily the fear of the physical pain that accompanies death? Indeed, Nazism's ideological system on the one hand reserves a central position for the body, for physical power, and on the other reserves an essential role for physical suffering. Whether it is in the form of *physical* services, "in the form of strong-arm methods and purges"[94] or that of "labor of childbirth"[95] which makes heroes where there are production records, *physical* power rises to the level of a principle.

---

[91] *Ibid.*, 44-45.

[92] Cf. Leo Löwenthal, "The Crisis of the Individual. Terror's Atomization of Man" in *Commentary* I (1946), no. 3, 1-8, re-echoed in *Schriften* III (Frankfurt-am-Main: Suhrkamp, 1982), 161-174; Hannah Arendt, *The Origins of Totalitarianism* (Cleveland: Meridian Books, 1962), 460-479.

[93] Horkheimer, "The End of Reason," 45.

[94] *Ibid.*, 38.

[95] *Ibid.*, 43.

At the same time and in opposition, *physical suffering* becomes the method and means by which domination can be carried out, as "leads the resistant and wayward, the phantast and utopian back to themselves."[96] Suffering reduces the individual to its body, to a part of the body, and reduces all men and animals to the same level. However, leaving aside the remarks that could be made to Horkheimer about this discourse on the leveling of suffering, and accepting with him the rehabilitation, via Nazism, of *physical suffering* through terror and torture,[97] it is clear that the principle of self-preservation once again appears in a different form. Indeed, is it not true that the reasons, or rather the "reason,"[98] for the physical violence imposed by Nazism is still the same — that which aims to touch the untouchable, self-preservation? Even if the foundation of bourgeois reason — the fear of death — has been destroyed, this does not mean that the principle of self-preservation does not endure. On the contrary, it changes its appearance. It takes on the form of a total terror, that of no longer mattering, of losing all individuality in the identity of the suffering inflicted in the concentration camps; the terror of being nothing more, in the end, than a tortured body or a "husk of pain."[99] The individual must "physically survive itself," says Horkheimer, as if the individual's remains, or perhaps of its self-preservation, can only survive in this afflicted and appalled corporeality. And while in the past physical torture was the *ultima ratio* to which society had recourse, with Nazi fascism it becomes the first and only reason capable of educating normal beings, of training social misfits and bringing to heel all those who dared to not believe in this reason of terror — in a word, all those who were "unreasonable."[100] It is also capable of eliminating all those who cause scandal, such as politicians, the Jews and the insane. Torture, then, becomes the sole reason to bring reason to the insane: "The new

---

[96] *Ibid.*, 46.

[97] Cf. the pages on torture by Jean Améry, *At the Mind's Limits: Contemplations by a Survivor on Auschwitz and its Realities*, trans. Sidney and Stella P. Rosenfeld (Bloomington: Indiana University Press, 1980), 21-40. Adorno quotes Améry and his analysis on torture in *Metaphysics*, 106.

[98] Horkheimer, *art. cit.*, 46.

[99] *Ibid.*

[100] *Ibid.*, 45.

order of fascism," explains Horkheimer, "is reason revealing itself as unreason."[101] And it does so in two ways: it is revealed as madness because it takes place under the unreasonability of the torture and torments inflicted on the enemies of the new order, and also because it turns against those who reveal not their own insanity, but the un-reason of fascist reason.

Thus, from this perspective, that of the fascist order, the apparent insanity or unreason of the Jews is sufficient reason for their persecution. As Horkheimer states in a profound and problematic passage, which leaves the reader a little unsatisfied, "the hatred of Jews, like the lust to murder the insane, is stimulated by their unintelligible faith in a God who has everywhere deserted them and by the unconditional rigidity of the principle they maintain even unwittingly. Suspicion of madness is the unperishable source of persecution. It originates from distrust of one's own pragmatic reason."[102] And yet although this passage leads us directly to Nazism's detestable logic in effectively murdering the insane and mentally handicapped in the euthanasia project preceding the Extermination, at the same time it says something significant which was outlined in the text "*The Jews and Europe*": essentially, hatred of the Jews is simply hatred towards a faithfulness and belief in a "principle" that is irreconcilable with the world, a principle that directly confronts what dominates and controls the world, a principle, perhaps, that is *other* in relation to the same principle of perseverance in being or self-preservation which guides instrumental reason and the world's reason. The Jews testify, despite themselves and despite the unconsciousness of their testimony, both to a transcendence and to an *other* reason. They are the "memory bearers" of a demanding transcendence — a God who would abandon his children — and are the spokespersons for a reason of madness. They are the spokespersons for a logic *other* than that of instrumental reason which has been used to dominate nature and men for centuries, and for a reason that names men and "animal[s]"[103] instead of imposing itself as mastery and domination. It seems to me that Horkheimer touches on something crucial here. Not only does he suggest an idea that would not be echoed for long afterwards, and perhaps not even yet — in other words, the idea

---

[101] *Ibid.*, 46.

[102] *Ibid.*, 45.

[103] *Ibid.*, 47.

that the Nazi hatred which eradicated the Jews is a way of eradicating along with the Jews the "principle" that they hold, Jewish law and its commandments, or the very "object" of their faith, this strange enigma of an absolutely transcendent God — but by this very path which draws on Jewish belief, he also foresees an *other* possibility for reason.

2. REASON AND NOMINATION

At the moment when he draws this essay's conclusions and makes the turn which takes his discourse from a criticism of *"today"* to the possibility of a tomorrow, Horkheimer resorts, albeit in passing, to this *other* reason, traces of which can be found in the second book of Genesis (*Genesis* 2: 19-20). If bourgeois reason's perseverance in being revealed all its limitations during the centuries of civilization and western society, and its damages in the fascist form "in which it culminates"[104] during Nazism, then a change of course is necessary. A change is needed which proclaims the truth of an *other* reason, and which aims not to dominate nature and life but to understand it; an understanding that means *nomination*. "As the faculty of *calling things by their name*, reason is more than the alienated life that preserves itself in the destruction of others and of itself. To be sure, reason cannot hope to keep aloof from history and to intuit the true order of things, as ontological ideologies contend. In the inferno to which triumphant reason has reduced the world it loses its illusions, but in doing so it becomes capable of facing this inferno and recognizing it for what it is. Skepticism has done its job."[105] To recognize the hell it contributed to creating by its ability to "rise above" history and nature, by acting as a spectator watching from above rather than head on; or, in contrast, by identifying with the principle of self-preservation and becoming absorbed in this principle peculiar to biological life — these are the two aptitudes that distinguish subjective reason from objective reason[106] in *Eclipse of Reason* — is therefore the last possibility for reason. To free itself of its own delusions, to face and recognize hell for what it is, to know how to *name* it, is the only hope for reason.

It is difficult to say to what extent Horkheimer refers directly to biblical verses, or if he tacitly refers to the essay "On Language as Such

---

[104] *Ibid.*

[105] *Ibid.* [my emphasis].

[106] Cf. Horkheimer, *Eclipse of Reason, op. cit.*, 3-5.

and on the Language of Man"[107] (1916), where Benjamin tackles the story of God naming creation and Adam naming the living creatures. If we consider the fact that Horkheimer's essay was part of a work in tribute to Benjamin, this second hypothesis seems equally plausible. In any event, and although hell has taken the place of the Garden of Eden, it is clear that in this text Adamic nomination gives reason another aspect than that of domination. And though the explicit reference to the first book of Genesis (*Genesis* 1:26) in *Dialectic of Enlightenment* demonstrates the sovereignty of man over nature, like that of the gods over man, i.e. the sovereignty of a "creator god" and of "organizing reason" dominating things like a dictator dominating men,[108] this reference confirms that man, like reason, can find another sense only in *nomination*.[109] This is because *naming* gives reason *another* possibility of *knowing*, *another* method of knowledge that, instead of manipulating its object, makes it reveal itself for what it is. It transfers its object into language, and thus reveals it, in the *name*.

Indeed, if we follow Benjamin's ideas in the quoted essay, "the name that man gives to language depends on how language is communicated to him."[110] In this communication, then, there is no aim, no decision, no intentionality on the part of the one who is naming, no "violence" towards the object by the subject. It is simply allowed to pass into speech, allowed to reveal *itself* through speech and the translation of the subject. The subject, *naming* and *knowing* through *nomination*, thus remains in a certain suspension or passivity, but an essential one, providing the object with the care needed to reveal *itself*. The subject fulfills the object and welcomes its appeal to become speech, to make itself language. But what is crucial in this discourse barely outlined by Horkheimer and developed by Benjamin is that in the *name*, the thing — that is, the object of knowledge — is known for what it reveals itself to be, for what it is,

---

[107] Walter Benjamin, "On Language as Such and on the Language of Man," trans. Edmund Jephcott, *Selected Writings I, op. cit.*, 62-74.

[108] See Horkheimer and Adorno, *Dialectic of Enlightenment*, 6.

[109] In *Dialectic of Enlightenment*, Horkheimer's (and Adorno's) position is different. He seems to give a purely nominalist function to the *name* and refers to the impossible nomination of God's proper name in the Jewish tradition. Cf., *op. cit.*, 17.

[110] Benjamin, "On Language as Such...," 69.

and not for what it is supposed to be or what it can be used for. This reason of nomination is therefore very close to objective reason, which must be distinguished from subjective reason that always aims towards particular goals and thus domination. In short, the *name* frees the object of knowledge from imposed finality and from the goal intended by the subject, or rather, it frees it entirely from its status as a single object. If we accept this suggestion of a reason as *nomination*, then we can understand that what is the *object of* knowledge becomes the *other in* knowledge through the *name*. It is not aimed or manipulated, known by what the subject demands it to be, but is welcomed and known in its being *other*, *other* than the intentions and aims imposed on it by the subject, *other* than the being as an object. Therefore, the instrumental reason criticized by Horkheimer, reason that is always implicated in intentional knowledge, is deposed by *nomination*, by this *other* knowledge, by this knowledge thanks to the *name*. And thus it finds another way, another sense.

However, to return to Horkheimer's text, all that remains to be known "*today*" is the hell that reason contributed to creating with its power and instrumentality. Simply knowing hell for what it is and calling it by its name gives reason a lucidity, even if "in the duration of a brief moment,"[111] that can free it from illusions, from ideology, and even from its "foundation," the ego.

And yet, it is precisely the *naming* of the hell or terror imposed by Nazism as "hell" and "terror" that gives men a lucid and crucial consciousness. Knowing them for what they are, according to the parameters of critical theory, produces an essential degree of consciousness. Paradoxically, terror makes men understand, by the mutilation of their identity through the concentration camps and the fragmentation of mass culture, that the principle of self-preservation is what must be annihilated in order for them to stop conflicting by limiting each other. In the extreme moment when terror is working to annihilate the "ego" that is the basis of all of reason's "intelligence" and "stupidity," in the extremity of hell and the state of emergency, in a lucid despair, men can understand that "terror which pushes reason is at the same time the last means of stopping it."[112] In other words, in the state of emergency and danger into which it throws men, terror offers an opportunity, even if it is only a moment of

---

[111] Horkheimer, "The End of Reason," 48.
[112] *Ibid.*

lucidity — the "now of recognizability"[113] as Benjamin says — for them to understand that they must finally free themselves from this principle of self-preservation or submit entirely to total domination. Nazi terror in short obliges men and their concept of reason to change.

Either terror becomes a revelation for reason itself, or it definitively seals its fate. There is no other way out. As Horkheimer says, "the progress of reason that leads to its self-destruction has come to an end; there is *nothing left but barbarism or freedom.*"[114] In doing so, Nazism created a radical caesura in history.

3. A JEWISH INTELLECTUAL *AFTER AUSCHWITZ*

When the death factories and the extermination system had opened their gates and doors to the whole world and silence gave way to reports, Horkheimer directly, but also very intimately, tackled the hell validated by instrumental reason and invented by the Nazis. And although (as I have mentioned above) he had already previously dealt with the existence of the gas chambers while writing *Dialectic of Enlightenment* with Adorno, to the extent that one could almost say that this reality is the starting point for their line of thinking, Horkheimer tackles it much more explicitly in the fragments from later years collected under the title *Notizen*.

In these critical notes on the present, aphoristic notes that precisely accentuate the breath and irregular rhythm of thought in time, the philosopher returns time and again to the difficult and unended recent past. He exposes the issue that steered his own work and life during the post-war years. While Adorno was developing his "Meditations on Metaphysics" and formulating his categorical imperative, Horkheimer concentrated all his pain and his discreet insight into the few lines of the fragment entitled "After Auschwitz," which expresses the most intimate essence of his thinking, and to which we must pay attention: "We Jewish intellectuals who escaped death by torture under Hitler have only one task: to help see to it that such horrors never recur and are never forgotten, in solidarity with those who died in unspeakable torments. Our thought and our work belongs to them; that we escaped by accident should make our solidarity with them not doubtful but more certain.

---

[113] Benjamin, *The Arcades Project*, 473.

[114] Horkheimer, "The End of Reason," 48 [my emphasis].

Whatever we experience must revolve around the horrors intended for us as for them. Their death is the truth of our life; we are here to express their despair and their longing."[115]

What more could be added? This fragment stands out like a tombstone for those who had none, a stone set discreetly in the pages of a book, as a visible memory trail for those of whom there is nothing left, and also as a sign of *testimony* to a work dedicated to bearing their memory. It is a stone, a sign, a trail to be discovered and deciphered among the pages of a book of aphorisms, among the scattered fragments, by a reader who is filled with the same *feeling* and the same obligation. This fragment, real and true as only a *truth of feeling* can be, i.e. a truth that is based on the immanence, materiality and fragility of human existence,[116] and conveying the intimate essence of the philosopher Horkheimer — this fragment leaves *us*, even the post-Auschwitz *us*, the task of understanding and comprehending it, of clarifying what is already obvious and clear as the words of this text are. At the same time, it also sets *us* the task of following the same trail; it invites *us* in turn, in the ignorance and distance of a life begun during the years when the philosopher was writing, to lay the same memorial stone.

Looking very closely at this fragment, or stone, we can decipher two strata or sections and one closing line. The first stratum, which can be defined as deontological, aims to declare what should or should not be *after* Auschwitz; the second, definable as archeological or etiological, shows the reasons and motivations for this duty; and the closure or synthesis draws both of these together and opens itself up to *us* who come *after*. The first stratum, then, says three things: act so that "such horrors never recur"; so that they "are never forgotten"; and ensure "solidarity with those who died in unspeakable torments." These three obligations, stated in three lines and closely connected, are addressed to the "Jewish intellectuals" who escaped death, the martyr's death by torture (*Martertod*) inflicted by the *Totenkopf* on millions of Jews who arrived in the camps. Here, the categorical imperative expounded by Adorno almost at the same time, and which applies to everyone, is limited to the escaped Jewish intellectual. This is not because the agony and death of the torture victims does not concern others, but because an alliance, an indelible union, was secretly sealed between those who should have died and those who did — before them, despite them.

---

[115] Horkheimer, *Notizen*, 273.
[116] Cf. *supra*.

Once again, as with Adorno's imperative before, the justification for these three obligations in one is the concrete and real fact of having escaped the death that engulfed others forever. It is only through the words and speech of the one who is left alive and through the life of the survivor that the obligations of "never again," of memory against oblivion, of faithfulness and of "solidarity" with the dead can be uttered without indecency and arrogance, without rhetoric and conceit. Despite the *paradox of testimony*, the survivor has the authority to say and utter them, not because this survival is guilty, as Adorno believes, but because it is the survivor that must and can *bear witness*. His survival, and with it his life, are summoned to *testify* to those whose lives were snatched away. It is their life, taken away, that appeals for and demands *testimony*. So it is the survivor, more than any other, who can tell of the death of those who died because his blood and breath are still warm. And though the sense of guilt overburdens and eats away at the philosopher's soul, we can say that only the *testimony* delivered by his life and also by his work can transcend this guilt. Certainly, the weight is so heavy that it could crush this same life: "I am supposed to find satisfaction and peace in myself, because my life testifies to an absurd, undeserved accident, to injustice and the blindness of life in general, so that I must be ashamed to still be here."[117] If this fact, the fact of being here, testifies to accident, injustice, the absurd and the blindness of life, then it also testifies, and *at least* by contrast, to the death of the drowned. To say that this survival testifies to their life would perhaps be too much for Horkheimer, but it is possible to say that it *at least testifies* to their death. Indeed, without the survivor's *testimony*, how would the "one task" of memory and of fighting against oblivion, which is the responsibility of the intellectual, be thinkable and possible? How would it be possible, if even those who escaped the "horrors" hide away from it?

Thus, Horkheimer, too, encounters the paradox and challenge of testimony: the guilt and shame of being here to speak by his very survival of "the innumerable death"[118] of the others who were there, and, at the same time, the necessity and obligation to tell — to tell of this death; to tell, above all, of the "unspeakable torments"[119] to which they were

---

[117] *Ibid.*, 202.

[118] *Ibid.*

[119] *Ibid.*, 273.

exposed and subjected; to tell of them, without knowing anything of them and being far from it all.

In the extremity of this impossible and necessary *testimony*, Horkheimer turns towards the singularity of suffering, and specifically towards the suffering inflicted on the Jews who died at Auschwitz. It is their suffering, their agony, their *Martertod* that the intellectual must impossibly express. And he tries to do so, in his own way and as far as he can, in the enlightened synthesis of these words that contain the history of European Jews through a micrological perspective: "People like me, not just generally speaking, but specifically, i.e. Jews, who looked and thought like Jews, like my father and mother and myself — simply because they were like this — were, after years of terrible fear, unspeakable humiliations, inconceivable forced labor, blows and torments, slowly tortured to death by their thousands and thousands in the concentration camp, because they were like my father and mother and myself, because they looked and thought like Jews. They were kept for years in a terrible fear and finally tortured to death."[120] With a bitter irony, Horkheimer gives us here a sketch of the sufferings that the Jews had to endure during the years of the Third Reich — the expropriation of goods, forced unemployment, ghettoization, slavery, concentration in camps, famine, forced labor, humiliations, beatings, physical torture, death by torture, mass murder. And at the same time, he clearly says that it is the specificity or singularity of being Jewish that was targeted in these torments and this death. Having been born a Jew, appearing Jewish in relation to models established and fixed by the regime, by attitude or by thought — all of this directly resulted in the Jewish death from which non-Jews also perished. It is to this death intended for Jews, death in the gas chamber, that others — homosexuals, gypsies, and above all the handicapped and insane — also succumbed. To the Jewish death. Furthermore, Horkheimer seems to say in this passage that suffering is what most distinguishes the Jewish people. He does so not to tie them once more to a fossilized and now intolerable image, or to stigmatize them with a tragic destiny, but rather to say that "Judaism has turned the suffering it endured [...] into a factor in its own unity and permanence."[121]

---

[120] *Ibid.*, 202.

[121] Max Horkheimer, *Critique of Instrumental Reason*, trans. Matthew J. O'Connell (New York: Continuum International, 1974), 122.

And though suffering is effectively the *leitmotif* of their history, this does not mean that the Jewish people are martyrs, but that suffering becomes a sort of "intelligence" or "collective experience" of the memory of death, a knowledge of memory[122] and mourning. "The Jews are not ascetical people," Horkheimer writes again, "they have never glorified or worshipped or sought or praised suffering but only experienced it. Yet more than for other peoples, suffering is inextricably intertwined with their memory of the dead. According to the Jewish law men cannot become saints through suffering, as in Christianity; suffering simply colors remembrance of the dead with an infinite tenderness that does not depend on the consoling thought of eternal life."[123] But what precisely is this "infinite tenderness"? What does it mean?

The crux of "After Auschwitz" can be found in this solidarity with the dead, this memory of their pain and grief, the *knowledge of mourning*. For as the text says, it is only in "solidarity" with those who died at Auschwitz that the survivor can and should live. It is only through the "solidarity" and the unity (according to the German version) linking the living and the dead that testimony can take place. It is a solidarity that is formed and sealed in suffering, in the "horrors intended for us as for them." It is a solidarity that, in the text, connects the obligation of memory to its explanation: ensure "solidarity with those who died in unspeakable torments," and "that we escaped by accident should make our solidarity with them not doubtful but more certain."[124] The life of the survivor makes this "solidarity" certain; it confirms it and ensures it. And yet, how could it be realized except thanks to the *communion* or the *sympathy* of those who testify and bear the memory? How can it be possible except in the remembrance of their suffering? A remembrance capable of sympathizing with their pain? A remembrance of what has not been known, and which nonetheless pleads, longs to be spoken of? How can the suffering of those who were never known be told by those who are alive except through a never-ending mourning?

Horkheimer's approach seems to move in this direction, in the sense of a *knowledge of mourning*, rather than that of the *remembrance* spoken of

---

[122] Cf. Yosef H. Yerushalmi, *Zakhor, Jewish History and Jewish Memory* (Seattle: University of Washington Press, 1982).

[123] Horkheimer, *Critique of Instrumental Reason*, 122.

[124] *Ibid.*, 273.

by Benjamin, capable of activating or actualizing the longings of the past in the present. It is the knowledge of an incurable mourning. Despite the paradox of *testimony*, he thus condenses all of his *thinking* and intellectual *work* into this "solidarity," into this *communion* or *sympathy* with and for those who died at Auschwitz, into this mourning. "Their *death* is the truth of our *life*," he writes in conclusion; "we are here to express their *despair* and their *longing*." Their *death* is the *sense* of our *life*; their *despair* and their *longing* are the profound *sense* of our *work*, of our writing, of our reflections, of our thoughts, of our breaths. Speaking of this *despair* and *longing*, expressing in words the unspeakable of their suffering and the inexpressible of their desires, is the *sense* of the Jewish intellectual's intellectual work — and that of the non-Jewish intellectual who *feels* the same obligation — *after* Auschwitz. Knowing how to listen and how to say what only silence can convey. *Knowing how to testify to this knowledge of mourning.*

But how can we avoid dying from it? How can we live with this mourning? And do they, the dead, find consolation in our words? In our memory? Or is this faithfulness a way of consoling us? A way of becoming more innocent[125] of a fault that we never committed? And above all, how do we transform this mourning into life?

Horkheimer achieves this point, this *knowledge of mourning*, this philosophical gesture of laying a gravestone for those who have no grave, and he imparts the same task to *us* in these conclusive words. By laying this stone, he leaves *us* a "knowledge," a trail to follow. He assigns it to *us* as a sign of a death to be communicated to memory — by our work — but above all as a sign of a life to be renewed — by our life. By giving *us* this stone, this mourning is opened and transmuted, and perhaps finds consolation and an end in this new life that is called to receive it and to carry it. *It is transmuted by being communicated.* And although *we* were born following something that cannot be followed, in the very empty yet very alive *afterwards, our life* becomes this "solidarity," this *connecting line* to those who no longer exist. Through *our life*, and those of the generations to come, their death can remain alive.

---

[125] Horkheimer writes: "Human mourning, by contrast, is more elevated [than that of animals] and more profound—through mourning, they themselves become more innocent," in *Notizen*, 42.

Chapter IV

"The presentiment and the memory of the Nazi horror": Emmanuel Levinas

We are all responsible for all and for all men,
And I more than the others.
Fyodor Dostoyevsky

"How to philosophize; how to write, in a memory of Auschwitz, about those who said to us, sometimes in notes buried near the crematoriums, 'Know what happened, do not forget, and at the same time you will not know.' It is this thinking that runs through and forms the basis of all of Levinas's philosophy, and that he suggests to us without saying it, above and beyond any obligation."[1] These are the words of Blanchot, a friend and close partner of Levinas, which can directly — and also profoundly — introduce the crux of the question.

How, precisely? How to ask this initial question? How to think *afterwards, after* this interruption of history and the *human fiasco* in this century of horror and pain? How to write, how to *tell*?

The fact that "the presentiment and the memory of the Nazi horror"[2] fill and haunt Levinas's thought; that this event runs through and eats away at his life; that it is the abyss in which his philosophical exodus towards "human utopia"[3] originates and takes shape; that it is the "lung" of his open, silent, direct and modest *testimony* — all of this is felt, recognized and absorbed by closely and attentively reading his texts and writing.

As a physical survivor, Levinas cannot forget. As a man and as one of the saved, he cannot erase or ignore this event. No one, he writes, can "look away from a suffering that is experienced as the abandonment of everything and everyone, a suffering at the limit of all suffering." No one can silence the cries of Auschwitz that will resound until the end of time — "can any human wash his hands of all that flesh turned to smoke?"[4]

---

[1] Maurice Blanchot, in *Textes pour E. Levinas*, edited by François Laurelle (Paris: J. M. Place, 1980), 87.

[2] Levinas, *Difficult Freedom*, 306.

[3] Catherine Chalier, *L'utopie de l'humain* (Paris: Albin Michel, 1993).

[4] Levinas, *Difficult Freedom*, 146.

The survivor, who is *other* than the martyrs, in particular cannot abstain from turning his soul towards the graveless dead, and so the most difficult thing for him is to be silent. He who is saved is "responsible and unable to remain silent. He is obligated to Israel for the reasons that oblige every man [....] It is impossible to remain silent. There is an obligation to speak" and, if necessary, an "obligation to cry out."[5] If political, historical and philosophical discourses on the Holocaust are distorted, falsified, manipulated, or trivialized, the survivor has the right, but also the obligation, to cry out.

To cry out, but with a cry attuned to silence, to the silences of those who can no longer speak.

For Levinas, who did not personally experience the extermination camps but prisoner of war camps, "to be a survivor" means to answer this initial question of how to think *afterwards* in words that are not rhetorical but *philosophical*. It means to say how the survivor, retaining a "burn on [his] sides," bearing "for ever the shame of having survived," the shame of being here in the place of another, bearing "the seal of the supreme test,"[6] the marks and stigmata of the "Passion of Passions,"[7] how this man, who is also a *philosopher*, can *think* and *tell* of it in another way.

While distancing himself from the rhetoric that, willingly or not, has often poisoned and continues to poison discourse on the Extermination, while never giving way to pompous complacency or contributing to a "widely-read literature," while never using wordplay to say the unspeakable, despite his brilliant writing, Levinas is wary of indecent, and therefore violent, language for a discourse that quickly becomes the ideology of survival's agony. The unspeakable must "be made word without being turned into literature."[8] It must be said, become *"saying,"* without absorbing the "forms of life that were still hot-blooded."[9] It must become his modest word, and at the same time his silent cry as a survivor who does not want to take the place of those who died, emerging from listening to their silences.

The central task in his philosophy is to give voice to these silences in *"saying"* and by thought that no longer makes a pact with the history

---

[5] *Ibid.*, 147.
[6] *Ibid.*, 236.
[7] *Ibid.*, 158.
[8] *Ibid.*, 237.
[9] *Ibid.*

CHAPTER IV. "THE PRESENTIMENT AND THE MEMORY OF THE NAZI HORROR"

of yesterday's, today's and tomorrow's conquerors, as Benjamin suggests. It is to give a place in the very history of thought to history's defeated, and to overtake the "virile judgment of history, the virile judgment of 'pure reason,'"[10] because this judgment is cruel — it damages, overwhelms and erases the uniqueness and singularity of human faces.

To fight against the tyranny of a visible and triumphant history which is always the history of the conquerors, to fight against the tyranny of a philosophy of the universal and the impersonal which is always oblivious to the singular, and to fight against the tyranny of a reason of the totality of the Same which always consumes the singularity of the Other — this is the explicit and implicit appeal in Levinas's thinking. The dedication in *Otherwise than Being* can only powerfully, respectfully, and also silently remind us of this: *"To the memory of those who were closest among the six million assassinated by the National Socialists, and of the millions on millions of all confessions and all nations, victims of the same hatred of the other man, the same anti-Semitism."* The block letters add to this dedication what other languages cannot say — the proper names of the victims — because persecution is untranslatable and "can only be told in the language of the victim."[11]

It is dedicated to the memory of those who were closest among the six million exterminated by the Nazis, to the memory of the victims of the same hatred of the other man, to the memory of all those defeated and persecuted on earth — to all of them. For at Auschwitz, a bond was forged "in blood and tears, with all the generations of Israel, wherever they are scattered, including the 'Jews of silence' behind the Iron Curtain and — in this immense communion — with all suffering humanity."[12] In the singular sufferings of this singular "Passion," a communion of pain was consecrated between all the sons of Israel, including the "Jews of silence," and all of humanity who suffer the same hatred and the same aversion to the other man. In this communion of tears, this bond of blood, a silent cry was to be received and retained; the cry of the "nameless."

---

[10] Levinas, *Totality and Infinity*, 243. Cf. *supra*, Chap. II, I, 2.

[11] Emmanuel Levinas, *In the Time of the Nations*, trans. Michael Smith (London: Athlone Press, 1994), 46.

[12] Emmanuel Levinas, "Séparation des biens," in *L'Arche*, no. 162-163 (Paris: September, 1970): 101.

I. PHILOSOPHIZING *AFTER AUSCHWITZ*: THREE LESSONS

And yet the book *Proper Names*, which opens with a resolute cataloging of the historical events that stained the twentieth century with blood — the two World Wars, National Socialism, Stalinism, de-Stalinization, the camps, the gas chambers, the atomic bomb — concludes with a chapter dedicated precisely to the "nameless," to all those drowned in history, but particularly to those whose names and faces were erased in the Annihilation.

Although blood has not stopped flowing since the end of this disaster, although hate remains merciless, although it continues to kill and to pay its toll in blood to some Minotaur, and although men are still exposed to contempt and destruction, at least the defeated of today — according to Levinas — "know whither to lift their dying gaze," where to look in their last moments. Perhaps. They are not left to the absolute drifting of their abandonment, to chaos and emptiness, as in the years 1940-1945.

Admittedly, everyone dies alone, and "everywhere the hapless know despair." But "among the hapless and forlorn, the victims of injustice are everywhere and always the most hapless and forlorn."[13] All the victims of injustice and those persecuted by hatred die in an extreme solitude and abandonment. All of them. And yet, what made the period of darkness under Hitler unique was the absolute neglect, the total desertion and the general abandonment into which the Jews were thrown. Those terrible years were a time of interregnum, of the suspension of being and of judgment, of the end of all institutions and opinion, a time of deadly silence, with churches, international human rights organizations, intellectual groups and private citizens all complicit in the same silence as nations.

"None to comfort them!" writes Levinas, taking inspiration from the verse in *Lamentations* [1:2].

And so "who will say the loneliness of the victims who died in a world put in question by Hitler's triumphs"?[14] Who will tell of the children's solitude? Who will name all this "unutterable suffering"?[15]

---

[13] Emmanuel Levinas, *Proper Names*, trans. Michael Smith (Stanford: Stanford University Press, 1996), 119.

[14] *Ibid.*

[15] Levinas, *Entre Nous*, 80.

I. PHILOSOPHIZING *AFTER AUSCHWITZ*: THREE LESSONS

Levinas does not answer — who could? — but he puts forward a hypothesis. In the few lines of this extraordinary text, from which emerges the personal drama of one who was privileged to have survived, the pain of keeping "that tumor in the memory," the impossibility of filling in this "gaping pit,"[16] he wonders if it is necessary, once again, to insist on making those who have come *afterwards* — those who did not know it, in other words *us* — part of this emptiness, this abyss.

Thus, Levinas turns his gaze from his own suffering, also present during this "grace period" of life that turns over and sews up its moments, to speak to the men born *afterwards*, to those who share a "humanity whose memory is not sick from its own memories." He does so not to remind them once more of the malignancy of this evil, the incommunicability of this passion, the hard fate and the difficult justice of the Jewish people, but rather to "awaken them to the sense of imperatives that turn the accusing and destructive burden of Nazism on its head,"[17] in Chalier's words, for if resistance was possible even in those barbaric hours, then it is even more possible *afterwards*. *Afterwards, retrospectively*. The philosopher's task, identical to that of the historical materialist for Benjamin, is to turn his gaze towards the past, to "brush history against the grain,"[18] to awaken to the hope of a past redeemed by the present's resistance, even if it is thanks to *remembrance*, or by opposition, in the present, to the destructive appeals of Hitlerism — an *inverted* yet necessary resistance, because "even the dead will not be safe from the enemy if he is victorious."[19]

Thus, for the conqueror and history to lose their "right to the last word,"[20] says Levinas, it is necessary to learn from the harsh reports of this disaster, *through* its cruelties, "*despite* these cruelties, *because* of these cruelties,"[21] that there are at least three paradoxical lessons to be communicated to future generations. Three lessons, or "truths," which the author sets out in this text, and which he tries to think of and pass on through the richness of all his works. Three lessons that can also be considered as points from which his thinking can be interpreted in three different directions.

---

[16] Levinas, *Proper Names*, 120.
[17] Chalier, *L'utopie de l'humain*, 60.
[18] Benjamin, "On the Concept of History," 392.
[19] *Ibid.*, 391.
[20] Levinas, *Totality and Infinity*, 243.
[21] Levinas, *Entre Nous*, 81 [my emphasis].

The first lesson, and first paradox, is that human beings, to live humanely, have infinitely less need of things than our magnificent civilization has made us believe: "one can do without meals and rest, smiles [and] personal effects."[22] And yet all of this, which was indispensable and whose relativity "suddenly became apparent," concerns human happiness. These "indispensable" things that provided — and still provide — many people with happiness deserve to be redeemed *despite* their relativity, *because* of their very relativity. After all, in the camps, meals, rest, friendly intimacy, smiles and landscapes were *indispensable* for resisting, even for just one more day.

Without wanting to be indecent, Levinas suggests by this paradox that, on the contrary, these "indispensable" things — earthly nourishments, pleasures, private joys, requests for attention — essentially share man's humanity, and that if there was a desire to attack this *very* humanity by depriving man of all this, then it must be *retrospectively* redeemed in this way, by this same path. This is particularly because not only must this path of "terrestrial nourishments," of happiness, not be rejected to return to the desert of an ascetic morality, but, quite the contrary, it must be travelled because it constitutes the "first morality,"[23] the first stage of a morality by which the subject opens itself to the *other*, entering a relationship with what is *other* in life, by enjoying the *other* in life. It is the first stage, certainly, but not the last.

The second lesson, and second paradox: "in crucial times, when the perishability of so many values is revealed, all human dignity consists in believing in their return. The highest duty, when 'all is permitted,' consists in feeling oneself responsible with regard to these values of peace."[24] When the logic of war seems to be the only one possible in a world at war, when "all is permitted," when we can do anything to men, then paradoxically all human dignity consists of believing in and hoping for a return to the values of peace, even if it is only the hope of a private peace, "to return to the shade of one's own vine and fig tree." But beyond this domestic and undoubtedly still too egoistical peace, the struggle not to give in to "the virile virtues of death" and murderous ideals when death alone seems to dominate every sense and sensibility *retrospectively* reveals a great strength, a height, and all human dignity. Not giving in to

---

[22] Levinas, *Proper Names*, 121.
[23] Levinas, *Totality and Infinity*, 64.
[24] Levinas, *Proper Names*, 121.

the temptation of despair, of nihilism, of anti-humanism — *precisely* when the overwhelmingly obvious violence of history makes all awareness incredulous, and when the silence of God, with its haunting echo, makes all lips dumb — is already an act of peace, an act towards peace.

However, for Levinas, the problems of peace and reason are closely linked, as though peace was a gamble, a challenge, and a test for reason; as though peace sought and called into question reason itself; and, conversely, as though reason has always had to vouch for peace, for a peace as closeness to the other.

By following this direction, by following this second tangent, we can interpret the totality of Levinas's philosophical work as a search for a new opportunity for reason, as an exodus "towards an *other* reason, towards the *other* as reason,"[25] towards a reason of peace, and on the other hand, as a *retroactive* struggle against the forces of war, a struggle by reason against its own "totalitarian" temptations.

The philosophical problem from which this consideration of the subject of peace as a test for reason emerges is thus created by the necessity of thinking *after* the caesura in history, *after* this "failure" of reason which was not met with an end to history or an end to violence. To think *afterwards* means to think *otherwise* with regards to rationality that is complicit with barbarity, rationality that is based on being and persevering in its *esse*, and *otherwise* in relation to the "ontology of war." This urgency undoubtedly stems from the fact that Levinas's thinking was affected and dominated by the Disaster, but also by the observation that reason and knowledge are *not sufficiently* insured against barbarity — an observation that Levinas shares, as we have seen, with Horkheimer and Adorno.

In the post-scriptum to *Reflections on Hitlerism*, he spells out: "the source of the bloody barbarism of National Socialism lies not in some contingent anomaly within human reasoning, nor in some accidental ideological misunderstanding. [...] [it] stems from the essential possibility of *elemental Evil* into which we can be led by logic and against which Western philosophy had *not sufficiently* insured itself."[26] Barbarity, which was revealed in all its horror during the disaster, and which may re-emerge at any time, does not stem from an "anomaly" of reason or

---

[25] Blanchot, *art. cit.*, 80.

[26] Emmanuel Levinas, "Reflections on Hitlerism," trans. Seán Hand, *Critical Inquiry* 17, no. 1 (1990), 64 [my emphasis].

chance circumstances of an "ideology." It is, much more underhandedly, one of the derivatives of rationality and its "logic." More precisely, "bloody barbarism" stems from a possibility of *"elemental Evil,"* evil in the primary element — the being — evil implicit in being, in its interest in being, in its *conatus essendi*, in its concern with being. This evil *can* be not only in and of the being, but *can* also take root in a logic based on the being; a logic that, in turn, is the structure of all comprehension and all knowledge. This evil *can*, again, gain a foothold in ontology, in the *logos* of the *esse*, and therefore germinate in the history of western philosophy if, as Levinas writes, "western philosophy has most often been an ontology."[27] This evil is one against which philosophy itself is *not sufficiently* insured, and against which it has *not* been *sufficiently* vigilant.

The "horror of being" and of war that animates Levinas's thinking thus accompanies vigilance towards the being's harmful opportunities connected to reason and the history of western philosophy. Starting by exposing these knots, yet without leaving the philosophical discourse, thus deconstructing it from within as highlighted by the legend of Odysseus, the philosopher centers this "anti-ontological revolt" around three major axes that are at the same time three branches of philosophy: gnoseology, the history of philosophy, and metaphysics.

The third lesson and third paradox: "we must henceforth [...] teach the new generations the strength necessary to be strong in isolation, and all that a fragile consciousness is called upon to contain at such times."

We must remember those who behaved "amidst total chaos as if the world had not fallen apart"; those who, inside, were already resisting the disintegration of a world, and a universe, of sense; those who, to resist, had "no other source but [their] own convictions and privacy."[28] We must remember them, these hidden and tacit resistors, to teach all who have come *afterwards* the hidden and secret strength of internal life. It is as if this vigilance in the storm, this celebration in torment,[29] was not the core of a self-enclosed consciousness but an opening to something *beyond* the self, an opening up to a call and to an awakening, to an "inner voice" coming from the infinitely exterior. It is as if this very consciousness,

---

[27] Levinas, *Totality and Infinity*, 43.

[28] Levinas, *Proper Names*, 121-122.

[29] Cf. *Célébrations dans la tourmente. La résistance spirituelle dans les ghettos et les camps de concentration* (Lagrasse: Verdier, 1993).

this "inner consciousness," this "precarious, divine abode,"[30] was already inscribed with every obligation of man towards the other man, already engraved with all ethics, already marked with the *in* of the *in*finite.

Levinas, however, explicitly clarifies what we must turn towards in order to better understand this paradox of a fragile power, an interiority called on to "contain" an exteriority, a transcendence, a "more" in the "less": "we must," he says, "through such memories, open up a new access to Jewish texts and give new priority to the inner life."[31]

By always keeping memories of the Catastrophe within him, Levinas therefore perseveres, like Horkheimer and Adorno, in the certainty that the task of thinking remains crucial. However, unlike them, Levinas believes that thought must also draw on Jewish sources,[32] frequently forgotten by philosophical rationality and too often fossilized by the Jewish tradition itself. It should access Jewish texts in a new way and create dialogue between philosophers and exponents of Jewish thought without deciding in favor of one or another, but always keeping a tension, a suspense, between the two.

While remaining attentive to this dialogue, the philosopher thus restores a new privilege to interior life in his own thinking, by his *saying otherwise* and using biblical and rabbinical sources he tries to express the *otherwise than being* of this interiority. He does so to the extent of considering the paradox of an "inwardness [that] frees itself from itself, and is exposed to all the winds,"[33] which is already called to this very exposure without any initiative. It is an inwardness that, in addition, is expressed in its *saying,* through a subjectivity of flesh and blood; an inwardness, in short, that is already exposed to the open and expressed in the materiality of a body.

By following this third direction, then, this tangent that becomes a sort of "hyperbola" carrying us towards the "outside" of the subject and implying a *beyond*, an "other shore,"[34] we can also touch or simply

---

[30] Levinas, *Proper Names*, 123.

[31] *Ibid.*, 122.

[32] Among several works by Catherine Chalier, see *La trace de l'Infini. Emmanuel Levinas et la source hébraïque* (Paris: Cerf, 2002).

[33] Levinas, *Otherwise Than Being: or, Beyond Essence*, trans. Alphonso Lingis (The Hague: Nijhoff, 1974), 180.

[34] *Ibid.*, 183.

look at "the openness of space," the "without a place," the "utopia"[35] that is the proximity of the other. We can finally look at the "excellence" of the "for-the-other," the excellence of this "Height," this "Heaven."[36]

II. A SUBJECTIVITY OF FLESH AND BLOOD

That the sense of a book such as *Otherwise than Being* lies in the attempt to think beyond the being and the essence; that this sense finds itself part of and stigmatized by a transcendent subjectivity; that the sense of this transcendent subjectivity is in turn that of an incarnate subjectivity; and that, finally, the beyond-being is reduced to a being for-the-other, where this "being" for-the-other has lost all the characteristics of the being except for those of being a body of flesh and blood that can give to the other — all this now seems to be obvious for several commentators. However, the centrality of a carnal subjectivity which marks out Levinas's itinerary, an itinerary which stretches from the an attempt of an "extraction from essence"[37] to a tearing from the ego and leads to "tearing away of bread from the mouth,"[38] should be considered more deeply. This is because, beyond the philosophical controversies which can arise again and again, this centrality which focuses on one precise point — on what is the most fragile and the most corruptible, on what, above all, is subjected to suffering and death, the body to be precise — reveals not only a certain unfaithful fidelity by Levinas towards the teachings of the phenomenological school in concentrating on what is tangible in the corporal experience, but above all a *testimony* to the trauma of history, which is the subject of my book.

As I have attempted to explain so far, Levinas's itinerary, starting with the eradication of the sturdiest Western philosophical roots and aiming to eliminate the buds of all war along with these roots, draws on the history of the years 1933-1945. It is in turning towards history that Levinas begins this book whose aim is "the destitution and desituating of the subject"[39] down to its "ashes." By taking these "ashes" as a starting

---

[35] *Ibid.*, 182.
[36] *Ibid.*, 183.
[37] *Ibid.*, 8.
[38] *Ibid.*, 64.
[39] *Ibid.*, 185.

II. A SUBJECTIVITY OF FLESH AND BLOOD

point, philosophy manages to deconstruct a certain subjectivity of the subject in *Otherwise than Being*. And it is precisely here, in turn, that my interpretation will be reoriented — because the Catastrophe, and what created it, are in the background for Levinas. They are the silent background to which the philosophical response is very particularly the idea of a subjectivity of flesh and blood, disinterested in its being *and yet* interested in the suffering of the other. The only option for a "still vacillating modernity"[40] is to show a human subjectivity whose crux is "attention to the suffering of others" and where this attention is expressed in the physical body.

Conversely, what is surprising in this extraordinary book is that the uprooting of the being, or even the *esse* or *essence*, is accomplished where one is supposed to achieve the greatest being, where one almost assumes a surplus of being: the body. Indeed, if the most unique modality of the *essence* is its *interest* and its *share* in being, by asserting itself in beings as *conatus essendi*, as an impulse to persevere in their being, as "the allergic intolerance of their persistence in being,"[41] then we could easily suppose that this *conatus* can be fulfilled above all by a body's self-will to live, i.e. where this perseverance is bent "in the midst of a Nature."[42] On the contrary, however, for Levinas it is in the body itself that this "tearing" from the being is accomplished and the "otherwise than being" materializes. Put another way, the surpassing of the being and escape or exit towards the "other-than-being" passes through the web of vessels, nerves and mucous membranes that is the body. It is important, then, to ask *how* a subjectivity's perseverance can be interrupted, obliterated or fractured precisely where the self-will to be materializes in the *physicality* of a body, and of what this would be a testimony, and to examine *why* Levinas believes that it is precisely the suffering body that allows this obliteration and fracture.

First, I will try to answer *why* with a hypothesis.

In 1933, in *"Reflections on Hitlerism,"* written in response to the rise in Nazism and undoubtedly also in response to Heidegger, the issue of the body was central because it was central to Hitlerism and "terribly dangerous," and on the basis of this question, according to Levinas, it

---

[40] Levinas, *Entre Nous*, 80.
[41] Levinas, *Otherwise Than Being*, 4.
[42] *Ibid.*, 68.

was necessary to work to eradicate the new concept of man from which Hitlerism derived its rallying cry. In this text, as we have seen, the body is no longer the eternal stranger, the obstacle or the tomb of the spirit, according to the classical interpretation that Levinas criticizes. Beyond the banal observations that could be made, he says, "there is the feeling of identity. Do we not assert ourselves in this unique warmth of our body long before the development of the Ego which will claim to differ from it?" This — the feeling of identity beginning with the perception of the body — seems to him to be evidence that should not be underestimated. It is evidence, however, that "traditional Western thinking" has always cast aside by consigning the body, and the feeling of identity which emerges from it, to an inferior level. Conversely, it is evidence that the "philosophy of Hitlerism" emphasizes — and does so on a large scale — through the precedence given to these "elementary feelings," which are increasingly revealed as a "bondage to one's own body" and where the very essence of the "new man" resides. In other words, the philosophy that forms the basis of Hitlerism and which makes it philosophically significant for Levinas is not a racism founded on the centrality of the biological, or on "the mysterious urgings of the blood," but on the centrality of this feeling of identity between the ego and its body — contrary to the analysis of Horkheimer and Adorno, who consider identification with the body as one of the driving forces of the dialectic between myth and Enlightenment — this "ineluctable original chain that is unique to our bodies,"[43] whose importance has been forgotten by so-called "classical" philosophy and which, by contrast, becomes the "heart" of the new concept of man with Hitlerism. And it is precisely this feeling of identity and chaining that must be taken into consideration in order to understand the significance and danger of Hitlerism, which threatens "the very humanity of man" beyond all political, social and anthropological thoughts that could be put forward. Without being able to develop the consequences in this article, Levinas therefore seems to reveal the best viewpoint from which to understand "the fundamental principle" of Hitlerism: the biological body, certainly, but also the feeling of identity arising from the body, and the chaining to which the body itself is destined to identify. Levinas stresses this point: "the body," he writes, "is not only a happy or unhappy accident that relates us to the implacable world of matter. *Its adherence to the Ego is of value in itself.* It is

---

[43] Levinas, *Reflections on Hitlerism*, 69.

II. A SUBJECTIVITY OF FLESH AND BLOOD

an adherence that *one does not escape*." And according to the new concept of Hitlerism, "the whole of the spirit's essence lies in the fact that it is chained to the body"[44] and in the impossibility of escaping this identification.

And yet is it not possible to think that it is necessary, precisely in this place or non-place of the body and of the *ego's* identification with the body and its chaining, forty years after these reflections, to respond no longer to the danger but to the scourge of Hitlerism which reduced the body of Israel to ashes? To think that this "elementary feeling," very close to "elemental evil," should not be neglected, and this evidence of the *ego's* identification with the body should not be rejected, but rather that we should change the signs of it and think of it *otherwise*, i.e. otherwise than by the structures of being and relative to the body of the other?

Indeed, as Abensour says, "as absurd as it would be to present Levinas's work as a response to Hitlerism, it seems equally legitimate to think carefully about the initial trauma which affected this philosophy." Here, "think carefully" means to consider "how this trauma revealed the structures of existence likely to cause 'the horror of being'; how this revelation inspired a revolt against this experience of being; how this anti-ontological revolt opened the way for a philosophy of evasion."[45] And how — I would add — this revolt leading to a philosophy of evasion takes place beginning with the body, by restoring to the body all its dignity, by thinking of it as essential — if this term has not already been compromised — for a subjectivity of flesh and blood, a subjectivity that no longer identifies with its corresponding body, but is considered in relation to the body's experience towards the other. This subjectivity happens, is established, and is expressed in the "having the other in one's skin." For Levinas, it is not a question of responding to Hitlerism after forty years, but of developing a great intuition sparked by the trauma of Nazism and aiming to attack it retrospectively at its very "heart"[46] and to completely reverse the details and parameters that drove it.

After having outlined with this hypothesis a possible response to the question of *why* it is the body that must allow an evasion of the being, my task is now to show *how* this subjectivity comes into existence and "is structured," and to illustrate, through interpretation of *Otherwise*

---

[44] *Ibid.*, 68 [Levinas' emphasis].

[45] Abensour, "Le Mal élémental," in *Quelques réflexions*, 98.

[46] *Ibid.*

than Being, that this subjectivity testifies to historical persecution. I will therefore analyze this subjectivity from a three-sided perspective that links it to sensibility, vulnerability and persecution, respectively, to show that this latter plays a crucial role and refers to the persecutions of Hitlerism.

1. SUBJECTIVITY AS SENSIBILITY

The subject, first described as "the other-in-the-same," evolves during the course of the book into the *self* by quickly leaving the paths of the Same and the *ego* and following those of the *self* and the *one* to arrive finally at the *here-I-am*. As the author states, "the subject will be described denuded and stripped bare, as *one* or *someone*, expelled on the hither side of being, vulnerable, that is, sensible, to which [...] the being cannot be attributed."[47] This passage, beyond the interweaving of concepts that become more refined and mutually define themselves, and where it sometimes becomes difficult to find a way out of Levinas's labyrinth of methodological style built on hyperbole, escalation, concreteness and analogy, shows the close connection between the three adjectives (expelled, vulnerable, sensible) which determines the passage from the *ego* to the *self*.

This passage from the *ego* to the *self* takes place through an *exile* of the *ego*, an *exile* where the essence is called into question, where the other indicts and robs the *ego* of its essence, strips it, accuses it and thereby bares it down to the skin. And yet, this "deposition" or desituating of the *ego* into a *self* that is "stripped" and accused despite itself takes place through and within the sensible and vulnerable body: "the reverting of the Ego into a Self, the de-posing or de-situating of the Ego, it is the very modality of dis-interestedness. It has the form of a corporeal life devoted to expression and to giving. It is devoted, and does not devote itself: it is a self despite itself, in incarnation, where it is the very possibility of offering, suffering and trauma."[48] The *ego* becomes the *self* by way of the body, because the body offers the possibility of giving itself, the possibility of giving, "an offering oneself which is not even assumed by its own generosity, an *offering oneself* that is suffering."[49] In other words, the body is the pre-requisite for all offerings and giving to the other;

---

[47] Levinas, *Otherwise Than Being*, 54.
[48] *Ibid.*, 50.
[49] *Ibid.*, 54.

II. A SUBJECTIVITY OF FLESH AND BLOOD

an offering that is not chosen or wanted but "devoted," "more passive than any passivity," according to Levinas's recurring phrase. Thus, the subjectivity of the subject is "the suffering of suffering — the ultimate offering oneself, or suffering in the offering of oneself," a sensibility which is passive and suffering at the same time.

But in what sense should we understand this passivity?

One could say, in fact, that the passivity of sensibility has two nuances in Levinas's discourse. Firstly, passivity is understood in the most manifest sense, i.e. as an offshoot of the subject's subjection to the other and, a little schematically, as the passivity of a subject that does not decide to give to the other but is called on to do so, is "compelled" by the other "anarchically," whereby this adverb implies all the themes of the *"Saying,"* "testimony" and "prophecy" which will be set aside here. Secondly, passivity can be considered as patience and suffering, as the body's suffering, to be precise. It should not be interpreted here as opposition to a matter that resists the body, nor as passivity endured under oppression, nor even as passivity of the effect in the relationship between cause and effect. The passivity of subjectivity is not assumed; it is "unassumability," like suffering. Thus, in the words of the author, the subjectivity of the subject is "adversity assembled in corporeality which is susceptible to pain called physical."[50] It is because I am physically exposed to the other, and exposed *despite* myself to physical suffering and pain, that this exposure is passive.

The passivity of the subject is therefore patience in the sense of physical pain. Moreover, it is possible because pain, in sensibility, targets the *ego's* enjoyment and well-being, enjoyment through which the *ego* arises, asserts itself and basks in its isolation. Pain — which emerges suddenly with the appearance of the other and obligation towards him — comes to interrupt and suspend this enjoyment, comes to tear me from this isolation and thus "tears me from myself."[51] This means, therefore, that passivity in giving is possible because the *ego* is suspended and interrupted in its most essential quality, the possession of its being and enjoyment of life.

Again, this enigmatic passage from the *ego* to the *self*, which does not pass from one substance to the other, in reality only suspends the enjoyment of the enjoying, savoring and relishing *ego*. Thus in this

---

[50] *Ibid.*, 55.
[51] *Ibid.*

suspension, enjoyment is transformed into suffering, into complaint and sacrifice. The other, with the demand and request that it makes of me and no other, asks me to "tear from myself" the most essential thing, to give it that which is most precious and not what is superfluous. It asks me to "give to the other even the bread out of [my] own mouth" or "the coat from [my] shoulders."[52] From this comes suffering, because there is no gift without sacrifice or offering without pain. We do not give the superfluous, the "superfluxion" as Levinas says, but only what is necessary. Tearing the bread from our mouths when we are starving, taking the coat from our shoulders when we are freezing; these alone signify giving. Thus, to feed the other by fasting, to warm it at the expense of my own warmth, these are sacrifices with a cost and implying *physical* pain. This pain is one that interrupts and inverts the *ego's* enjoyment, that tears the most essential quality, expropriates the proper, lacerates the flesh. Giving therefore has no meaning other than "as a tearing from oneself despite oneself,"[53] i.e. as a tearing of oneself from self-indulgence in enjoyment. Only in this tearing does the *ego* become the *self*, the subject in subjection and passivity. "The immediacy of the sensible," writes Levinas, "is the immediacy of enjoyment and its frustration. It is the gift painfully torn up, and in the tearing up, immediately spoiling this very enjoyment. It is not a gift of the heart, but of the *bread* from one's mouth, of one's mouthful of bread. It is the openness not only of one's pocketbook, but of the doors of one's home, a 'sharing of your bread with the famished,' a 'welcoming of the wretched into your house' (*Isaiah* 58)."[54]

In attempting to move Levinas's thinking away from any suspicion of masochism, it is necessary to recall that in *Totality and Infinity*, sensibility is also interpreted on the basis of enjoyment and the enjoyment of life, and that there, too, this enjoyment is closely linked to corporeality and carnal enjoyment. However, there the subject is again an *ego* that remains at home in its enjoyment and that barely begins to open itself up to the other — to the world, the first other that it encounters, to the other that does not yet have a face — whereas in *Otherwise than Being*, this opening of the subject, this exodus, is carried to its extreme consequence: the subject is nothing more than the for-the-other, in the immediacy of the flesh, in physical materiality, in sensibility. To simplify, perhaps,

---

[52] *Ibid.*
[53] *Ibid.*, 74.
[54] *Ibid.*

the subject — now accused and "under indictment" — does not lose its body and, with it, its enjoyments. It opens itself, despite itself, even despite its enjoyments, to the other man. It opens itself without any act of freedom.

2. SUBJECTIVITY AS VULNERABILITY

As some of the quoted passages have indicated, the two adjectives "sensible" and "vulnerable" always come as a pair when relating to subjectivity. Thus, we can also approach subjectivity from this perspective, different and at the same time identical, revealing subjectivity as *vulnerability*, whereby vulnerability is merely a demonstration of *sensibility*, but also a declension of *maternity*. Indeed, in the section on vulnerability, subjectivity is defined, adapted and modeled on the semantic register of maternity, the figure of the feminine which signifies "having-the-other-in-one's-skin."[55]

Maternity — in its integral being-for-the-other, in its life which is in itself given to the other, in its infinite patience — allows access to the sense of an existence entirely dedicated to the life of the other. "Having the other in one's skin" or bearing it "in my breast as the nurse bears the nursling,"[56] are two images which represent the "being-for-the-other" of the carnal subjectivity conceived by Levinas. To bear the other in "one's entrails"[57] like a mother, or to carry it in one's arms like a nursing mother, to feed it like a nursing father[58] — according to the masculine translation of the biblical verse (*Numbers* 11:12)[59] — presumes and requires all the sensibility of a body — a body made of flesh and blood, of sweat and secretions, "of hemorrhaging," of "a hemophiliac's hemorrhage."[60] It is a body capable of giving, certainly, and of giving in suffering, but above all a feminine body, wrought by the female, a maternal body, as during gestation he — she — exposes, and says in his *saying*, "the gestation of the other in the same."[61]

---

[55] *Ibid.*, 115.
[56] *Ibid.*, 91.
[57] *Ibid.*, 75.
[58] *Ibid.*, 91.
[59] *Ibid.*
[60] *Ibid.*, 92
[61] *Ibid.*, 75.

Thus, the subject is exposed "to tend to the other's needs" like a mother, in the fragility of the body that feels and suffers. In Levinas's terms, maternity "is already the corporeality which the philosophy of the conscience wishes to constitute on the basis of it. The corporeality of one's own body signifies, as sensibility itself, a knot or a denouement of being, but it has also to contain a passage to the physico-chemical-physiological meanings of the body."[62] Here, the author specifies that sensibility or maternity is linked to corporeality; not to a corporeality that is indebted to the conscience, and that is only a perception or a glimpse of this same conscience, but to a "signifying corporeality one's own body," i.e. one that signifies itself and the entire physical, chemical and physiological dimension of the body. This material dimension of the body is therefore crucial, because the very significance of all signification and all sense is based on it. Moreover, it is the key to understanding the "intrigue" of the corporeality in question here and towards which my analysis turns. As Levinas explains a few lines earlier: "the sensible experience of the body is already and from the start incarnate. [...] I am bound to others before being tied to my body."[63] Sensibility, like maternity, does not appeal first to an *ego*'s consciousness, but is already incarnate in a body which is already tied to the other, to the body of the other, even before being tied to an *ego*, to me, to the essence of me, to the archetype of me, to my body. Although this may seem excessive, this intrigue of incarnation — which furthers the other to the extent of giving it priority over the intimate core that the subject still maintains itself, with its own body and with the consciousness of its body — curls up, takes shape, and is played out precisely in corporeality. And it is here, in the incarnation of the body, in its material immediacy, that the signification of the *sense* emerges.

By taking this idea to the extreme, Levinas also seems to say that the "one-for-the-other" — that is, *signification* — cannot occur without passing through corporeality and its materiality. The tearing from the *self*, caused by the invasion of the other which goes as far as the *ego*, tearing me from my enjoyment and my body, invading me in the most intimate privacy of my body, in my entrails and skin, can be justified uniquely in that "giving to the other the bread from one's own mouth is being able to give up one's soul for another."[64]

---

[62] *Ibid.*, 77.
[63] *Ibid.*, 76.
[64] *Ibid.*, 79.

Sensibility, then, conceptually evokes vulnerability. This in turn evokes persecution. Indeed, vulnerability calls to mind "the absence of protection and cover,"[65] an anxiety apparently without reason, "a pre-original not resting on oneself" and the "anxiety of the persecuted,"[66] as Levinas writes. Although he has not yet explained how, it seems clear that vulnerability calls to mind maternity, i.e. the concrete carrying of the other, the "groaning of the wounded entrails," according to the author's biblical reference (*Jeremiah* 31:20). And this physical pain and these entrails remind us that vulnerability is also connected to persecution. But why, then, do vulnerability, maternity and persecution go together? In what way are they related?

Firstly, we can understand that vulnerability, like maternity and persecution, is defined by passivity — different from inertia or the effect produced by a cause — in the sense of exposure to injury, pure subjection and suffering. However, this suffering arises from "having been offered without any holding back," as Levinas says. Similarly to maternity, vulnerability takes its sense from the implicit passivity of the passive form of "having-been-offered," from the offering's passivity, without choice and without holding back. Besides the passive form in this "having-been-offered," the past infinitive indicates the absence of any present and any beginning, any choice, act or initiative, which presumes a pre-original, a before time and a before nature.

Secondly, we can understand that vulnerability, maternity and persecution are linked by the author due to the suffering that they presume and cause. They are not only related by their passivity, but also by physical pain. Levinas explains the anxiety of the persecuted through the anxiety of ubiquity and identity — "where to be? how to be?" — that only the persecuted or the stateless know, and through the suffering that they feel, suffering that is comparable only to the "groaning of the wounded entrails"[67] of the mother. The analogy between maternity and persecution lies in the pain of the "wounded entrails," injured by those — the others — they will one day carry or those they have already carried. It is internal pain, whether already suffered in the past or still possible in the future. It is injury, sickness and bleeding for the coming of the other.

---

[65] *Ibid.*, 75.

[66] *Ibid.*

[67] The expression "maternal entrails" (*Humanism of the Other*, 75) evokes the Hebrew term "*rakhamim*" (mercy), which contains a term with as little neutrality as "*rekhem*" (uterus).

But there is an even more crucial issue. Vulnerability is therefore obsession with the other, suffering for him, support of the other without taking anything, knowledge — without knowing — of how to support the other, knowledge of how to carry him, to pine for him, but also, as the author said in his first attempt to define this concept in *Humanism of the Other*, "it is the aptitude — that any being, in its 'natural pride' would be ashamed to admit — for 'being beaten,' for 'getting slapped.'"[68] In other words, vulnerability is exposure to persecution in general, but beyond any affectation of suffering or humiliation, beyond any masochism. However, Levinas states something unprecedented, where the terms maternity, responsibility and persecution mix and mutually define themselves, and where the subject is called on to take the responsibility of the persecutor: "in maternity, what signifies is responsibility for others — to the point of [...] *suffering both from the effect of persecution and from the persecuting itself in which the persecutor sinks. Maternity, which is bearing par excellence, bears even responsibility for the persecuting by the persecutor.*"[69]

3. SUBJECTIVITY AS PERSECUTION

One question is raised, then: by whom is the subject persecuted? By the being? By the other? Or by the Other?

This question takes us onto very unstable but important ground. Indeed, in *Otherwise than Being*, persecution sometimes seems related to the subject's *ego*, i.e. to its being, as if the *esse* were persecuted in its *conatus essendi* which the subject is called on to suspend; as if it were persecuted by its very being, by the being, by the "there-is." But sometimes, and in fact most often, it is persecution inflicted by the other, by others, by the neighbor that invades the subject's body, his entrails, his skin. It is persecution by the other in the excess of responsibility that the subject is called on to bear, an excess that goes as far as "responsibility for the persecuting by the persecutor," persecution in always being behind the other, persecution in substitution etc. In short, the persecution's perpetrator is also the Other, the Infinite, the Good "before any beginning." It is what "anarchically" requires and inspires the subject's obligation towards its neighbor before this other person makes his appearance, as if the true

---

[68] Levinas, *Humanism of the Other*, 63.
[69] Levinas, *Otherwise Than Being*, 75 [my emphasis].

II. A SUBJECTIVITY OF FLESH AND BLOOD

persecutor was in fact He who commands in the commandment and inspires in the spirit.

In Levinas's vocabulary, persecution by the neighbor-other is designated as "obsession,"[70] while persecution by the Other-Infinite-Good evokes "testimony," or *"Saying,"* or "Glory," where we rediscover the theme of the anarchic, the pre-original. However, these two concepts, persecution-obsession and persecution-testimony, are only two sides of the same structure. As I am not able to tackle both here, I will focus on the first, which is crucial to my subject.

Obsession as a derivative of persecution is not introduced by Levinas to express the negativity of the difference between the other and the *self*, a difference which is expressed by "non-indifference" and responsibility towards it, but to say that persecution-obsession goes beyond consciousness. Obsession paralyzes the consciousness because it does not recognize the weight of having to take on and bear the other. It is a "seed of folly"[71] or "delirium." "Obsession is irreducible to consciousness," writes Levinas, "even if it overwhelms it. [...] Obsession traverses consciousness countercurrentwise, is part of consciousness as something foreign, a disequilibrium, a delirium. It undoes thematization, and escapes any *principle,* origin, will or αρχή, which are put forth in every ray of consciousness."[72] "The-one-for-the-other" is thus a "one-way relationship"[73] and beyond consciousness. However, this "beyond consciousness" of persecuted subjectivity is possible only because there is never synchronization between the subject and the other. The two never in fact meet, and there is no possibility of giving or suffering reciprocally, i.e. at the same time. This is because there is always a gap between each one: first a temporal gap because one is always too late to meet the other; then a gap of responsibility because one always has an excess of responsibility with regards to the other; and finally a gap in suffering because one suffers a surplus of suffering in its suffering for the responsibility of the other. The philosopher remarks that obsession is different to cognition or knowledge; in other words it is beyond — or before — consciousness, and it is precisely in this "beyond consciousness" that proximity-obsession is "unassumable like a persecution."

---

[70] *Ibid.*, 77.
[71] *Ibid.*, 91, 101.
[72] *Ibid.*, 101.
[73] *Ibid.*, 84.

And yet, in a note relating to another passage, Levinas explains the sense of this "beyond consciousness" — very close to a before, the before of the unconscious to be precise — which involves a slightly "unnatural"[74] suffering and allows it to be associated with persecution. In a few lines, the philosopher explains that if obsession is suffering, this is due to the fact that there is no "natural benevolence" in proximity-obsession. There is no altruism, no approval, no will or freedom, but rather something "unnatural" — the suspension of enjoyment, specifically, something "unassumable," like the unassumability of all suffering, something "anarchic." Here "anarchic" signifies a state of disorder where persecution brings the *ego* back to the *self*, placing it in the accusative and under accusation, accused of an absolute charge, imputed with a fault that it neither committed nor willed. Levinas explains: "[P]ersecution is a trauma [...] Persecution leads back to a resignation not consented to, and consequently crosses a night of unconsciousness. That is the sense of the unconscious, a night in which the reverting of the ego into itself under the *trauma of persecution* occurs."[75] Thus, the "beyond consciousness" is similar to the "before" of the unconscious, and the trauma of persecution affects or touches the unconscious. But regardless of any potential reflections drawing on psychoanalytical theories, which I will leave to the experts, I would like to stress that despite the violence, despite the lack of "logic" and "knowledge," despite the impossibility of defence or shrinking away, here *it is persecution that "builds," or even "teaches" the subject, because it is persecution that "brings the ego back to the self."* Put another way, persecution, *despite* and *because of* all this, allows the unconscious passage — and passage through unconsciousness — from the *ego* to the *self* by *teaching* the subject the non-consented resignation which is a passivity more passive than any other passivity, the first act — without action — of the subject's subjectivity.

However, although the first part of the phrase signifies that persecution, without consent and without consensus, travels the paths of the unconscious, the second part — "this is the sense of the unconscious, a night in which the reverting of the ego into itself under the trauma of persecution occurs" — is less clear. Indeed, why does Levinas need to specify "the sense of the unconscious," and to do so based on the "trauma of persecution," a sense which also gives a true sense to the sense of

---

[74] *Ibid.*, note 1 [my emphasis].

[75] *Ibid.*, 197-198.

proximity, in this first movement of the *ego*'s reverting to the *self*? Moreover, is the "night" of which he speaks only that of the unconscious — without the rays of consciousness — or does this "night" also evoke another night, that which invades the unconscious each night, a "night" of an unconsciousness stigmatized by the "trauma of persecution"? In other words, does this *"trauma of persecution"* not also evoke, albeit in a veiled manner, the trauma that the night of history exerted on his unconscious? I do not mean to suggest by this that Levinas's unconscious is obsessed with the Disaster — which would be out of place and irrelevant — but that the trauma of historical persecution was also able to affect not the philosopher's unconscious but his thinking, to the extent that in this key phrase he confirms that passage from the *ego* to the *self* — a passage that is crucial to his analysis — *takes place in the unconscious and under the "trauma of persecution."* And though it would be too simplistic to think that the association here between the persecution of the neighbor-other and the historical persecution of the Jews is based on the equivalence of the term "persecution," it would be equally wrong to think that Levinas uses this term superficially and without any reference to the anti-Semitic and racial persecution exercised by the Nazis. Consequently, I would like to show that *testimony* to the trauma of persecutions under Hitler — a trauma whose traces can be found in some of the more relaxed pages, in some very strong expressions we have already encountered — is revealed in a moment that is theoretically crucial to Levinas's reasoning. Here, at the heart of the philosophical reasoning on the otherwise than being, i.e. in the inner workings of the book — in this passage from the *ego* to the *self* that heralds the birth of an other subjectivity — we can find repercussions and traces of the trauma of persecution. Indeed, this little note, closely related to other equally crucial passages in the book, shows that something happened under "the trauma of the persecution" of the Jews in the twentieth century not only in Levinas's thinking that was affected by this trauma, but also in the particular idea revealed in the passage — the "reverting" from the *ego* to the *self* which takes place in a "beyond consciousness" that is certainly very close to the unconscious, but also marked by and stigmatized by historical persecution.

Thus, under the *"trauma of persecution"* — pure violence where someone, but also a people, is accused of "a fault it has not committed or willed" — this passage took or takes place, transforming an *ego* that is free, active, enjoying and persevering in its being, into a *self* that is ordered or commanded, suffering, passive, disinterested in its being *and yet* interested in the other.

All that is important in Levinas's analogical and ethical reversal is at stake in this *and yet*. The passage from the *ego* to the *self* occurs at the same time by analogy and in a reversal of historical persecution. Indeed, the persecuted subject is persecuted by the neighbor-other, and not by the tormentor-other or the enemy-other whose terrible violence has been revealed by history. Furthermore, it is not a case of active persecution, i.e. one administered voluntarily by the other, but a persecution that the other exercises passively against me and which I suffer in complete passivity. It is a persecution that is passive for the other and passive for me. This, at least, is the initial interpretation. On a second level, however, the passivity is that of the subject, and the other is the persecutor who strikes violently: "to undergo from the other," writes Levinas, "is an absolute patience only if this by-the-other is already for-the-other. This transfer, other than interested, 'otherwise than essence,' is subjectivity itself. 'To tend the cheek to the smiter and to be filled with shame' (*Lamentations* 3:30): to demand suffering in the suffering undergone (without producing the act that would be the exposing of the other cheek) is not to draw from suffering some kind of magical redemptive virtue. *In the trauma of persecution it is to pass from the outrage undergone to the responsibility for the persecutor, and, in this sense, from suffering to expiation for the other.*"[76] Here Levinas explicitly and strongly states what was alluded to and relegated to a footnote in the section commented on above.

This quote, which evokes biblical sources and in particular the prophet Jeremiah, once more reveals the hyperbole at work in Levinas's thinking. The subject's responsibility must be distinguished from "altruistic will," the instinct of "natural benevolence" or "love." On the contrary, it is, in its madness, exposition even as far as expiation of the persecution inflicted by the persecutor who this time strikes and smites. Here, the suffering endured in the persecutor's blows is transformed into suffering for the smiter's neglected responsibility — guilt, then? In the end, this suffering redeems nothing. It remains suffering. *And yet* there is "expiation" in this passage or "reverting" or "transfer."

But why exactly "expiation" if it redeems nothing and if we speak of a subject that has committed no fault, except perhaps that of always being indebted to the other? And, on the other hand, if we consider the point of view of the other, what fault has the persecutor-other committed

---

[76] *Ibid.*, 111 [my emphasis].

except that of non-responsibility towards the other man, that of forgetting or, worse, of persecution of the other? But if this is the case, according to Levinas's logic, is it not his own business, the business of the other who does not care about what is other to him? Unless this expiation evokes another expiation, one that is much more difficult, *where the subject expiates the evil of the persecutor, the persecuting of the persecutor, the persecuting of persecutions under Hitler.*

In persecution and driven by the current of persecution, then, the passage from the *ego* to the *self* takes place; one which, above, occurred through physical sensibility and the gestation of maternity, then in the unconscious, and now in the "transfer" — again a term relating to psychoanalysis — or *passage* where one passes from "the outrage undergone" to "the responsibility for the persecutor," where suffering produced *by* the other is transformed into suffering *for* the other, even if this other is the "neighbor in its persecuting hatred."[77]

It is a passage that is also accomplished at a more general level, in the book as a whole and in the reversion made by Levinas, by a hyperbolic, even dizzying inversion that transforms sufferings caused *by* persecuting hatred — aiming to annihilate man's humanity during the Catastrophe — *into* the sufferings of a subject called on to answer for the suffering of the other man. It is a *reverting* that transforms the pain inflicted on the bodies of those persecuted by Nazism *into* the passive suffering of a subject of flesh and blood caused by the physical suffering of the other, even to giving him the last mouthful of bread.[78] The model, or the anti-model, of this "subjectivity of the subject as *persecution* and *martyrdom*"[79] applies to all those persecuted on earth, to all the "victims of the same hatred of the other man," but most particularly to "those who were closest among the six million assassinated by the National Socialists," as the book's dedication reads. In the end, inexorable evil can be interrupted, *retrospectively* suspended — "expiated" — only by the gesture, even if only an elusive tear, of "being torn from oneself for another in the giving to the other of the bread from one's own mouth."[80]

It is *testimony* to an otherwise than being, or saintliness.

---

[77] *Ibid.*

[78] Levinas's emphasis on the piece of bread and the bareness of the skin is a *trace*, a *testimony*, of this *reverting*.

[79] *Ibid.*, 146.

[80] *Ibid.*, 142.

III. A HUMANISM OF THE "SUFFERING SERVANT"

The parabola of Levinas's thinking reaches this point, transforming the sufferings undergone due to Nazi persecution into sufferings of the subject by this dizzying reversal — a subject of flesh and blood, of madness, or holy subject, the nerve center of this extreme book *Otherwise than Being*. But as Levinas wrote almost at the same time as the book was written (1973), "all this *bears witness*, not to some sort of masochism belonging to persecuted people looking for a haven for the source of their unhappiness," but to a humanism capable of keeping alive "the persecuted man's human essence — that is to say, to act in such a way that in his rebellion or patience, he does not himself become a persecutor and mistrusts resentment."[81] In other words, all this testifies to a "humanism of the suffering servant,"[82] to use another of Levinas's favored expressions, or to a "humanism of patience" that evokes "the history of Israel," which in turn testifies to the singular sufferings of the Extermination and, with them, includes all the suffering that still "demands justice until the end of time."[83]

1. AUSCHWITZ AS A PARADIGM OF USELESS SUFFERING

And yet, Levinas more explicitly tackles the problem raised by suffering in general and by that endured during the Extermination in the revealing article "Useless Suffering" (1982). This is one of the rare cases where the philosopher openly deals with the "tumor" of his personal memory and also the "tumor" of the collective Jewish, European or universal memory. This memory, the *testimony* of the suffering of European Jews that is important to him is, as I have attempted to show, at the very heart of his thinking.

The first stage of this essay is a phenomenological analysis of suffering, where it is interpreted as an "excess," an "unassumability," a "too much," after which it moves on to investigate the possibility or impossibility of a theodicy "after Auschwitz." According to Levinas, the most revolutionary fact for the European consciousness, whether religious or atheist, is the destruction of the balance between all theodicy and the forms that suffering took during the twentieth century; between,

---

[81] Levinas, *Difficult Freedom*, 297.

[82] *Ibid.*, 186. This expression clearly evokes Isaiah 53.

[83] *Ibid.*, 302.

on the one hand, theodicy attempting not only to vindicate God, but also seeking a justification to save morality and make suffering bearable, and on the other hand, all the "useless suffering" inflicted by humiliation, torture, murder and annihilation in the sinister sites invented in this century of modern barbarity.

This testing of the idea of theodicy is all the more necessary in light of the phenomenal pain endured in the death camps. Among all the events staining this century with blood, "the Holocaust of the Jewish people under the reign of Hitler," writes Levinas, "seems to be the paradigm of gratuitous human suffering, in which evil appears in its diabolical horror."[84] And although all the victims of the places of torture and all those who died in the gulags are present when we utter this place name, Auschwitz, as Adorno believes too,[85] it is not only a "subjective feeling" to maintain that Auschwitz is the "paradigm" of useless suffering and of the malignancy of evil. Why?

In attempting to answer this difficult, thorny question, the source of so much equivocation then as now, Levinas endorses the views of Emil Fackenheim, showing once again how truly difficult it is for him to deal with this subject in the first person. For both men, the genocide of European Jews was different from other genocides, and from other persecutions of the Jewish people, precisely because this massacre was perpetrated without any reason, whether conceivable or horrifying, but instead solely to achieve annihilation, "massacre for massacre's sake, evil for evil's sake."[86] Moreover, the aim was not annihilation for annihilation's sake, but rather pain for pain's sake. In other words, what is unique in this evil is also, and certainly not only, the perpetration of sufferings "for nothing," "useless suffering."

It is well known, through many testimonies, that pointless violence was inflicted at Auschwitz and at all the other places of torture and

---

[84] Emmanuel Levinas, "Useless Suffering," in *Entre Nous, op. cit.*, 83.

[85] Indeed, Adorno writes, "and by that [Auschwitz] I mean not only Auschwitz but the world of torture which has continued to exist after Auschwitz and of which we are receiving the most horrifying reports from Vietnam," in *Metaphysics*, 101.

[86] *Ibid.*, 108. Cf. Emil Fackenheim, *God's Presence in History: Jewish Affirmations and Philosophical Reflections* (New York: New York University Press, 1970).

death implicit in this name. It is enough to recall the account by Levi, this familiar witness who, almost in the same period as Levinas, admitted that to speak of "useless violence"[87] may seem offensive, even obscene. And yet, according to him, it is indeed necessary to distinguish a useful violence — that is, violence that is on the margins of being justifiable by various reasons — from a violence that is absolutely useless, a violence for nothing, with no other *sense* than to inflict suffering "for nothing" or to humiliate those who endure it. But can we not say that it is possible to find a sense or a utility in humiliation? Aside from the large-scale violence that will be part of history from now on, there is a whole series of "small" abuses, useless violence causing useless and gratuitous sufferings that are nonetheless indelible in the memory of the deportees. There is useless violence that reveals a character that is gratuitous, nonsensical, "too much," "excessive," a character of malignancy that marks the evil and pure pain suffered by those who arrived in the camps. There is useless violence and suffering, like that of the sealed wagons, of constantly violated modesty which conditioned of life in the *Lagers* through the prolonged obligation of nudity, and in some camps, the useless violence of tattooing, gratuitous violence, "pure offence."[88] In short, there is useless and extreme violence against the dead and their remains.

And yet, what theodicy, in either the wide or strict sense of the term, could "apply" in the face of this unjustified and unjustifiable violence, of imposed suffering and humiliation, of torments before waiting for the end to come? What justification could there be for all this evil? For all the *malignancy* in this evil?

Moreover, *after* this suffering it is impossible to believe, following a theodicy as old as the Bible, that the tragedies of the Jewish people can be justified by any culpability. And this is without counting the fact that, as Levinas explains, "the inhabitants of the Eastern European Jewish communities constituted the majority of the six million tortured and massacred; they represented the human beings least corrupted by the ambiguities of our world, and [that] the million children killed had the innocence of children."[89] What theodicy could be invented to justify the abandonment of children?

---

[87] Cf. Levi, *The Drowned and the Saved*, 118

[88] *Ibid.*, 119.

[89] Levinas, *Entre Nous*, 84.

2. ETHICAL RESISTANCE *AFTERWARDS*

The philosophical problems posed by this "pain that appears in its fundamental malignancy," this "suffering for nothing,"[90] concern the *sense* that human morality on the one hand, and religiousness or faith on the other hand, can have after the end of theodicy. Two directions are opened up: one towards the pursuit of an *other sense* of morality itself; the other towards an *other sense* to be given to faith, or rather, towards another way of uttering — or not uttering — the name of God. These are two directions that Levinas constantly keeps parallel and superimposed throughout his book, and two directions that also do not yield to the temptation of once again becoming theodicies, i.e. that never transform into a justification of a cheap morality or into a justification of a slightly primitive God. But the questions raised remain open.

Indeed, as far as faith is concerned — and particularly the Jewish faith — it is still unknown whether it is necessary to "renounce after Auschwitz this God absent from Auschwitz."[91] And as far as morality is concerned, we must ask what morality this is. Like Levinas, we must ask "the humanity that, during all these horrors, breathed — already or still — the smoke from the ovens of the 'final solution' crematoria where theodicy abruptly appeared impossible — will it, in indifference, abandon the world to useless suffering [...]? *Or*, incapable of adhering to an order — or a disorder — that it continues to think diabolical, must not humanity now, in a faith more difficult than before, in a faith without theodicy, continue to live out Sacred History; a history that now demands even more from the resources of the *I* in each one of us, and from its suffering inspired by the suffering of the other, from its compassion which is a non-useless suffering (or love), which is no longer suffering 'for nothing,' and immediately has meaning? At the end of the twentieth century and after all the useless and unjustifiable pain which is exposed and displayed therein without any shadow of a consoling theodicy, are we not all committed — like the Jewish people to their faithfulness — to the second term of this alternative?"[92]

The two directions merge in the second term of this alternative, in this "or," because these directions are comprehended in their super-

---

[90] *Ibid.*, 84-85.
[91] *Ibid.*, 85
[92] *Ibid.*, 85-86 [my emphasis].

imposition — one based on the other, one explaining the other. The possibility of a faith *afterwards* in fact depends whether it is possible for an *ethic* to survive *afterwards* too; an *ethic* "of the inter-human,"[93] which envisages in man the responsibility and remedy for the sufferings of the other man. It is an *ethic* that certainly draws on the biblical message. Therefore, this faith *afterwards* can only be a demanding way of "loving the Torah more than God,"[94] a way of prayer embodied in giving, in giving the other the aid he asks for. This faith, then, can only coincide with an "inter-human" *ethic*.

The Jewish faith *after* Auschwitz, faith in God and in the ethical message of the Torah, is therefore necessary so that the "final solution," which aimed to eliminate the Jewish people and with them the message that they carried, does not come to fruition, so that the malignancy of evil does not have the last word. Furthermore, according to Levinas, through generations of renewal and communication of this message, the Jewish faith carries a "universal signification," a signification valid for all humanity. More precisely, this faith, persevering in its life and rebirth, continuing the "Sacred History," even and especially *afterwards*, brings to humanity the *ethical* signification of the perseverance of good, which uses the resources of the *ego* in each person and the *ego*'s *compassion* towards the suffering of the other. It brings the *ethical* signification of a "humanism of the other man" and of the "inter-human" commandment of *compassion* for the other — perhaps also for the world — allowing it (the other, the world) to not be left to the excesses and the harmful powers of evil by abandoning it to useless suffering.

This *compassion*, or love, or kindness that is a "non-useless" suffering in the *ego*, can suspend the useless suffering of the other, even if only for a moment. And in this suspension it can bring aid, remedy, relief, and goodness.

While the intrinsic character of suffering is a "too much," an "excess," an unassumability, it also paradoxically implies a call for exteriority, for a transcendence.

Without any desire to explain and justify the suffering of the other, and also without intending to take the place of Job's friends, the *ego* — I – can however lean towards the sufferer and make an opening for him in consolation and remedy, in attention and compassion, and bear the

---

[93] *Ibid.*, 81.

[94] Levinas, "Loving the Torah more than God" (1955), in *Difficult Freedom*, 142-146.

weight of suffering *with* him — yet without enduring it *for* him. It can, quite simply, open up a horizon to him, elusive like that of a caress,[95] fleeting as hope.

More than ever *after* Auschwitz, then, communication of the *ethical* message of the Torah is not only a way of remaining faithful to it despite everything, but a possibility for humanity to resist the malignancy of evil, of this evil that wanted to annihilate both the people of Israel and the word to which they testify. Thanks to Jewish perseverance and faithfulness to the biblical word, and through the model it offers, humanity can have access to "a new modality"[96] of *both* morality *and* faith. If Auschwitz indeed revealed the fundamental uselessness of all suffering — particularly of that undergone by the inmates of the ghettos and camps — and at the same time the end of all theodicy, then especially *afterwards, ethical resistance* to malignancy *can* and *should* be applied against this uselessness, against this "too much" of suffering. To ensure that the diabolical plan that was supposed to be accomplished in the death camps is not completed, man *can* act retroactively — through an action that remains passive, being a response to an appeal by the other — so that the suffering of the other man is what concerns *him* (or *me*), so that the remedy is *his* (*my*) duty. Thus, in this inter-human perspective "there is a radical difference between *the suffering in the other*, where it is unforgivable to *me*, solicits me and calls me, and suffering *in me*, my own experience of suffering, whose constitutional or congenital uselessness can take on a meaning, the only one of which suffering is capable, in becoming a suffering for the suffering (inexorable though it may be) of someone else. *It is this attention to the suffering of the other that, through the*

---

[95] In *Existence and Existents* (1947), trans. Alphonso Lingis (London: Kluwer Academic Publishers, 1988), written—we must recall—during the years of imprisonment in a camp, Levinas writes: "The caress of a consoler which softly comes in our pain does not promise the end of suffering, does not announce any compensation, and in its very contact, is not concerned with what is to come with afterwards in economic time; it concerns the very instant of physical pain, which is then no longer condemned to itself, is transported 'elsewhere' by the movement of the caress, and is freed from the vice-grip of 'oneself,' finds 'fresh air,' a dimension and a future," 55.

[96] Levinas, *Entre Nous*, 86.

cruelties of our century (despite these cruelties, because of these cruelties) can be affirmed as the very nexus of human subjectivity, to the point of being raised to the level of supreme ethical principle."[97] This attention to the suffering of others, this suffering for the suffering of the other, or *"compassion,"* or "love," can thus become, according to Levinas, the "supreme ethical principle" of a modernity that is "still vacillating,"[98] still hesitating *after* all this and *despite* all this. But it can also express another idea of faith, or rather, in another way, *tell* of God's proximity despite His silence.

Is it not indeed in this attention to the suffering of the other, in this obligation with regards to him, that "the idea of God"[99] occurs to us? And that we, on our part, can have an idea of His suffering? It is as if paying attention to and caring for the pain of others was *also* a contribution to the easing of God's suffering, and as if our suffering, "suffering in me," was *also* a suffering for His suffering. It is as if His silence, in the extreme hours, was the silence of one who was silent not because he was abandoning his children, but because he was crying and suffering over all the sufferings inflicted on them. It was the silence of one who cried their tears.

In this way, Levinas manages to think very modestly of a God who was absent and silent at Auschwitz because He was suffering, and perhaps opens philosophical thought to another significance of sense — not only to that of ethics — attached to the sense of hope, hope for the "reparation of the irreparable," so that "no tear is [...] lost, no death [...] without a resurrection."[100]

---

[97] *Ibid.*, 81 [my emphasis].

[98] *Ibid.*, 80.

[99] The placing of the "idea of God" in our minds is a "descent" of God. Cf. "Transcendence and Intelligibility," 157. For a development of this topic, please also refer to my article "Humilité de Dieu, prière de l'homme" in *Levinas et les theologies*, edited by Danielle Cohen-Levinas and Shmuel Trigano, no. 42 (Paris: In Press, 2007), 155-169.

[100] Levinas, *Existence and Existents*, 55.

Conclusion

I called upon thy name, O Lord,
out of the low dungeon.
Thou hast heard my voice: hide not thine ear
at my breathing, at my cry.
Thou drewest near in the day that I called upon thee:
Thou saidst "Fear not."

Lam., 3:55-57

"There is no getting out of this, no more than out of the electrified barbed wire around the camps. Perennial suffering has as much right to expression as a tortured man has to scream; hence it may have been wrong to say that after Auschwitz you could no longer write poems."[1] This phrase by Adorno refers to another of his phrases, more well-known, which made the German philosopher unpopular and whose echoes are still resounding today: "to write poetry after Auschwitz is barbaric. And this corrodes even the knowledge of why it has become impossible to write poetry today."[2] This famous aphorism on the prohibition of the *ars poetica*, dating from 1949 and understandable only as part of the dialectic between culture and barbarity (initially envisaged by Benjamin), is relativized, but not completely rectified, by his assertion in *Negative Dialectics* almost twenty years later.

This assertion re-echoes Adorno's paradox, in whose wake we still find ourselves today, a paradox whose issue lies between the absurdity of a culture re-emerging from the ashes of disaster and the necessity of this same culture. "Even the most extreme consciousness of doom threatens to degenerate into idle chatter,"[3] he writes. On the one hand, there is the awareness that any culture, art, literature, poetry and philosophy "revived"[4] *afterwards* is only idle chatter or "rubbish," "including its urgent critique,"[5] and on the other, the awareness that this very culture, even if it is only rubbish, is nonetheless necessary and urgent — necessary because it helps us to understand the past and to make sure that the

---

[1] Adorno, *Negative Dialectics*, 362.
[2] Adorno, *Prisms*, trans. Samuel Weber (Cambridge: MIT Press, 1983), 34.
[3] *Ibid.*
[4] Adorno, *Critical Models*, 43.
[5] Adorno, *Negative Dialectics*, 367.

horror will never be repeated; urgent because devastations continue to ravage our present. *We* find ourselves, then, caught in the impasse and paradox of not being able to escape the "circle" that calls for a constant critique of culture *after* Auschwitz and for the necessity of contributing to its reformulation from within. Auschwitz has brought culture and, as far as the subject of this book is concerned, philosophy and philosophic thought to an insurmountable impasse.

However, this insurmountable impasse could be overcome if culture were pushed to re-travel the path that led to its failure, to reconsider its stages, images, myths, illusions, and also its solutions, in short, to rewrite its history through the perspective of a "critical self-reflection" entrusted to philosophy, or even through art, which according to Adorno is an unconscious writing of history where the "authentic artists [...] are those in whose works the uttermost horror still quivers."[6]

Thus, an opening would be made in this culture of *afterwards*, because after the disaster philosophy on the one hand and art on the other can also find their *raison d'être*, or a sense, in the lucid self-critique of philosophical thought and the concept that is the prerogative of the former, and in the echoes of "the uttermost horror" attributed to the latter. However, although the "price to be paid" is high (because we risk producing rubbish or idle chatter); although conformity and reification threaten the critical spirit of one and the potential of the other, remaining with Adorno, it seems that art is entrusted with the role of freeing culture from this impasse, finally promising the realization of what is unrealizable. If Adorno's interpretation of the work of art takes place, following Benjamin, in light of a philosophy of history and society, it is precisely to art, in its various forms including poetry, to which the role of deliverance, the role of opening up to utopia or redemption, seems to be entrusted. And so, in these last lines, I would like to follow Adorno to this point.

All of the above was explored in order to show that in being trapped by the "electrified barbed wire around the camps" which entangles the culture or the philosophy of *afterwards*, we find ourselves obligated to get out of this rut. My analysis has therefore attempted to explain that this plunge can be taken by *testimony*.

---

[6] Adorno, *Critical Models*, 47.

Indeed, what other word could be used to represent this solution, which is also a challenge given by philosophy to philosophy itself, a solution pursued by Adorno, by his "master" Benjamin, his colleague Horkheimer and by Levinas in the desire to confront "the extremity that eludes the concept"[7] and to give suffering the "right to expression"? But if philosophy — so as not to invest all culture with this same duty — does not tackle the absolute exteriority of suffering, it risks being, according to Adorno, "in the nature of the musical accompaniment with which the SS liked to drown out the screams of its victims."[8] In other words, it risks compromising itself and becoming mixed with barbarity, albeit a barbarity disguised as culture like the music reducing the voices of tortured victims to silence.

Giving suffering the "right to expression" is thus the intention of Adorno and the other philosophers covered here, an intention that falls under the heading of *testimony*, that becomes *testimony* without being explicitly thematized as testimony. It is an aim that I also took as a priority, even though it may seem pretentious, or even impossible, and that I propose to further explain and clarify at the end of this path.

The reader will have understood that these reflections are part of an examination of the conditions that make philosophical thought possible after the Catastrophe; a thought that holds memory, that is capable of bearing the testimony of disaster and making use of the opening made by these authors, by listening to their testimony on a very specific point — the suffering of history's victims, and most particularly that of those persecuted and killed in the Annihilation.

More precisely, these reflections did not intend to show that the work of these authors as a whole was stigmatized by the horror of Nazism and the hell that it caused, nor did they wish to entrench these thoughts in the period when they were developed, i.e. in the context of Nazi Germany or the post-war atmosphere. Using a hermeneutic and exegetic method, these reflections preferred to concentrate on the texts, to analyze the core ideas, to study and attest to how these philosophers express *testimony* within the web of their thinking, in crucial passages and sometimes also in interruptions and aporia as I have pointed out. It is the testimony of dark times, certainly; times which physically shattered their lives, as for all Jews in those times — the testimony of the victims and the defeated

---

[7] Adorno, *Negative Dialectics*, 365.

[8] *Ibid.*

in history, as in the case of Benjamin, but above all the testimony of evil and of the suffering that destroyed the victims of the Extermination. It is the testimony of the tragic hours, then, but above all the testimony of this singular suffering, this unique death, imposing itself on thought like a barricade, an obstacle, or a philosophical problem.

The following objection could be made to my approach: is the testimony of those who were not a part of the Disaster, like Benjamin, or who were fortunate enough to escape through exile, like Adorno and Horkheimer, or even those who were able to save themselves through the protection of the French uniform, like Levinas, a legitimate *testimony*? In their case — that of surviving Jews who were not deported — can we speak of *testimony*? But then how should we interpret Benjamin's suicide, or the fact that Adorno, Horkheimer and Levinas felt the necessity of bearing witness to Auschwitz and their "shame"[9] of having survived, in the form of some kind of impulse? More generally, is it possible for those who escaped, those who did not see the Gorgon, to bear witness for those who, unlike them, saw its horrible face and touched bottom? If the true witnesses are only the "drowned," as Primo Levi highlights more than any other, how is it possible to testify on behalf of those who are absent? How can their silence and suffering be told and expressed? And is it possible to speak of a *philosophy of testimony*?

In the *Interlude,* I attempted to address these questions more closely by turning to Lyotard's reflections on the differends and silences of the absent, and also by turning to the words of Levi. I concluded that the impossibility of testimony of the Extermination is coupled with its necessity, and considered the paradox of the duty to express the silence of the true witnesses who have all disappeared, and at the same time considered the impossibility of doing so except in a language that is also interrupted, shattered and fragmented. But the *Interlude*, elaborating this gap between the silence of the absent and the words of the saved, and further investigating with Ricœur the possibility of a *philosophy of testimony*, discovered that another term could be added to the binomial. A third party, or rather parties, is added to those of the "drowned" and

---

[9] Adorno speaks of the "drastic guilt of him who was spared" in *Negative Dialectics*, 363; Horkheimer says: "I must be ashamed to still be here," in *Notizen*, 202; Levinas: "the unjustified privilege of having survived six million deaths," in *Proper Names*, 120.

the "saved." It showed the necessity of an *other* implicit in testimony, a third *other*: *us*. *We* are this *other* because the silence of the true witnesses, like the words of the saved, summons *us*, calls on *us*, and begs *us* to testify, even if only to expound the paradox of testimony. This interruption by the *Interlude* revealed, in the difficulty of telling, that testimony is addressed to *us*, and it is precisely on this *us* that the voices of the philosophers in this book agree. It is in the sense of an *us* whom they address, an interpreting *us* and an *us* communicating testimony, that *we* can interpret their thinking as *testimonies of disaster*.

Of course, the case of Benjamin posed several difficulties, the first and foremost of which was that of justifying the decision to give him an important place in awareness of the fact that he never knew the ultimate effects of the Nazi devastation. However, I found a "place" for him, a "place" that is a passage: a passage for reading and interpreting his thinking as a *threshold*, to read it in the double sense of the *threshold* — from *before* to *after* the Catastrophe, and from *after* to *before* it. And this was not to suggest a further interpretation of Benjamin or to forcibly introduce it into this line of thinking, or even to highlight the influence of his thinking among the Frankfurt School, but to *take note of* and *carry out* his "Copernican revolution," according to which *nothing is lost in history's past*. And again, this was to learn from him the *knowledge* that is *remembrance*, the *knowledge* of how to listen to the silent pleas that link *us* to the past, the *knowledge* of how to respond to the "secret agreement" that they ask of *us* in the unique moment of *our* present.

It is in this way, through a "secret agreement" with the past and by the path that attempts to lend an ear to the suffering of the absent and to tell of them with a philosophical voice that addresses an *other*, a voice that speaks in the first person and addresses *us* — through *testimony*, then — that I initially found the first attestation of testimony among these philosophers, and thus picked up the message-in-a-bottle that they cast into the sea for someone else to find. Adorno in particular addresses *us* in the famous categorical imperative of "After Auschwitz," contained in the last part of *Negative Dialectics*.[10] It is an imperative that I analyzed very closely, because it is built on the physical feeling that *we* feel in the face of the horror of the "unbearable physical agony" of those who died. Horkheimer, for his part, also communicates an imperative to *us* that dictates the necessity of preventing the horror from re-occurring, but

---

[10] Adorno, *Negative Dialectics*, 365.

above all he entrusts to *us*, a little like Benjamin, the task of communicating a *knowledge* through *our* memory, *our* life, *our* work: "*knowledge of how to remember* those who disappeared and their suffering."[11] He entrusts it to *us* in the fragment "After Auschwitz," marked by signs of personal suffering and a conscious and committed Judaism, where the "despair" and "longing" of the dead *"in unspeakable torments"* becomes the truth of the Jewish intellectual's life and work. Although Horkheimer seems to limit the duty of testimony to the Jewish intellectual, in contrast to the more universalist attitude of Adorno's imperative, for him too it is the physical suffering of the massacred that prompts testimony. As for Levinas, he also raises the issue of the necessity of communicating a lesson to those who were born "following the Liberation," to the "new men" of *afterwards*. He too addresses *us*, putting forward three paradoxical lessons that once again confirm the necessity of preventing this horror from reoccurring and, in a way that is different to the others, the necessity of new access to texts from the Jewish tradition. But what appears more unusual is that the task of a renewal capable of opening up a horizon for those who come *afterwards* is achieved through the idea of an other subjectivity, a *physical subjectivity* where one is called into question by the suffering and death of the other, and where each person is called to be responsible for the suffering of the other.

Next, and simultaneously, I noted as a strong indication of this testimony that the thoughts of Adorno, Horkheimer and Levinas revolve around the physical. All three reveal themselves as sensitive to physical suffering in general, and to the pain inflicted in the extermination camps in particular. Thus, I commented on the articles and paragraphs where this suffering is dealt with or thematized and attempted to decipher the key concepts in each, discovering the central thread, the taut nerve that links them.

Consequently, as part of *a testimony that addresses us and a testimony of the physical suffering of those who died in the Extermination*, the analysis in this book was able to bring together authors that are sometimes very far apart and rarely subjected to a comparison[12] on the same issues, and

---

[11] Horkheimer, *Notizen*, 273.

[12] An exception is the book by Hent de Vries, *Minimal Theologies: Critiques of Secular Reason in T. W. Adorno and E. Levinas* (Baltimore: Johns Hopkins University Press, 2005).

allowed an idea to be put forward of a possibility for philosophy to create an opening in the ruins of *afterwards* by making itself and calling itself the *philosophy of testimony*. It is the *philosophy of testimony* in the sense of a hermeneutic of testimony — hermeneutic because it offers a *given* to be interpreted (for these philosophers, the suffering of Auschwitz; for their interpreter, the texts that attempt to express them); hermeneutic because it requires an interpretation, by calling on an *other*, *us*, *me*. It is a *philosophy of testimony* which therefore cannot be told or written except in the first person, and thanks to the singularity of the witness and of the signatory (and thanks to the hermeneutic movement), can only in this way interrupt and suspend conceptual logic and the linearity of philosophical discourse. It is a philosophy, then, that thanks to the *here* and the *now* of the witness, exceeds the boundaries of the concept and attempts to approach and express what eludes it. It is a philosophy, lastly, that can only respond personally and through a personal work, through the *here* and *now* of this breath, to the plea of the dead and their injuries.

But is there not too much attachment to wanting to respond with one's — my — breath to the pleas of those who no longer have breath? Does this not boil down to collaborating once more in the rhetoric of reconstruction? Cooperating in the "idle chatter" that Adorno talks of? Once again piling rubbish on rubbish while giving the illusion of contributing, by this accumulation, to re-establishment and to reconciliation with a false consciousness? And if we consider, as I have done here, that it is possible to respond to *their* plea, even if it is in the form of a *philosophy of testimony*, and despite its limits and paradoxes, is this enough? Does this restore anything to *them*?

The *feeling* of insufficiency, followed by a certain discomfort that constantly surfaces but is well reined in within this book, now re-emerges at the end.

At the end of a journey, like this one, that was known to be difficult from the outset and was intended to be fractured and interrupted, there is a great temptation to yield, for once and definitively, to the end, to silence. Not to justify the unutterable and the inexpressible — that would make no sense after the preceding pages — but because, as Levinas says, "is not its interruption its only possible end?"[13] If we must think of interruption as the only possible way to close all philosophical discourse,

---

[13] Levinas, *Otherwise Than Being*, 20.

as Levinas suggests, or think of complete interruption as an essential part of thought, according to Benjamin, then it is all the more necessary to do so in this work that, since its first pages, has been interrupted at each stage, unfulfilled at each end, without end. It is without end, not in the sense that it could be interminable, but in the sense that it never finds an end or closure. What is there to say at the end? *How* can we speak, once again but differently, the end of this never-ending End of the Disaster?

Perhaps we could follow Adorno's suggestion above: "the concept of a cultural resurrection after Auschwitz is illusory and absurd, and every work created since then has to pay the bitter price for this. However, because the world has survived its own downfall, it nonetheless needs art to write its unconscious history."[14] Thus, in returning to art, and particularly to poetry, in correcting Adorno's so well-known and so poorly understood aphorism, a way out of the impasse can take shape, and this end can finally be spoken and written.

The writing of an "unconscious history" that is entrusted to art, according to Adorno, and in particular "the thought of the disaster," as in Blanchot's words, can take place here in unison with and echoing the philosophical voice of the authors who fed and directed these lines of thinking thanks to poetry because it "is called on to weave and interweave this essential and irreducible link between *dying, surviving* and *writing*."[15] It is poetry's task, then, to speak at the end, to testify to this passage between the kingdoms of death and life peculiar to the testimony of the Extermination, to overcome the aporia peculiar to a *philosophy of testimony* and to find the solution for a culture of *afterwards*.

It is to poetry, which was once essential to resistance in the camps, like the song of Odysseus for Levi, and singularly to the poetic and prophetic voice of Nelly Sachs[16] that I entrust the role of a *tragic chorus* at the end of this conclusion.

---

[14] Adorno, *Critical Models*, 47.

[15] Rachel Ertel, *Braiser de mots* (Paris: Liana Levi, 2003), 279. Cf. also *Dans la langue de personne, poésie yiddish de l'anéantissement* (Paris: Seuil, 1993).

[16] Nelly Sachs (1891-1970), discovered by Stefan Zweig, and a friend of Selma Lagerlöf, who enabled her escape to Stockholm in 1940 (where she lived until her death), and of Paul Celan, winner of the Nobel Prize for Literature in 1966

Her feminine voice emerges, longed for, to grasp and communicate what the philosophical voice attempted to say and to unearth, without being able to say it entirely: the words, silences, breaths, and suffering of those engulfed in the night.

This voice, also of Jewish origin, also exiled, also a writer, composing poems while the death chambers were still working, is therefore in harmony with the philosophical voices of Benjamin, Adorno, Horkheimer and Levinas in the discretion of this end — almost a murmur — like a *sensu stricto lament*, crying over the inconsolable suffering of the body of Israel and serving as a counter-melody to the *lament* proclaimed by these philosophers over the twilight of reason and the desolation of disaster.

This voice is raised, and at the end and *retrospectively*, its poetic and prophetic words enlighten, illuminate and inspire the philosophical discourse of this book, which stumbles on aporia, paradoxes and questions that are difficult to consider and resolve, or more simply, on interruptions. To her, to her songs and choruses, to her *Chorus of the Rescued* and *Chorus of the Dead*, belongs the responsibility of *saying* what cannot be said through philosophical language and concepts and what could not be said in the reasoning developed here.

To her, a voice that is one of the most discrete and sensitive to the disaster, I entrust the role of expressing the insufficiency of the philosophical concept and thematization in the face of the extreme. Again, it is for her to say what can only be said in poetic language and to invent another idiom to express the interruption of language; it is for her to open up the text, my text, beyond its limits and insufficiency; it is for her to *testify to another testimony*. Finally, it is for to her to write the end, and to sing her — and my — *lament* on Israel's suffering at Auschwitz:

(with Shmuel Yosef Agnon), author noted for *In the Habitations of Death, Eclipse of the Stars, Glowing Enigmas, But in the Night* and *Eli: A Mystery Play of the Sufferings of Israel*.

CHORUS OF THE RESCUED

We, the rescued,
From whose hollow bones death had begun to whittle his flutes,
And on whose sinews he had already stroked his bow —
Our bodies continue to lament
With their mutilated music.
We, the rescued,
The nooses wound for our necks still dangle
before us in the blue air —
Hourglasses still fill with our dripping blood.
We, the rescued,
The worms of fear still feed on us.
Our constellation is buried in dust.
We, the rescued,
Beg you:
Show us your sun, but gradually.
Lead us from star to star, step by step.
Be gentle when you teach us to live again
Lest the song of a bird,
Or a pail being filled at the well,
Let our badly sealed pain burst forth again
And carry us away —
We beg you:
Do not show us an angry dog, not yet —
It could be, it could be
That we will dissolve into dust —
Dissolve into dust before your eyes.
For what binds our fabric together?
We whose breath vacated us,
Whose soul fled to Him out of that midnight
Long before our bodies were rescued
Into the arc of the moment.
We, the rescued,
We press your hand
We look into your eye —
But all that binds us together now is leave-taking.
The leave-taking in the dust
Binds us together with you.

CHORUS OF THE DEAD

We from the black sun of fear
Holed like sieves —
We dripped from the sweat of death's minute.
Withered on our bodies are the deaths done unto us
Like flowers of the field withered on a hill of sand.
O you who still greet the dust as friend,
You who, talking sand, say to the sand:
I love you.

We say to you:
Torn are the cloaks of the mysteries of dust,
The air in which we were suffocated,
The fires in which we were burned,
The earth into which our remains were cast
The water which was beaded with our sweat of fear
Has broken forth with us and begins to gleam.
We dead of Israel say to you:
We are moving past one more star
Into our hidden God.[17]

---

[17] Nelly Sachs, *Collected Poems 1944-1949* (Los Angeles: Green Integer, 2007), 101-103 and 113. Translations by Michael Roloff (Chorus of the Rescued) and Ruth and Matthew Mead (Chorus of the Dead). The two poems, written between 1940-1944, were originally published in German in Berlin in 1946.

Indicative Bibliography*

Anders, G. *Wir Eichmannsöhne: offener Brief an Klaus Eichmann.* Munich: Beck, 1964.

— *Die Antiquiertheit des Menschen. Bd. 1, Über die Seele im Zeitalter der zweiten industriellen Revolution.* Munich: C. H. Beck, 1980.

Antelme, R. *Textes inédits sur* L'espèce humaine. *Essais et témoignage.* Paris: Gallimard, 1996.

Arendt, H. *Eichmann in Jerusalem: a report on the banality of evil.* New York: Viking Press, 1963.

— "The Jew as Pariah: A Hidden Tradition." *Jewish Social Studies* 6 (1944), 99-122.

— "On the Nature of Totalitarianism." *Essays in Understanding, 1930-1954.* New York: Harcourt, Brace & Co., 1994.

— *Nach Auschwitz: Essays & Kommentare I* and *Die Krise des Zionismus: Essays & Kommentare II.* German translation by Eike Geisel. Berlin: Tiamat, 1989.

Ascheim, S. *Culture and Catastrophe: German and Jewish confrontations with National Socialism and other crises.* London: MacMillan Press, 1996.

Bauman, Z. *Modernity and the Holocaust.* Cambridge: Polity Press, 1999.

Bataille, G. "Reflections on the Executioner and the Victim" (1947). English translation by Elizabeth Rottenberg. *Yale French Studies* 79 (1991), 15-19.

— "Ce monde où nous mourons" (1957). *Œuvres complètes.* Paris: Gallimard, 1988, 457-66.

Bensoussan, G. *Auschwitz en héritage?: d'un bon usage de la mémoire.* Paris: Mille et une nuit, 2003.

---

* Titles quoted in this book are not listed here; non-quoted works by the authors studied and critical literature are not included in this selection of critical studies and essays on the subject in general.

Blanchot, M. *The Infinite Conversation*. English translation by Susan Hanson. Minneapolis: University of Minnesota Press, 1993.
— *The Step Not Beyond*. English translation by Lycette Nelson. Albany: State University of New York Press, 1992.

Bloch, E. *Heritage of our Times* (1935). English translation by Neville & Stephen Plaice. Berkeley: University of California Press, 1991.

Chalier, C. "Dieu sans puissance." Postface à H. Jonas. *Le concept de Dieu après Auschwitz*. Paris: Payot & Rivages, 1994, 45-69.
— "Ils ne furent pas les derniers... Réflexions sur la Choa et la civilization." *Bulletin de la Société Suisse d'Études Juives* 5 (1996), 5-16.

Chaumont, J. M. *La concurrence des victimes: génocide, identité, reconnaissance*. Paris: La Découverte, 1997.

Coquio, C. (ed.). *Parler des camps, penser les génocides*. Paris: Albin Michel, 1999.

Derrida, J. *Margins of Philosophy*. English translation by Alan Bass. Chicago: University of Chicago Press, 1985.
— "Faith and Knowledge." English translation by Samuel Weber. *Acts of Religion*. New York: Routledge, 2002, 42-101.
— *Pardonner: l'impardonnable et l'imprescriptible*. Paris: L'Herne, 2005.
— "Poetics and Politics of Witnessing". *Sovereignties in Question: the poetics of Paul Celan*. New York: Fordham University Press, 2005, 65-96.

Diner, D. *Beyond the Conceivable. Studies on Germany, Nazism, and the Holocaust*. Berkeley: California UP, 2000.

Faye, J.-P. *Langages totalitaires, critique de la raison, l'économie narrative*. Paris: Hermann, 2005.

Forever in the shadow of Hitler?: original documents of the Historikerstreit, the controversy concerning the singularity of the Holocaust. English translation by James Knowlton & Truett Cates. Atlantic Highlands: Humanities Press, 1993.

Gorny, Y. *Between Auschwitz and Jerusalem: Jewish Collective Identity in Crisis*. London: Vallentine Mitchell, 2003.

Jankélévitch, V. *L'imprescriptible. Pardonner? Dans l'honneur et la dignité*. Paris: Seuil, 1986. (A section published as "Should We Pardon Them?". English translation by Ann Hobart. *Critical Inquiry* 22 (Spring 1996), 552-572.

Jaspers, K. *The Question of German Guilt*. English translation by E.B. Ashton. New York: Capricorn Books, 1961.

Jonas, H. "The Concept of God after Auschwitz: A Jewish Voice". *The Journal of Religion* 67 (Jan 1987), 1-13.

Levi, P. *The Voice of Memory: Interviews 1961-1987*. English translation by Robert Gordon. New York: New Press, 2001.
— *Auschwitz Report*. English translation by Judith Woolf. New York: Verso, 2006.

Lyotard, J.-F. *Heidegger and "The Jews."* English translation by M.S. Roberts & A. Michel. Minneapolis: University of Minnesota Press, 1990.
— *The Inhuman: Reflections on Time*. English translation by Geoffrey Bennington & Rachel Bowlby. Stanford: Stanford University Press, 1991.
— *Misère de la philosophie*. Paris: Galilée, 2000.
— *L'exercice du différend*. Paris: P.U.F., 2001.

Kofman, S. *Smothered Words*. English translation by Madeleine Dobie. Evanston: Northwestern University Press, 1998.
— *Rue Ordener, Rue Labat*. English translation by Ann Smock. Lincoln: University of Nebraska Press, 1996.

Nancy, J.-L., with Lacoue-Labarthe, Philippe. "The Nazi Myth." English translation by Brian Holmes. *Critical Inquiry* 16 (Winter 1990), 291-312.
— *L'art et la mémoire des camps. Représenter. Exterminer* (ed.), *Le genre humain* 36. Paris: Seuil, 2001.

Neher A. *Exile of the Word, From the Silence of the Bible to the Silence of Auschwitz*. English translation by David Maisel. Philadelphia: Jewish Publication Society of America, 1981.

Rabinbach A. *In the Shadow of Catastrophe: German Intellectuals Between Apocalypse and Enlightenment*. Berkeley: California University Press, 1997.

Ricœur P. *Evil: A Challenge to Philosophy and Theology*. English translation by John Bowden. New York: Continuum International, 2007.
— *Memory, History, Forgetting*. English translation by Kathleen Blamey & David Pellauer. Chicago: University of Chicago Press, 2004.

Sartre J. P. *Anti-Semite and Jew*. English translation by George J. Becker. New York: Schocken Books, 1948.

Segev T. *The Seventh Million: The Israelis and the Holocaust*. English translation by Haim Watzman. New York: Hill and Wang, 1993.

Steiner G. "Comment se taire?" and "La longue vie de la métaphore. Une approche de la Shoah", *Ecrits du temps* 14-15 (1987), 3-33.
— *In Bluebeard's Castle*. New Haven: Yale University Press, 1971.

Todorov T. *Facing the Extreme: Moral Life in the Concentration Camps*. English translation by Arthur Denner & Abigail Pollak. New York: Metropolitan Books, 1996.

Traverso E. *The Origins of Nazi Violence*. English translation by Janet Lloyd. New York: New Press, 2003.
— *La pensée dispersée: figures de l'exil judéo-allemand*. Paris: Leo Scheer, 2004.

Trigano S. (ed.). *Penser Auschwitz*. Paris: Cerf, 1989.
— *The Democratic Ideal and the Shoah: The Unthought in Political Modernity*. English translation by Gila Walker. Albany: SUNY Press, 2009.

Wiesenthal S. *The Sunflower*. English translation by H. A. Pichler. New York: Schocken Books, 1998

Wiesel E. *Night*. English translation by Stella Rodway. New York: Bantam Books, 1982.

www.ingramcontent.com/pod-product-compliance
Ingram Content Group UK Ltd.
Pitfield, Milton Keynes, MK11 3LW, UK
UKHW021848140426
5217IPUK00022B/1657